BELOW THE STARS

BELOW THE STARS

*How the Labor of Working Actors and
Extras Shapes Media Production*

KATE FORTMUELLER

UNIVERSITY OF TEXAS PRESS
Austin

Requests for permission to reproduce material
from this work should be sent to:
Permissions
University of Texas Press
P.O. Box 7819
Austin, TX 78713-7819
utpress.utexas.edu/rp-form

♾ The paper used in this book meets the minimum requirements of
ANSI/NISO Z39.48-1992 (R1997) (Permanence of Paper).

Library of Congress Cataloging-in-Publication Data

Names: Fortmueller, Kate, author.
Title: Below the stars : how the labor of working actors and extras
shapes media production / Kate Fortmueller.
Description: First edition. | Austin : University of Texas Press, 2021. |
Includes bibliographical references and index.
Identifiers: LCCN 2020047423
ISBN 978-1-4773-2307-6 (cloth)
ISBN 978-1-4773-2308-3 (library ebook)
ISBN 978-1-4773-2309-0 (non-library ebook)
Subjects: LCSH: Extras (Actors)—United States—History. | Motion
picture actors and actresses—United States—History. | Television
actors and actresses—United States—History. | Motion picture
industry—United States—History. | Television broadcasting—United
States—History. | Precarious employment—United States—History.
Classification: LCC PN1995.9.E97 F67 2021 | DDC 791.4302/80922—dc23
LC record available at https://lccn.loc.gov/2020047423

doi:10.7560/323076

CONTENTS

v

ABBREVIATIONS

4As or AAAA	Associated Actors and Artistes of America (1919–present)
AEA	Actors Equity Association or Equity (1913–present)
AFRA	American Federation of Radio Artists (1937–1952)
AFTRA	American Federation of Television and Radio Artists (1952–2012)
AGMA	American Guild of Musical Artists (1936–present)
AGVA	American Guild of Variety Artists (1939–present)
AMPP	Association of Motion Picture Producers (1924–1964)
AMPTP	Alliance of Motion Picture and Television Producers (1964–present)
CEA	Chorus Equity Association (1919–1955)
DGA	Directors Guild of America (1936–present)
MPPDA	Motion Picture Producers and Distributors Association (1922–1945)
MPPU	Motion Picture Players Union (1918–1920)
SAG	Screen Actors Guild (1933–2012)
SAG-AFTRA	Screen Actors Guild-American Federation of Television and Radio Artists (2012–present)
SEG	Screen Extras Guild (1947–1992)
SWG	Screen Writers Guild (1933–1954)
TVA	Television Authority (1949–1952)
WGA	Writers Guild of America (1954–present)

ACKNOWLEDGMENTS

*B*_{*elow*} *the Stars* is, among other things, about ecosystems of labor and the many different networks that support creative pursuits. This book has benefited from the work of my delightful editor Jim Burr, helpful archivists, actors, union workers, colleagues, friends, and family—I am appreciative of all the help along the way and hope these acknowledgments can offer insight into my own labor, networks, and pathways.

I relied on archival research from the Margaret Herrick Library, New York University's Tamiment Library, the New York Public Library's Performing Arts Library, the SAG-AFTRA Archive, University of California–Los Angeles's Special Collections, the University of Southern California's Warner Bros. Archive, the University of Texas's Ransom Center, and the Wisconsin Center for Film and Theater Research. Special "shanks" to Valerie Yaris, who allowed me to share her office over the course of two separate summers. I am also immensely grateful for the generosity and enthusiasm of the actors who sat down for interviews for this project. My understanding of the work and creative fulfillment of acting is much richer as a result of these conversations.

The faculty at the University of Southern California's School of Cinematic Arts provided me with a broad overview of film and media history that empowered me to believe I could undertake a project of this historical scope. This project has grown and changed significantly since graduate school, but many of the questions and concerns in this project were born out of my dissertation. I continue to be tremendously grateful for the insights and questions posed by Ellen Seiter, Priya Jaikumar, David James, Richard Jewell, Laura Isabel Serna, and Steven Ross at various stages of my graduate education and dissertation process.

The Department of Critical Studies (now Cinema and Media Studies) also introduced me to a tremendous pool of smart and supportive colleagues. The Ellen Seiter dissertation group provided a wonderful source of like-minded scholars in Patty Ahn, Ghia Godfree, Eric Hoyt, Shawna Kidman, and Taylor Nygaard. A very special thank-you to Luci Marzola, who in addition to being a great friend has been a devoted reader of chapters, a wonderful collaborator, and an essential sounding board for talking through labor histories.

My years in Los Angeles were enriched by the fact that I was surrounded by smart and funny people who have challenged my thinking about film, television, and pop culture (all of whom are also *excellent* movie and television watching companions), like Elizabeth Affuso, Alessandro Ago, Michael Bolton, Lara Bradshaw, Emily Carman, Rob Cavanaugh, Kristen Fuhs, Chris Hanson, Daniel Herbert, Carlos Kase, Alison Kozberg, Luci and Michael Marzola, Ross Melnick, Michelle Neale, Taylor Nygaard, Luke Pebler, Paul Reinsch, Jennifer Rosales, Brett Service, Suzanne Scott, and Laurel Westrup. Special thanks to "the Ladies," aka "the First Wives Club," Elizabeth Affuso, Kristen Fuhs, and Suzanne Scott. From dinner parties to pandemic Netflix parties, I am grateful for a group of friends who are supportive, engaging, and quick to offer professional solidarity and advice across time zones.

I am appreciative of the support of my colleagues across the University of Georgia. The Willson Center for Humanities provided me with funding to travel to archives around the country. In the Department of Entertainment and Media Studies, James Biddle, Matthew Evans, James Hamilton, and honorary department member Andres Rosende (who invited me to see Ray Wise in action at his table read) have all been enthusiastic and supportive colleagues. Special thanks to Shira Chess and Anne Gilbert (aka the other two original members of the "EMST Women's Caucus") for humor, encouragement, and of course, fire pits. In Film Studies, Richard Neupert brought me into the fold of the Athens Film Arts Institute; he and Rielle Navitski have often provided me with opportunities to share my work in Film Studies. Christopher Sieving has also been a generous reader of several chapters.

Athens has also provided me with a truly wonderful community of friends in Alexa Bankert, Katie and Joe Ehrlich, Monica Sklar, and Kristen Shockley and Jay Winters. My life has also become so much richer with the O'Brien and O'Neil pack (Katy, Michael, Jonas, Ronan, your entire extended families, and of course the fur family, Ginny, Harry, and Albie)—from the bus on the new faculty tour to napping in the Griffith Park Observatory to floating at the Tropic of Cancer—thanks for helping keep me human during the writing process and being our Athens family.

I am obviously indebted to my mothers, Beth Fortmueller and Jeanne Holden, who have always instilled in me that we are a union family and told me stories about my resourceful grandfather that made it into the introduction of this book. They have inspired my thinking and supported this project in countless ways.

Film and television shows often use the "and" credit to specially call out important actors. The "and" credit in my acknowledgments belongs to David Lerner, who has been living with this project for as long as I have. Thank you for your insights, careful reading, constructive feedback, pep talks, and cheerleading, but most importantly, thank you for reminding me to take breaks and enjoy the writing process.

BELOW THE STARS

INTRODUCTION

In 1933 my twelve-year-old grandfather, William (Bill) Fortmueller, had to figure out how to contribute to his household. He was already selling newspapers on Hollywood Boulevard between Grauman's Chinese Theater and industry hot spot Musso and Frank's, but he needed to contribute more to help his single mother. When a Musso and Frank's regular spotted him selling papers and took note of his red hair, freckles, and somewhat mischievous smile, he offered to give Bill a bit of work as an extra. Working in the movies was not Bill's life's dream, but he was happy to earn the additional income from his jobs in the movies, and he even invested in a set of headshots to submit to casting departments. Extra work presented an opportunity for a young boy growing up in Hollywood to earn some extra money—at least until he was old enough to take a more lucrative and steady job.

At the young age of twelve, my grandpa Bill was working two part-time jobs in Los Angeles, a living that closely corresponded to a lot of other LA denizens—he was ostensibly a working freelancer. As an adjective, the term "freelance" dates back to 1854, when it was used to describe a mercenary soldier, but as a verb, freelancing has its origins in the early 1900s to describe professional work without a contract, initially deployed when referring to journalists and later used for actors and many other professions. The practice of retaining workers when and if needed applied to an array of workers in media fields and was part of how these fields kept costs low. These two jobs, newsboy and extra, share a surprising number of characteristics. In both jobs, employees face poor working conditions and low pay, each of which drew the attention of social reformers at various points.[1] Despite their connections to the professional media industries, neither job historically presented clear opportunities for growth or advancement, nor did they offer long-term career prospects. In 1933, Bill Fortmueller participated in both of these industries as one of five hundred

William Fortmueller, full-length photo for casting,
1933. Photograph from author's collection.

thousand newsboys and seventeen thousand extras working casually in the United States.[2] My grandfather, as it turns out, was an unexpected trailblazer, embodying the "gig economy" well before this term became a buzzword for labor practices of the twenty-first century.

Freelance work has a long history in the film industry. Unlike my grandfather and many others who do extra work without harboring grander ambitions in entertainment fields, even serious aspirants and professional actors below the level of stardom string together different jobs out of necessity to support their creative aspirations, dreams of fame, or love of the craft. The reason for this professional uncertainty and endemic rootlessness is that some core aspects of the industry have remained constant: the supply of labor has always exceeded the demand to cast roles, and for studio heads and producers concerned with the financial bottom line, this vast array of hopefuls willing to work without the security of full-time employment creates a large, diverse, and competitive pool of talent that helps keep costs low while maintaining efficiency. In addition to working on multiple projects and across media venues, many actors find themselves taking on jobs that interfere with their career trajectory as actors and perhaps end up displacing acting as their primary career. The necessity of cobbling together disjointed opportunities and jobs often leaves actors feeling disempowered, but what actors might lack in decision-making clout they have often made up for in influence on the media industries.

Below the Stars: How the Labor of Working Actors and Extras Shapes Media Production is a work of film and media history that cuts across media and industrial boundaries to look at major industrial changes from the perspective of screen actors and positions their labor, union organization, and shifting industrial position as the primary focus of history and analysis. "Below the stars" is a reference to where the actors in this book fall in the credit scroll in film and television shows, but it also signals the association between extras and the below-the-line workers who represent fixed costs on budget sheets. Many working actors and all extras have very different professional experiences from stars, but their professional lives are intertwined. Stars, and their importance to media production and marketing, provide additional leverage in negotiations and make actors' strikes more visible. Despite the importance of thinking about stars separately from other on-screen talent, it is never entirely possible to eliminate the presence of stars who always seem to hover over conversations about actors.

Stars are central both to audience understandings of actors and to scholarly research on screen talent. Many formative works on stars remove agency from them either by focusing on them as part of a star system, or, following in Richard Dyer's model, by considering the star as text and image.[3] Noteworthy exceptions such as Adrienne McLean's work on Rita Hayworth and Emily Carman's study of female stars who negotiated their own freelance contracts have been instrumental in contributing to the understanding of star labor and career management beyond their publicity and screen performances.[4] Individual star contracts can establish important precedents for future contracts, but they do not establish widespread professional norms and practices like those created through collective bargaining. Stars help to raise the profile of the union, but working actors and extras push for bargaining agendas that have helped shape the industry.

3

As a visual piece of the mise-en-scène, actors often seem to be part of the on-screen magic rather than part of the labor contributing to the infrastructure of the media industries. By examining actors as a labor group rather than focusing on the nuances of individual performances or training methods, I approach acting as a profession and explore how the labor history of actors influences industrial structures and practices more broadly in four historical moments of industrial and technological upheaval. Actors and extras do not decide what gets made or determine how on-screen stories are told, but their influence on the media culture of Los Angeles and the business of Hollywood has been substantial.

My methodological approach toward actors and extras is one that Eric Smoodin has described as "film scholarship without films."[5] This can describe many industrial, historical, and material approaches toward the study of media, but in the case of this book it is a way of thinking about film and television that begins with questions about labor, which it sees as integral for understanding media form and politics. I rely on archival research from the Margaret Herrick Library, New York University's Tamiment Library, the New York Public Library's Performing Arts Library, the SAG-AFTRA Archive, University of California–Los Angeles's Special Collections, the University of Southern California's Warner Bros. Archive, the University of Texas's Ransom Center, and the Wisconsin Center for Film and Theater Research. To extend the project to the present, I conducted one- to three-hour in-person interviews in Los Angeles from 2014 to 2018 with more than twenty-five aspiring and working actors, casting directors, and owners of other ancillary businesses that target actors. In addition to archival research and interviews, I sat in on a contract information session, registered for extras work with Central Casting, observed table reads, audited a casting workshop, toured the facilities of ancillary businesses, and sat in on an automated dialog replacement (ADR) session. My experiences and interactions with different aspects of the business gave me both a granular understanding of the bureaucracy of acting and a broad perspective on the lived reality of actors. Understanding contracts, rehearsals, the casting process, and fixing dialogue are not elements of the business where "the magic happens," but these are essential parts of acting as a profession. Although this is a media history without texts, the activities in boardrooms and behind the camera shape the culture of productions, the development of technologies, and, inevitably, textual meaning. As such, actors provide a lens for considering the relationships between policy, texts, infrastructure, and labor.

Acting is an ecosystem. By focusing on Hollywood history independent of media texts, I focus on labor, professional stratification, and the structures that organize Hollywood's largest population of workers. For many actors there has always been a tremendous amount of work and activity beyond what audiences see on screen. Much of an actor's work involves interacting with agents, managers, acting coaches, instructors, casting directors, union representatives, and various administrators who determine work and opportunities. Each actor has a network around her—ideally these are people she has hired in order to help enrich her career, but for many the surrounding network might be composed of opportunistic producers or small businesses offering services of questionable use or value. Although these various aspects of an actor's network operate on the periphery, they are essential for understanding the context of an actor's creative work and professional identity, regardless of her level of fame. Breaking down the barriers between the stratified divisions separating types of actors also reveals distinctions between professions, practices, and different forms of media—between extras and character actors, film and television, video games and commercials, studio and independent. Changes in opportunities and contracts for stars impact opportunities for actors lower in the hierarchy. Decisions made in union negotiations impact all actors and can shape production practices, budgets, locations, and the media objects themselves. All of these aspects of acting and labor reveal how the treatment of actors is integral to understanding Hollywood's business practices.

A STAR ISN'T BORN

By approaching media history from the perspective of workers who are often marginal from the decision-making process, *Below the Stars* intervenes in some of the basic assumptions of media historiography. Media histories tend to focus on the influence and power of executives, directors, writers, or others with financial or creative control, and the parallel influences and insights of audiences and their active relationships to media, culture, or textual forms. These broad categories are not necessarily discrete, and many scholars of industry and unions stress that an understanding of infrastructure and labor is essential for a complete understanding of media and more nuanced criticism.[6] However, for labor and industrial histories, these approaches tend to be structured as either top-down histories of executive decision-making and authorship in Hollywood or persuasive and recuperative arguments about a particular worker's or group's creative power. If we interpret the value of media workers strictly through lenses of creativity and authorship, we naturally exclude a wide array of media workers from scholarly study and restrict our understanding of how the media industries function and who shapes media infrastructure.

Although media studies as a field is often highly critical of Adorno and Horkheimer's conceptualization of top-down power in the media industries, histories of industry decision-makers do little to complicate our understanding of entrenched power in Hollywood. Recent historical and contemporary studies have ushered in more varied histories of marginalized workers, but even those centralize the creativity and authorship of these marginalized groups. Of the works focusing on media labor, especially those of below-the-line workers, there is a tendency to emphasize "creative control" or creativity as the justification for why the workers being studied are important.[7] Although some works attempt to take a broader view of labor in order to understand who is recognized as "creative" and how work deemed "noncreative" has been gendered, in both cases scholarship on marginalized workers is contingent on the assumption of creative contributions.[8]

Hollywood union histories offer an alternative model for studying and thinking about marginalized workers and their place within the industry without resorting to textual influence or creative practice. Histories of unions present organizational histories and analysis of internal union politics, as in Nielsen and Mailes's *Hollywood's Other Blacklist*.[9] Miranda Banks's *The Writers* integrates oral history into a history of writers and their guilds to account for the development of screenwriting as a professional identity.[10] In *Liberating Hollywood*, Maya Montañez Smukler weaves a discussion of unions into a broader history of the struggles of women directors in the 1970s. Essential to these analyses is an understanding of fragmentation and internal conflicts within unions. For Banks and Smukler, the unions are part of professional identities that can sometimes be at odds with smaller groupings within a large union. The unions were often microcosms of the structural inequities that permeated Hollywood, but they also provided the institutional setting for writers, directors, and actors to strategize ways to combat racism and sexism in Hollywood.[11]

The protagonists of this book are not the protagonists of the films they make, but rather the supporting actors and the background performers who serve as a lens into the evolution of creative labor in the twentieth and twenty-first centuries. Although actors are frequently the primary point of identification for film viewers, they are not as central to scholarly work on film and media. Danae Clark explains that the absence of scholarship on acting, labor, and professional norms stems from a tendency within film studies to center conversations about subjectivity in work on spectatorship.[12] Since Clark published her work on actors in 1995, there have been numerous works of media history and others in media industry and production studies that have placed media workers' subjectivities at the center of their analysis.[13] Despite the shift in the field toward increased analysis of the identities and subjectivities of workers, however, there has been little scholarship on actors beyond Clark's book, which she herself admits is more theoretical than historically grounded in voices due to the "lack of information available on specific actors/stars in relation to specific events."[14] As such, Clark understands screen actors' subject formation through evidence from their unionization process in the early 1930s. In subsequent decades the increased precarity of the work, the addition of media forms, new methods of distribution, and the growing importance of other forms of screen performance all contributed to an evolution in actors' collective subject formation.

Below the Stars weaves together individual accounts and union documents to develop an idea of the actor's perspective on the media industries throughout Hollywood history. Because lesser-known actors and extras do not make substantial narrative contributions to films, few of these non-star and background actors have donated collections to archives, although there are some important exceptions. For example, Leo Rosencrans's letters (featured in chapter 1) provide insight into the cost of living and difficulties of life as an extra in 1916, Arnett Williams's correspondence with Gregory Peck (also in chapter 1) underscores one individual's struggle against the barriers for black actors, and Alan Hewitt's files (which inform chapters 2 and 3) in the New York Public Library's Performing Arts Library demonstrate how actors worked across media and navigated multiple unions. Unfortunately, these personal collections are rare and only make up a portion of the stories and archival material I use. In addition to individual accounts, documents from unions and individual production files help clarify the structural and professional dimensions of acting as a career. Hollywood differs from other creative industries because it has a long history of unionization. Minutes from meetings, correspondence between union leadership, letters from concerned members, and transcripts from meetings all help to construct a picture of the key concerns of working actors over time. The negotiations, strategies, and communications among union membership provide material records of actors' concerns and struggles and are essential to understanding their working lives and the evolution of screen acting as a profession.

THE LABOR OF ACTING

"Casual employment," Hugh Lovell and Tasile Carter write, "has typified the industry since the very beginning."[15] Although Lovell and Carter's study was released in 1955, contract, rather than casual, has been the dominant characterization of Hollywood labor, especially studio system labor. Casual labor describes the short-term contracts of temporary work arrangements that were common for many actors, as well as craft workers. Although casual employment is typical, there is a tremendous amount of additional labor that actors perform as part of the process of finding work. An actor's work can include acting classes, reading casting notices, auditioning, discussions about acting in unions, and the myriad activities that have constituted professionalization. All of these actions and processes contribute to an actor's ability to help convey character and textual meaning, and they need to be included in how we talk about an actor's labor. The nature of freelance work, and the gaps in employment it creates, should be central to how we think about the professional subjectivities of actors and other freelance careers in the media industry. Scholarly work on precarity and freelance work spans multiple disciplines, but in *Below the Stars* I show how precarity is a defining aspect of screen actors' careers regardless of the stability of the industry surrounding them.

In relation to actors, precarity describes some of the ways that actors might feel disempowered. As Nicole Cohen points out, precarity is not used to describe simply low-income workers, but also those who experience income and scheduling uncertainty, as well as an increasing blurring of boundaries between work and home life.[16] Actors, much like the journalists Cohen writes about, accept precarity because they like flexibility and the creative fulfillment of the job. For actors, the creative rewards are often tempered by the lack of control over many aspects of the casting process and the kinds of roles they are offered. Short-term contracts offer actors flexibility, but not autonomy.

Film historians and sociologists have identified the tendency toward project-based rather than long-term contract-based work as a defining characteristic of the post-studio system in Hollywood as well as many other industries under late capitalism.[17] Freelance work is not necessarily disempowering for the employee—as Emily Carman identifies, many stars in the 1930s and 1940s who were not on long-term studio contracts were able to leverage their fame to negotiate advantageous freelance contracts.[18] When we look at the long history of actors as contract workers, it allows us to see where studios, networks, and producers have ceded some of the control of their artistic vision and, often with the assistance of external agencies, brought in short-term workers. In the case of working actors and extras, this means considering the significance of casting agencies, talent scouts, agents, and managers as various labor brokers or gatekeepers who help to determine the careers of actors. In broader terms, it means that we should be reconfiguring how instability and labor precarity inform the process of media production.

Many sociologists and political theorists have analyzed the role of precarity in worker cultures throughout history. Sociologist Robert Castel argues that the history of wage labor is a history of insecurity.[19] Wage insecurity is also characteristic of how political theorists have defined and explored precarity as a mode of imposing social order, as distinct from offering social securities.[20] Political theorists Brett Neilson and Ned Rossiter argue, "Precarity appears as an irregular phenomenon only when set against a Fordist or Keynesian norm. . . . If we look at capitalism in a wider historical and geographical scope, it is precarity that is the norm and not Fordist economic organization."[21] In practical or organizational terms, they argue that the notion of precarity should be built into any kind of solution or plan to address capitalist development. Neilson and Rossiter explain that by challenging the periodization of precarity and understanding it as the cultural norm of labor, scholars need to rethink our understandings of labor hierarchies, spatialization of labor, and the international division of labor.

Working or journeymen actors, who have in previous eras also been called "character actors," are those actors who create characters, deliver lines, and help move plot yet fall beneath the most visible level of actor in terms of both fame and compensation. A character actor, as defined by David Thomson, is "someone who is not at the heart of a film, or, if at the center, not someone whose decisions are the crux of the drama."[22] This tier of actor has gone by a number of different names and contractual designations; whether they were called stock players, freelance actors, or character actors, this group encompasses the expansive middle ground between stars and extras. Casting directors Janet Hirshenson and Jane Jenkins identify this tier of actor as, "you've probably never heard of them, though you may well recognize their faces."[23] This middle category is much more nebulous in its definition than stars or extras. Successful character actors receive screen credit, potentially receive residuals (payment for reuse of material), and might be able to make a living from their work, but their names are not bankable enough to launch a project or guarantee its funding.

Actor Vincent D'Onofrio has been forthcoming about the life of a working actor and the limits of that success. In one interview he explained that despite his famed performance as Private Pyle in *Full Metal Jacket* (1987) and his long-running role as Detective Goren on *Law and Order: Criminal Intent* (2001–2011), his name is not "big enough" to guarantee film funding or success.[24] Speaking to this phenomena on Twitter in 2018, D'Onofrio commented to a fan, "They said I would always be Private Pyle. . . . Now I'll always be Fisk. . . . What's next? I'll always be looking for a job."[25] As these comments suggest, despite D'Onofrio's fame, he is still aware, and perhaps a bit self-conscious, that none of his past successes are guarantees of future work.

The middle class of actors constitutes a wide array of experience and financial success. D'Onofrio, despite his claims to be constantly look-ing for work, demonstrates the diversity of the "working actor" category. D'Onofrio's career has been long, and he has starred as a well-known character in a network television show in frequent syndication; many people would likely recognize his name as well as his face, but industrially speaking he does not sell a project, especially a big project for a global audience. Although Vincent D'Onofrio is by most metrics a successful actor, frequently these are the actors who rely on and benefit the most from their union.

Although jokes about actors who work as waitresses permeate popular culture, the specific stories of actors who struggle to make a full-time living are less commonly known. One example of this is Misty Upham, an ac-tress with speaking roles in *Frozen River* (2008) and *August: Osage County* (2013). While Upham regularly took auditions and got parts, she could only pay her rent by working as a housekeeper. Upham explained, "Most actors in Los Angeles, even those of us who you may vaguely recognize from a film or TV show, generally have very modest incomes. It's a secret kept alive by a media that equates all things Hollywood with decadence and fortune. In reality, many working actors live with considerable un-certainty, moving from job to job, often paid minimum fees, and if we're lucky, sporadic residuals. Health coverage is patchy, and the ability to fo-cus solely on our craft is a luxury we simply can't afford. Most of us have 'rent jobs' to make ends meet."[26]

Upham's experience of job uncertainty and journeyman work is com-mon for actors trying to build their careers while also meeting minimum work hours to maintain their union health benefits. For many women, surviving in Hollywood is not solely about making ends meet, but also surviving harassment and assault. Upham was a victim of sexual violence, living with the memories and effects of both a childhood sexual assault and an alleged rape by Harvey Weinstein's associates at the 2013 Golden Globes.[27] Even as she pursued her career, Upham was in and out of psychiatric care until her death in 2014. She died under mysterious circumstances after falling down a ravine. Her life and death are a testament to the fact that precarity, even among the glamorous actors on screen, is not just an economic condition, but can also be a serious matter of mental and physical health.

In contrast to character actors, extras, or background actors, are uncredited screen performers, a distinction with material, symbolic, and historiographic implications. There are some who do not consider background work to be acting, nor would they consider extras to be part of the story of actors. Indeed, the history of extras runs in parallel to the history of other screen actors, but there are crucial moments in which the history of extras and actors have intertwined in meaningful ways for both parties. The human background is realized in a variety of ways, but one of the most important jobs of the background actor is to work in service of the central action on screen. On set, background actors are usually managed as a group and interact with the assistant director; they need to do their jobs and, perhaps more importantly, not interfere with or slow down the film production. Although in contemporary films and television many scenes are computer-enhanced, this does not necessarily change the work of the background actor. As one *Game of Thrones* background actor, Stephen Presley, explains: "[Shooting with] the Unsullied was brutal because of the VFX tiling, where you make about 70 guys look like 100,000. You stand locked up in different positions for hours, creating this giant force . . . so they can composite it later. . . . If you stepped out of line, you could ruin the whole thing and they'd have to start over. I wound up with a slight crisp of the early stages of frostbite on my nose."[28] Presley's work in these scenes contributed to what made *Game of Thrones* cinematic and engaging for audiences, but the process of creating rich visuals was frequently boring and physically demanding.

Even though extras play an important role in realizing the mise-en-scène of a screen image, the term "extra" signifies precisely that which is additional and in excess of a film or television program. Although a mass of extras might embody certain plot points, individual extras do not propel the narrative forward. Campbell MacCulloch, general manager of

Central Casting in 1939, summed up this tension for extras, stating, "In Hollywood, no one is willing to admit that he is in the 'excess class'—no matter what his earnings or lack of earnings might be—and as a result, the situation never attains anything near balance between demand and supply."[29] This statement from 1939 sheds light on the negative implication of the term "extra" and provides insight into why, since the 2000s, this group has preferred to be designated as "background actors" within the Screen Actors Guild–American Federation of Television and Radio Artists (SAG-AFTRA).

As the examples of these actors and extras demonstrate, all actors shoulder a degree of risk to keep themselves employable in this sporadic profession, but precarity is not experienced equally by all actors. Previous success as an actor is not necessarily an indicator of stability or longevity, and even successful actors like D'Onofrio might feel uncertain about the availability of future roles (even though older men are more employable than older women). Some actors, whether through family support or because their physical characteristics make them more versatile in casting, experience precarity less acutely. Other actors, such as Misty Upham, must rely on a professional support system that offers inadequate protections and securities.

UNDERSTANDING ACTORS, UNDERSTANDING HOLLYWOOD

Below the Stars spans the history of Hollywood, showing how actors have traversed the boundaries of the media industry across media. While there are excellent historical studies that trace the cooperative relationships between film and television or other industrial synergy between media, actors offer a different view of the permeable boundaries between media.[30] The history of US media production from the perspective of actors shows how industries and institutions often viewed as separate have historically been interconnected.

The ecosystem around actors can include an array of individuals (teachers, coaches, fitness trainers, and agents) who provide services and support to actors, but it also includes organizations such as casting services and unions that provide broader and more systematic support. Unions, in addition to their function as bargaining representatives, are one of the primary forces for defining professional norms and workplace standards for actors. As such, unions have an important role in the construction of actors' labor through the development of contracts, residual processing, and professional training, which are all part of this discussion of actors. Although these bureaucratic processes are not part of the creativity, these are the means by which, in a Marxist context, labor power is transformed into a commodity. Film, art, and culture in the twentieth and twenty-first centuries are not simply produced by creative practices—they are also produced through the legal and social relations of unions and professional organizations.

The history of actors is also the history of the industrialization of Hollywood and the often-haphazard professionalization of the arts. For actors and other white-collar workers, professionalization often occurs through a process of self-definition. Both actors and extras have struggled to assert their professional identities within the media industries. In relation to media industries, Vicki Mayer has noted that the concept of the "professional" or "professionalism" is hard to define. "Unmoored from any objective criteria," she writes, "the word professional . . . has rather served as a historical articulation of status and privilege in relation to changing labor markets and their organizing hierarchies."[31] In the absence of universal ideas of what defines a profession, workers develop a professional identity collectively. Sociologist Martin Oppenheimer explains, "A profession is an occupational grouping that defines itself as a profession, declares membership limited to those meeting qualifications set by itself . . . , creates for itself a 'rationale.'"[32] Oppenheimer points out that many professions use education (and specialized degrees) as a barrier to access for jobs. Casting calls do not list criteria such as "BFA required," but they do specify whether a job is union or nonunion as a tangible barrier to entry. Although union membership helps actors claim and define a level of professionalism, membership has historically been one of the ways that the Screen Actors Guild (SAG) and the American Federation of Television and Radio Artists (AFTRA) have been successful gatekeepers to professional acting jobs.

Unions maintain their strength in the film and television industry by their ability to represent members and collectively bargain with the Alliance of Motion Picture and Television Producers (AMPTP). SAG and AFTRA (and now SAG-AFTRA) negotiate the minimum contractual terms for actors under a basic agreement. For actors, these are important documents that dictate scale (minimum compensation rates), explain what they are entitled to for their services, and define how they will be treated on set. These are different from star contracts, which are negotiated for payment beyond the basic agreement. Changes in contracts from year to year offer a history of bargaining priorities, or as Jane Gaines explains, they can "offer something significant about the history of labor relations in the film and television industry."[33] This function of contracts as a history of interests is particularly evident in the discussion of residuals, which, as chapters 2 and 3 demonstrate, underwent significant transformation from the 1950s to the 1960s as the unions transitioned from focusing on creative aspects of performance to the distribution and circulation of media.

Each chapter of this book looks at actors at four key junctures in Hollywood history, each of them a moment of industrial crisis during which the responses of on-screen labor provide a window into understanding the larger media industry economy. As several of the chapters show, technological change is frequently an important condition that sparks worker reflection and industrial change. As such, I agree with labor scholars Lois Gray and Ronald Seeber, who contend that "technology has been the source of conflict both between unions and between unions and employers."[34] I do not argue that technology determines the practices of labor, but as I make evident in this book, it is a disruptor. Acting as a craft is not dependent on technology or technical skills, but new technologies shape collective priorities and professional practices, and actors' existing cultural practices contribute to the adoption of new technologies. Lisa Gitelman's definition of technology as both a delivery system and a set of cultural protocols is particularly useful for considering how labor relates to and uses new technologies.[35] New technologies act as trigger points for laborers who need to figure out how to use them and be appropriately compensated. The fact of constant technological change is an essential feature of Hollywood as a business, and one that puts labor at a strategic disadvantage.

From the 1910s through the 1930s, creative producers and studio executives developed the efficient and well-oiled Hollywood studio system. While many actors were kept under contract—this is often identified as one of the central characteristics of the studio system—in fact, most worked as freelance actors. From extras to character actors, professional organizations in Hollywood developed around these freelance conditions. Chapter 1 looks at the emergence of Central Casting and later the SAG and Screen Extras Guild (SEG) as divergent solutions to manage the oversupply of actors. These organizations were part of the agglomeration of businesses that shaped the professional and industrial norms for actors, but they also present a fragmented history alongside Hollywood's industrial organization.

Chapter 2 looks at the heated debates among the actors' unions over television jurisdiction and presents a worker-centered history of television that contrasts with television histories focused on the expansion of infrastructure, creation of new programming, or development of a mass audience. Assumptions about television as a technology shaped many of the negotiations over television contracts. Labor discussions in the 1940s used medium-specific language to understand the nature of television work. Although the language of these conversations frequently emphasized technology, I demonstrate how these debates served to carve out cultural territories and distinctions. Archival materials inform my analysis of the debates between the East Coast and West Coast labor unions that helped establish television acting's professional standards and compensation, as well as some of the key distinctions between film and television at the precise moment when television was developing its industrial niche. Whereas the practices and norms for the film actor largely developed in response to the demands of Hollywood producers and directors, the unions and the numerous bicoastal disputes played an active role in shaping the conditions for television actors.

Since the earliest days of television negotiations, actors and union leadership expressed concerns about how recorded media would be replayed and continue to generate profit. This unease was rooted in the troubling idea that improvements in technology would lower the demand for labor. The importance of second-run syndication, commonly known as reruns, emerged when there was a new market for second-run material in the 1950s and expanded with new markets in the coming decades. The period of economic recession in the 1970s and 1980s and the culture of deregulation helped to expand the number and influence of cable networks. Old content found new life on broadcast, newly expanded cable networks, and later home video. While studios and producers profited from new distribution avenues, actors negotiated, struggled, and struck to get a share of these profits. Chapter 3 considers how actors came to understand the importance of residuals and incorporate a formula for profit participation into their collective bargaining agreements. The ever-expanding industry and changing technologies encouraged the reuse of media content and shifted actors' conversations to emphasize the monetary value of a performance over time.

The availability of digital tools, increased demands of "flexibility" and "multitasking" in digital workplaces, and the expansion of digital content distribution have posed significant challenges to cultural and contractual definitions of work in media union cultures. In chapter 4, I look at the relationship between actors and digital content by considering voice actors and the transformations in the casting process. Online casting sites and the increased accessibility of media-making tools and distribution platforms have created new opportunities for aspirants to maintain public visibility and connect with industry players. The availability of digital technology has impacted all actors and placed greater demands on them to multitask and self-promote, but, as this chapter demonstrates, this transformation in auditioning, casting, and booking roles has been especially evident in the field of voice acting, where many actors work on some of the least-regulated types of projects.

Below the Stars traces bottom-up histories of Hollywood through its largest and most visible workers. Since the demise of the vertically integrated studio system, Hollywood, like many other industries, has moved toward an increasingly flexible workforce. Hollywood's demand for a wide pool of potential actors is undoubtedly why many people have stories like that of my grandfather; stories of family members, friends, or their own personal experiences acting in television shows or working in the background of a film. These interpersonal connections to media perpetuate the myth that anyone can find fame, or at least visibility, in Hollywood. As media scholars and audience members, we should take seriously the kind of ideological work that this performs; it deepens our personal relationship to media content, but it also works against the idea that on-screen work is a job strictly for professionals.

ONE

HOLLYWOOD FREELANCE

How Actors and Extras Shaped the Film Industry

*I do not find it democratic to put 50 percent of our actors on a
yearly contract—providing them and their families abundantly
with food and shelter, while the other 50 percent, just as
good actors, have to go with their families to the gutter.*

BELA LUGOSI TO SAG EXECUTIVE SECRETARY
KENNETH THOMSON, FEBRUARY 26, 1938

In the film industry's earliest decades many actors moved between work
on the stage and work on screen. For those working in different performance venues, such as Wallace Beery, this was a juggling act requiring
shifts in performance styles, genres, and locations. In its section on "Brevi-
ties in the Business," *Motography* observed, "Wallace Beery, the 'Sweedie'
of Essanay's comedy company, made a lightning jump into the leading
part in a dramatic production. . . . In just one hour and fifteen minutes
he had familiarized himself with his part. . . . He finished the week in the
part without neglecting his screen work."[1] This description is indicative of
much of Beery's career as he filled in on the stage, took on bigger theatrical roles, played comedic characters in the film industry, and later gained
prominence as a "heavy" in genre films.

After performances around the country, a career in the circus, and
numerous well-known roles in silent shorts, Beery, who was dubbed by
an Oklahoma paper as "the greatest free lancer of them all," eventually
signed a studio contract with Paramount and set down roots as an actor
in Hollywood. This article marks the first newspaper usage of the term
"free lancer" to describe a person in the film industry available for projects
rather than someone working under contract. Beery was an exceptional
case because he eventually transitioned from freelance performer to star
actor—by the 1930s, he was a regular on the *Motion Picture Herald*'s list of

top box-office draws.[2] However, his early career experience was exceedingly common, in that freelance work was a condition of labor so firmly established by 1924 that it necessitated a special noun. In the early twentieth century the term "freelance" provided a shorthand to distinguish short-term from long-term contracts, but it was also a way of describing how actors navigated their career paths and built their livelihoods by moving between roles on stage to roles on screen and taking on multiple, short-term, project-specific contracts. For actors like Beery, a freelance life was not a hindrance to a successful career, but a privilege that allowed him professional flexibility akin to bigger stars.[3] However, those who had freelance careers included a range of "classes" of actor, from extras to working actors to stars, each with distinct and different professional needs. Those who never attained star status influenced how Hollywood management talked about and surveilled actors in future decades and ultimately why actors unionized.

From the late teens and through the studio era, screen actors could work for the major studios or find work with small independents producing B-movies. Aspirants with no experience moved from around the country alongside experienced actors who left the theater in New York to work on screen in Hollywood. The primary challenge facing these actors during the formative years of the studio system was breaking in—which many assumed they could do through extras work. However, the competition for background spots and small roles was fierce. Depending on the source, there were between eleven thousand and eighteen thousand extras throughout the 1920s, which means approximately 2 to 3 percent of Los Angeles residents during that decade were registered as extras.[4] Some actors worked their way up through the studio system; Iris Adrian initially took roles as a chorus girl and continued to get small roles in subsequent decades, while others were discovered by scouts or from extra work.[5] By the 1920s, agents were playing a more significant role in vetting and placing talent.[6] Regardless of how actors got their starts, they likely passed through one or several studio gatekeepers that were often invisible to the general public. In the 1910s and 1920s, various private companies emerged to provide additional services for those freelance actors and extras who were still on the margins of the studio system. Actors and extras who tried to get a toehold in the industry found themselves faced with exploitative schemes and somewhat dubious middlemen. Those who were working sporadically faced a different set of challenges, as they navigated the industry without a formal support network that would allow them to air grievances or hold studio heads, producers, or directors accountable for their abuses. It is in these gaps outside of studio control that we can begin to see the business of filmmaking transform away from control by studios and toward a future of independent producers and contract workers.

The businesses and services that emerged in Los Angeles developed in part to serve working actors and aspirants, but frequently actors' services, such as Central Casting, developed in response to audience concerns about social welfare. In Hollywood's early decades many professional standards and norms were in flux and often hotly contested by industry forces, but acting was unique because there was tremendous public interest in this profession. Central Casting is a key example of a company that emerged from public outrage and subsequent studio concerns about Hollywood's public image rather than the problems that actors faced. In the 1920s, the major studios were embroiled in an array of public scandals, some of which were linked to the perceived safety and well-being of Hollywood's oversupply of labor, specifically the ubiquitous Hollywood extra girl. Feminist historians of Hollywood have shown how concerns for the safety and well-being of the extra girl, a modern woman navigating the big city, captured the popular imagination.[7] Public outcry over the safety of the extra girl reached a tipping point after Roscoe "Fatty" Arbuckle's alleged rape and murder of starlet Virginia Rappe. The Arbuckle-Rappe incident had a direct impact on actors, specifically, how they found work and how they reported labor grievances. In the aftermath of the trial, the studios attempted to consolidate management and cooperate across studios to manage actors and oversee the supply and demand of on-screen labor. The solutions did not organically emerge from actors, but came instead from studios looking for ways to minimize public controversy. Adrienne McLean has noted that the Arbuckle-Rappe scandal is often cited as an example of how Hollywood manipulated current events to justify creating institutions like Central Casting to control and keep the regulation of extras within the industry (rather than ceding power to unions).[8] The formation of Central Casting demonstrates that the challenges facing actors generated wide-ranging interest beyond the regional confines of Hollywood, and that the professional infrastructure for actors has been historically determined alongside broader responses from outside interests.

The infrastructure that surrounded screen actors is a significant part of the development of Los Angeles as a place and Hollywood as an industry, but one that complicates the assumptions of the studio system as a Fordist mode of mass production dominated by hierarchically organized film studios. In contrast to this characterization, geographer Allen J.

Scott identifies the development of Hollywood as "an idiosyncratic super-structure of institutions in response to diverse needs for coordination and collective order" as a key characteristic of the formation of "industrial clusters."[9] Scott's analysis of business clusters primarily focuses on how groupings of businesses emerged to enhance industrial efficiency, and in the case of media, how these clusters incidentally offer a space for creative collaboration. Many smaller businesses emerged to address precarity among the bloated labor force of screen actors, but these businesses, led by what Andrew Dawson describes as a "class of petty entrepreneurs," often failed to resolve the infrastructural problems they addressed.[10]

In the 1930s, actors contributed to the development of professional standards and norms through their newly formed Screen Actors Guild. Although studios attempted to thwart unionization, SAG and later the Screen Extras Guild often aligned with Stanley Aronowitz's critique that unions in the United States essentially function as "a force for integrating the workers into the corporate capitalist system."[11] The Hollywood studio system was dominated by white men, from the decision-makers to the below-the-line workers.[12] In essence, while SAG (and later SEG) helped establish essential contract minimums and safety standards, and occasionally expressed concern for the lack of work for black actors, they did not consistently try to change structural inequities in the Hollywood system or their own union. As actor Frances Williams noted, "The Screen Extras Guild had black members who were almost never hired."[13] What Williams observed was a function of Hollywood filmmaking reflecting racism of the era, but also union policies that restricted black members. Thus while unions ushered in some important professional standards, they also affirmed Hollywood's systemic whiteness.

The story of actors during the studio system is one of inefficiencies both in relation to studio dealings and intra-actor conflicts. Actors and extras traversed Hollywood oftentimes with minimal interactions with the studios, yet in the public eye the studios were the ones accountable for the well-being of these underemployed workers. Actors and extras also frequently navigated unemployment with minimal connection to other actors who might offer support during this process. This chapter looks at Central Casting, which sought to provide public accountability for the perceived problems facing extras, and the Screen Actors Guild, which united actors in their shared experiences. Central to the industrial story of actors in Hollywood is how the powerful but often disinterested studios tried to create new systems to rationalize the work of freelance actors and extras in a way that allowed studios to efficiently monitor these workers.

Actors seeking work in this period maintained frequent communication with employment companies, union organizers, and other representatives of their newly formed union. As such, archival documents from these institutions and organizations produce records of actors' ideas about their creative and working lives as they unfolded. Material from the Margaret Herrick Library, SAG-AFTRA Archive, and the Wisconsin Center for Film and Theater Research provide much of the archival foundation in this chapter. Documents relating to Central Casting have been more elusive. SAG-AFTRA maintains a scrapbook of newspaper clippings about Central Casting that illustrate the relationship between the union and this service. Although Central Casting was important to the membership, the unions did not oversee the casting from this office. Central Casting was administered by the studios until it was purchased by Production Payments, Inc. in 1976.[14] As a privately owned company, its archival materials remain unavailable to public archives. Similarly, there is little or no material on some of the failed unions discussed in this chapter. For these records, I rely largely on newspapers and, where possible, publicity documents, to understand where these organizations fit within the larger ecosystem of actors, with the understanding that the public face of these organizations offers a limited and often rosy perspective on decisions and efforts made on behalf of actors and extras. The histories of a studio-funded casting company and a worker-led union are fundamentally different and illustrate how Hollywood's industrialization was a fragmentary process shaped by studio leadership and workers.

ACTORS' INEQUITY

While many studies of classical Hollywood and the studio system stress the ways that filmmaking became more modernized from the 1910s through the 1930s, the experiences of extras and freelance actors tell a different story. Despite Hollywood's increasingly standardized and rationalized business practices, many actors on the fringe of the industry experienced work in variegated ways. Descriptions and accounts from nonstar actors are necessarily anecdotal and fragmented. The specific details of how actors navigated Hollywood, casting calls, and film productions in the 1910s and 1920s—actors' experiences and stories—provide an important foundation for how executives and unions understood performers' challenges and hardships, and how they shaped industrial responses and business strategies to negotiate them.

The working conditions and struggles for extras were well documented by journalists of the time. Although journalists were fascinated with the plight of the extra, there are scant personal accounts of this experience, with one notable exception in the Leo Rosencrans Collection at the Margaret Herrick Library. Several of the struggles faced by extras are encapsulated by Leo Rosencrans's brief foray into the movie business, which he recounted in letters to his parents. Like many men and women in the 1910s, Rosencrans had what he referred to as a "malady after the movies."[15] He did not want to live a fast or glamorous lifestyle. He had a college education and was a religious man who often wrote home to his family in Ohio about Sunday Bible classes and his hopes that California would ban alcohol and become a "dry" state. But he was also an avid reader of motion-picture magazines, and it was his love of movies that drove him to Hollywood with the hope of directing motion pictures. Rosencrans was not naïve—he did not think it would be easy to break into the film business. His first order of business when he arrived in 1916 was to meet with a friend of a friend, a production manager named Nash.[16] Nash worked at the Selig Polyscope Company, an Edendale studio that made numerous jungle films and westerns from 1896 to 1918 (and notably launched "Fatty" Arbuckle's career). Nash promised Rosencrans that he would call him if any work opened up at Selig, but advised the inexperienced twenty-year-old aspiring director that he should find work as an extra and observe as much as possible before trying to find a permanent job in the film industry.[17]

Rosencrans's positive attitude toward the movie business was not enough to help him find employment or sustain him through a lengthy job search. On an average day he would wake up in his downtown apartment at 6 a.m. and walk to the nearby Free Employment Bureau, an organization that posted film and nonfilm jobs. After checking the work notices, he would take a car to Hollywood and solicit six different studios before catching the bus for Universal City. At 3 p.m. he would return to Hollywood and revisit all the studios in search of work.[18] When Rosencrans was unable to find work at the studios, he paid to join the California Motion Pictures Producers and Actors Exchange (which claimed to be an employment agency for numerous studios). These employment agencies often oversold their services; as Rosencrans explained: "the Exchange . . . although claiming to be in touch with 16 studios, in reality had but that one, so they really acted as an employment agency for Signal."[19] Leo Rosencrans seemed to be doing everything correctly. He was using his connections, diligently checking job postings, and making his rounds of the studios. Unfortunately for him, getting work in the film industry was not simply about hard work or persistence.

In 1916, work in the film industry was competitive, and for extras trying to launch careers in the industry, it was not only hard to come by but also poorly compensated. If an aspiring actor was lucky enough to get work, he or she still might not be able to pay basic expenses. Rosencrans claimed he could have made between one dollar and three dollars per day (plus lunch and car fare)—or up to five dollars per day if he was willing to do dangerous stunts (which he was not willing to do)—but these rates were unreliable.[20] In a letter home to his parents, Rosencrans explained, "The wages paid to extras have been cut at least 1/2 in the last two or three months. Instead of $3, they now pay $1.00 and $1.25 and dinner, and carfare. I have earned altogether thus far $5.25—not so much, but as Mr. Nash said—I am going to school (practically) and getting experience, and being paid for it at the same time."[21] When Rosencrans found work, his compensation was meager and unpredictable, with little transparency as to what determined the fluctuations. When wages were cut, extras received no explanation; they simply had to make do. Even though Rosencrans's letters suggest a frugal lifestyle, his wages as an extra were not sufficient to rent a room at the YMCA (which cost between $2.50 and $5 per week). According to letters, his savings, work as an extra, and supplementary job earnings barely covered the rent of his small room (one dollar per week) and his food.

Despite his struggles, Rosencrans maintained an optimistic outlook. Since work as an extra was inconsistent and underpaid, he supplemented his income by working briefly in a printing office and later by stuffing newspapers at the *Los Angeles Times*. However, after almost a month of life as an extra, Rosencrans was beginning to exhibit signs of frustration. In a letter to his parents in November 1916, he explained, "I've lost a lot of the 'romance' I entertained concerning the Movies, and probably could settle down now into some 'real work.' I should like this business if I was one of the big ones, but the life of the extra is mostly, in the parlance of the crew—'coffee, and ———.' They mean, you have to live on coffee and doughnuts."[22] Ultimately, working as an extra could not support the lifestyle Rosencrans wanted. Like many of his contemporaries, he struggled to find stable work and establish a professional identity in the film industry, and after four months he returned home to Ohio.

Leo Rosencrans is simply one example among thousands of extras who tried to break into Hollywood in the 1910s. Rosencrans's attempts to find work were usually unsuccessful, but many of those who were able to work consistently as extras found the work demanding. As Sean Holmes points out, extras were often "required . . . to do more than an extra's work, refused . . . payment for retakes, or cut . . . from the payroll without compensation when a film was running over budget."[23] Extras accepted these terms based on the assumption that there was no other alternative for those who were trying to break into the business during these early decades.

As Rosencrans traveled from studio to studio looking for work, there was nothing he could do to distinguish his skill or ability; he had to rely on whether his appearance suited the needs of the film. For extras, physical appearance was of central importance for finding work. Several decades later a 1930s pamphlet bluntly declared, "Generally speaking, extra work does not need TALENT; it needs TYPE."[24] Type, as Richard Dyer has explained, is "any simple, vivid, memorable, easily grasped and widely recognized characterization in which a few traits are foregrounded."[25] Pamela Robertson Wojcik expands on Dyer's definition of type to clarify that it can mean a stereotype, social type, or regional type; however, with respect to unspeaking extras, type typically relates to physical characteristics or markers of identity such as race or gender.[26] Emphasis on type underscores the importance of specialization and division of labor in the industry's formative years; Hollywood producers needed not only bodies for the background, but also access to diversity that would suit any and all creative needs.

Extras were primarily in demand for large crowd scenes, which meant that Hollywood films needed people to fill in a neutral background. In 1926, only a year after opening, Central Casting reported that within a six-month period, thirty out of the six thousand registered female actors averaged three days of work per week, in contrast with the sixty-four (out of five thousand) registered male actors who reached this average.[27] A few years later, Central Casting reported increases to their placements, but a significant gender disparity persisted between 140,901 male roles versus 67,515 female roles.[28] This disparity in casting is largely due to the fact that men were in higher demand for neutral background scenes. Although women came to Hollywood in droves, opportunities for extras work were scarce.[29]

Despite limited job opportunities, industrial discourse was often inclusive, emphasizing Hollywood's need for a variety of people of all races, sizes, ages, and skills for their changing aesthetic and entertainment demands. In one of the earliest scholarly treatments of Hollywood unions, Murray Ross offers an explanation for why Hollywood welcomed all aspirants with open arms: "To turn back an aspiring extra who is probably an enthusiastic fan and thereby antagonize all his friends is bad business."[30]

While this is partially true, Hollywood did in fact need a range of extras to fill roles. As Anthony Slide notes, people of color were often used in specific genre cycles, for example, Native Americans in westerns. When studios failed to find enough "types," as was the case in 1913 when director Thomas Ince needed more Native Americans for a western, studios recruited nonactors to work and fill these roles.[31] For many people of color, this was the only work in Hollywood that was readily available. Although there were hundreds of black actors looking for work in Hollywood in the 1920s, Charlene Regester explains, "For African-Americans, being employed in white Hollywood meant being employed as an extra."[32] Studios seeking out a variety of different appearances and narrowing extras to type effectively helped create a surplus of labor. From the perspective of those seeking work, this could be particularly disempowering, because actors could not assert skill or experience as leverage.

Since extras work was determined based on physical characteristics, producers and directors could offer it as a perk available to those with connections in the industry or those who lived in Los Angeles but harbored no larger aspirations in the film industry. Producers and directors would cast family members or friends or sometimes find kids off the street (including my own grandfather, William Fortmueller) for background roles rather than holding casting calls or consulting employment bureaus. Those in charge of casting "background," including production assistants like Leigh Smith (who worked with D. W. Griffith), kept notes of their favorite extras with names, ages, and phone numbers for quick reference.[33] Getting work as an extra favored those who were known within the system, whether that was through familial relationships, friendships, or social networks. The importance of personal relationships and connections as a means for actors to gain entry in the industry established a dangerous culture and precedent for women seeking roles. The late 1910s saw a variety of "casting couch" scandals, in which directors and producers used their positions to take advantage of aspiring stars, positioning Hollywood as a predatory environment, with young women as the prey.[34] The lack of any clear path for a successful career meant that actresses often misunderstood (or perhaps understood all too well) what it would take to find success in Hollywood.

In the absence of clear entry points for employment, screen-acting aspirants looked for anyone offering potential assistance. In the 1910s and 1920s, extras earned low wages (occasionally for dangerous work) and frequently spent the little money they earned paying into exploitative agencies like the California Motion Pictures Producers and Actors Exchange that Leo Rosencrans joined, which claimed to have relationships with studios that could help actors find work. Stories about these agencies seem to indicate that they were largely unhelpful for extras, but they did provide the important service of handling studios' nonessential hiring for individual projects. Off-loading the responsibility of this task was ultimately more efficient for the studios, even if these agencies generated problems for workers. The decision to cede control to external networks provides further evidence how studios eschewed the Fordist system. Staffing agencies in Hollywood worked for-profit, and they worked for the benefit of the studios rather than the workers. These businesses retained power in Hollywood because extras were desperate for work and there were few alternatives offering guidance to find it.

The extras' casting agencies—including the two largest examples, the Service Bureau and Screen Talent—claimed that they could help people find extra work, but extras usually found their own jobs, with these agencies primarily functioning as check-cashing facilities. Studios refused to pay extras legal tender (cash or checks) and instead compensated extras with vouchers. Extras' agencies acted as middlemen between the studios and the extras, since the only way to redeem these vouchers was to go to one of the agencies, which would, for a fee, exchange the voucher for cash.[35] By paying extras in this way, studios effectively sustained the existence of these agencies that failed to provide the additional job and casting services they claimed to offer. Extras recognized the exploitative strategy behind this system, but they did not have any other options for redeeming the vouchers. Despite complaints, the Service Bureau continued to charge extras service fees for voucher redemption (regardless of whether extras used them as a casting service or not), and frustration with the Service Bureau mounted. As evidenced by internal memos and newspaper articles, many industry leaders, union organizers, and journalists were aware of extras' working conditions in the 1910s and 1920s, which resulted in several attempts to organize extras between 1914 and 1924. However, despite recognition of the problems, even active attempts to change the system were entirely unsuccessful.

In contrast to extras, character actors and supporting players faced issues with work hours and overtime that paralleled struggles between workers and management in other professions. Producers often engaged in some creative juggling to make sure they did not overuse actors on short-term daily or weekly contracts. Actors retained under freelance contracts were only paid while they were shooting. As Sean Holmes remarks, these contracts included clauses that required actors to be available for reshoots or new additional scenes, and "studios often took advantage of such clauses, laying actors off with the full knowledge that they would need their services again and calling them back later for what they claimed were 'added scenes' so that they did not have to pay them for the duration of a shoot."[36] Actor Wedgwood Nowell complained that studios would lay off actors to stop paying them and later call them back for new scenes.[37] Actors had very little leverage in setting the terms of these freelance contracts, and it would also seem they had even less control over their work on set. Working freelance actors were frequently subject to different creative scheduling practices aimed at maximizing work time within the bounds of an actor's daily or weekly contract. Speaking to the speed of filmmaking, Anita Garvin remembered making two-reel films at Christie Film Company in two to three days.[38] In a letter to Actors Equity Association (AEA) Nowell described the process of "rotation shooting," writing,

> Various "sets" in the picture are erected in such order as to permit the studio to absolutely "clean up" all scenes with a given actor or actress who receives, say, $2,900 weekly. This player is "railroaded" right through those sets which are ready and waiting . . . Just as they are concluding the scenes with the $2,900 player, then and only then do they start the next highest player . . . then they take up the next salary. If these two have scenes together these scenes are the *last* played by the *first* player and the *first* played by the *second* player.[39]

Whether or not this was a widespread practice, what Nowell observed reflects the values of efficiency in the Fordist film industry. This process unmistakably resembles an assembly line practice, in which goods (such as a Model T Ford) move through different stations or specialized machines on the way to completion. In this case, however, actors functioned as the object moving down the line. Rather than bringing the product to the workers, Hollywood workers were tasked with going to the action. Whereas each step along an assembly line could be completed in mere minutes, each scene and take could stretch on for much longer, and the entire shoot might be a physically exhausting process that could go on for hours. This type of scheduling allowed producers to maximize an actor's workday and avoid paying them beyond their contracted time.

Representatives of management also clearly understood these practices to be a problem. In a letter to Will Hays, the chairman of the Motion Picture Producers and Distributors Association (MPPDA), Fred Beetson, secretary-treasurer of the Association of Motion Picture Producers (AMPP), reported his understanding of an actor's working conditions after meeting with a small group of actors (Wallace Beery among them), explaining, "the freelance actor, especially the smaller fellow, does get a pretty raw deal . . . some cases of a man starting on Sunday and finishing on the following Sunday, working one or two nights, and being paid for a week [actors should have been paid overtime for Sundays and nights]. These poor fellows are fearful of reporting the matter to this office due to the imaginary bogey of the black list."[40] Beetson's remarks are consistently sympathetic to actors and their working conditions, even though he offers no solutions and goes on in the letter to sympathize with the need for producers to keep costs of productions low.

These individual stories construct a grim picture of labor conditions in which extras and actors had very little autonomy over their careers. Hollywood's emphasis on "type" meant that a wide array of hopefuls navigated Hollywood with the hope that they could bring something unique to the movie business. Those left out of the studio mode of production fended for themselves as they navigated exploitative businesses masquerading as part of the film industry. The problems of the extras were compounded by the fact that they were being exploited by several organizations simultaneously, including casting agencies, employment bureaus, and acting schools, which all falsely claimed to help actors find work while charging them a fee or a percentage of their earnings. As outsiders looking for an entryway, most of their contact with the industry came through ancillary businesses acting as gatekeepers. Many of the studios benefited from these businesses and had no interest in changing the system. Those actors who found themselves with semiregular employment were unable to advocate for themselves out of fear that they would be thrust into the realms of unemployment. As the stories of extras and actors in the early decades of the film industry demonstrate, unemployment was a common experience, with unique dynamics for each actor. This culture provided a fertile landscape for ancillary businesses and employment brokers to sprout up, offering promises of assistance and future employment. The relationship between precarious labor and exploitative external agencies is an important element of Hollywood history and an example of how the ecosystem of film-related businesses grew around Los Angeles.

ORGANIZING EXTRAS

Long hours, inconsistent work, low pay, and shady ancillary businesses were some of the pressing issues facing freelance actors and extras in the burgeoning Hollywood studio system. In the 1910s and early 1920s, amid strikes by studio workers and unionization attempts among workers in other industries, labor organizers sought to unionize extras. Efforts were focused on extras because this group seemed to collectively suffer the worst labor abuses, and organizers assumed they would be receptive. One of the unique challenges to organizing extras was that they faced abuses from studios as well as ancillary businesses that decentralized some of the work of casting extras. What organizers also failed to account for in their efforts was that some extras, especially aspiring actors, often saw more differences than similarities between their experiences and those of more established actors, and were thus willing to endure the normalized hardships of a competitive industry. Although extras were one of many groups striking, extras were less committed to unionization, and these efforts were less successful than those of studio craft workers, a fact that reveals how the aspirational nature of extras work undermines their collective identity as workers.

The attempts to organize Hollywood workers were part of a larger labor effort to organize workers in the staunchly "open shop" or nonunion city of Los Angeles.[41] As a city that lured many businesses with the promise of cheap nonunion labor before the 1935 passage of the Wagner Act, which protected unions and the right to organize, the fights for better working conditions were violent and often unsuccessful. Unionization would inevitably mean that workdays would be shorter and actors would receive higher pay, but this would result in higher production costs—and studios were strongly opposed to anything that would impact their financial bottom line. Steven Ross notes that given these high financial stakes, the studios hired spies to infiltrate (and undermine) union meetings.[42] The meetings and strikes that were part of unionization efforts were risky, and as a result they were often initiated by organizers working with a variety of unions rather than by working extras.

Union organizers took note of the conditions for the extras who wandered between the Free Employment Bureau, California Motion Picture Producers and Actors Exchange, and other private employment placement agencies in downtown Los Angeles to find background work. The Industrial Workers of the World (IWW), which, as Steven Ross points out, attempted to unionize extras at Universal Film Company as early as 1914, led the extras to strike after Universal refused to increase wages from one dollar to two or three dollars per day.[43] The IWW's efforts to unionize extras were unsuccessful. One of the challenges for extras was that they were organizing against the decentralized power of private employment agencies and studio management, which created unique challenges for strikers addressing multiple entities.

The Los Angeles local of the International Alliance of Theatrical and Stage Employees (IATSE), despite having to contend with multiple jurisdictional disputes, was more successful in its efforts. Only a few years later, World War I generated increased film production and some labor shortages throughout the industry.[44] These conditions allowed some workers and nascent unions to leverage themselves into more powerful positions in relation to management. The results from strikes and labor organizing, however, were mixed. Emboldened by the increased demand for labor and the diminished supply of available workers, the Los Angeles local of IATSE led a successful strike in 1918 that won their membership of theater workers an increase in wages.[45] However, studio craft workers still made less than construction workers in Los Angeles.[46] Disputes between management and labor erupted throughout the film industry in the period after World War I, and actors were no exception to this trend. In 1918 a new group, the Motion Picture Players Union (MPPU), rallied extras under the leadership of union organizer A. B. Dale, who had previously attempted to organize railway workers.[47] The MPPU was particularly concerned with inconsistent wages; it advocated for a standard three dollars per day rate and criticized the casting agencies that were taking a percentage of extras' minimal wages.[48] In their October 1919 resolution (which had also been presented at the American Federation of Labor [AFL] Convention in June 1919), the members of the MPPU came out against two particular agencies, the Motion Picture Producers Service Bureau (known simply as the Service Bureau) and Screen Talent, both of which took a 7 percent cut of actors' wages and provided little by way of job support.[49] The MPPU wanted to eliminate exploitative casting agencies, but the union had its own struggles garnering enough support to maintain their status as an autonomous union. Although the MPPU advocated for changes in the casting process and an increase in wages, they were not able to facilitate job placement for extras, which for many was the most pressing concern.

As less essential than actors with speaking roles, extras had less power than members of the crafts. Within the film industry, the lack of leverage made it difficult for a union of extras to find a place at the bargaining table with the studios. Even though extras shared the screen with stars, they had a dramatically different experience of the industry. Sam Stoloff writes about stars in the 1920s, "[stars'] work cannot be reduced to an abstract labor power precisely because their value as 'stars' depends on qualities that they uniquely possess. They are simultaneously workers and branded products: their labor is worth what their brand image will sell."[50] Stoloff's analysis of stars and their value provides a counterpoint to the labor power of extras. Unlike stars, extras do not possess unique qualities or brands. In fact, the labor of extras only has value if extras can blend seamlessly into the background. As such, their only power could come from collective efforts. For extras to achieve their collective goals, they would need the help of actors with more power. Thus the MPPU's work as a separate entity for extras was short-lived. By February 1920 the theater actor's union, Actor's Equity Association (AEA), had subsumed the MPPU and taken on the struggle to advocate for extras in the face of these exploitative labor agencies, although with minimal success.[51]

AEA's primary goal was to help extras find jobs and obtain their full daily rate. The problem for AEA was that they were forced to compete with the exploitative casting agencies. In many cases these casting agencies undercut the rates that AEA was trying to establish. For example, a studio would ask AEA to provide a list of actors for ten dollars per day, and the Service Bureau would then swoop in and find people to work for five dollars per day.[52] Rather than taking a firm stance to advocate against these agencies, AEA offered essentially the same services, but at undesirable rates for the studios. As a union that was established for and by theater actors, AEA was ill-equipped to work with screen actors and underestimated extras' willingness to work for low pay.

The failures on the part of organized labor meant that extras were still struggling to gain a toehold in the industry in the early 1920s. Feeling disenfranchised, extras filed complaints with the California State Labor Commission, mostly against the Service Bureau and Screen Talent.[53] The State Labor Commission began its investigation in January 1923, resolving two months later that these agencies needed to reform in order to maintain their business licenses. However, this mandate had no effect on business practices. On March 15, 1923, two hundred extras went to the Service Bureau offices in downtown Los Angeles to collect their daily wages. When they arrived, they were told that they were going to receive three dollars instead of five dollars for their work. The angry crowd began to protest outside the Service Bureau. The anger eventually led to gunfire and several injuries; one of those wounded, Earl L. Davis, was shot in the back.[54]

The strikes and violence were bad enough to raise the attention of state officials and industry leaders, but this did not translate into clear collective action on the part of actors. The conflicts between workers, extras agencies, and studios could have galvanized workers and led them to AEA, but that was not the case. AEA's failure to effectively unite its base against industry abuses demonstrates that this theatrical union was ineffective for film actors, and that no other union or organizer had emerged to compete with AEA for jurisdiction over extras. These early unionization failures underscore the unique challenges of organizing and representing a population with no real leverage—even when they are being exploited.

FROM THE CASTING COUCH TO CENTRAL CASTING

Actors struggled through myriad workplace abuses throughout the 1910s and 1920s related to job availability, hours, and compensation, but the sexual exploitation of aspiring actresses, which would later be known as "casting couch" scandals, were the ones that captured the national imaginary and would come to expose Hollywood's pervasive labor problems.[55] In the 1920s, amid growing societal concern for women's virtue in the modern city, the issue of morality, rather than wages and working conditions, was what jolted the studios into short-lived action. As Denise McKenna observes, "The question of a daily wage was one of the central problems for extras, yet this issue emerges more frequently in relation to male extras as a question of a living wage, while for female extras the issue of wages was still tied to questions of morality."[56] McKenna's astute comment about the uniquely gendered problem of labor could perhaps help to explain why the studio solutions to labor problems, like Central Casting, were deeply unsatisfying for decades to come. Rather than focusing on labor conditions, Hollywood preoccupied itself with its symbolic moral image to the world in ways that remained tangential to the material realities of labor conditions in the screen industry.

In *Hollywood Babylon*, filmmaker Kenneth Anger juxtaposes real-life Hollywood sex scandals and the sordid gossip which emerges out of a system of artistic production that exploits both the land and the masses of aspiring stars. For Anger, much of Hollywood excess stems from the availability of workers and the abundance of money. The 1920s was a rich and unchecked breeding ground for potentially deviant behavior: Wallace Reid's heroin overdose, William Desmond Taylor's murder (and affairs with both Mabel Normand and Mary Miles Minter), and the alleged bigamy between Mary Pickford and Douglas Fairbanks all contributed to the city's and industry's growing image as a cesspool of immorality. While these scandals influenced public perceptions of Hollywood films and Hollywood as an industry, the infamous Fatty Arbuckle scandal was the one that most contributed to the transformation of labor practices and policies for extras and Hollywood hopefuls. In 1921, Arbuckle went to San Francisco with two friends, director Fred Fishback and actor Lowell Sherman, to escape Hollywood and carouse. Virginia Rappe, a former model and aspiring star, made the same trip with two friends (Alfred Semnacher and Maude Delmont) for a weekend getaway. Fishback knew Rappe, and when he realized that Rappe was also in town, he invited her and her friends to a party in Arbuckle's adjoining suites. The party lasted throughout the evening, and during the revelry Rappe ended up in a locked room with Arbuckle; what happened in that locked room has since been a source of distortion and conjecture. The day after the party Rappe became very ill, and she died three days later. The cause of death was later determined to be peritonitis, or a ruptured bladder.[57] The press perpetuated the story that Rappe's peritonitis came from being raped with foreign objects (including champagne bottles), a story that generated apprehension about the safety of the young women who traveled to Hollywood to work in what was beginning to seem like an immoral industry. The scandal surrounding Rappe's death was also tied up with broader societal fears about the role of women in modernity; as Hilary Hallett explains, "Standing in as modernity's scapegoat, Hollywood represented the most powerful force luring the nation's daughters far outside the home."[58] Whereas other Hollywood scandals seemed to be examples of bad behavior among the wealthy Hollywood establishment, what happened in San Francisco was different because Rappe was not a star, and she was perceived as a victim of this corrupt environment.

The Arbuckle-Rappe scandal exemplified the perceived fate of the vulnerable, small-town, and easily exploited "movie struck girl" wandering the streets of Los Angeles (despite the fact that the alleged crime occurred in San Francisco). The scandal put actors and their off-screen lives on display for the national audience and seemed to confirm that women's participation in modern culture (especially Hollywood culture) would inevitably lead to sexual exploitation. The details of the evening were heavily publicized and embellished, but the result was an increased public concern for women's safety—especially those who were not working under the watchful eye of the studio.

Studio leadership interpreted the Arbuckle-Rappe scandal as evidence of a need for greater control over all facets of the industry, and thus for a consolidation of studio power. The studios' logic was that greater studio efficiency and stronger management, all of which would be mediated by new and existing technologies, would solve the industry's public image problems. The main challenge was implementing new procedures across the studios (whatever they might be) and acclimating actors to new professional norms and routines. Although studio heads were clearly aware of the problems, they did not immediately look to reform existing Hollywood practices. Three years after the Arbuckle-Rappe scandal, the Russell Sage Foundation, an organization established to study working conditions across the United States, generated a report, "Outstanding Problems in the Human Relations and Employment Conditions in the Motion Picture Industry," that jump-started the industry and forced it to find a solution. The report called for a mechanism to track available workers and available jobs in the film industry. Through the Motion Picture Producers and Distributors Association (MPPDA), studio leadership used the scandals and the Russell Sage Foundation study as justifications for greater controls and moral safeguards over workers in the film industry. Studio heads, worried about their business's public image and potential union interference, attempted to resolve problems with their own resources as swiftly as possible.

As labor tensions continued to mount alongside Hollywood morality scandals, the industry looked for new ways to manage the image of their business, but not to the extent that these changes would disrupt Los Angeles's status as the "open shop" center of the United States or undermine production costs. In April 1925, Association of Motion Picture Producers secretary Fred W. Beetson sent a letter to all members of AMPP. He had met with the California state labor commissioner and determined that the studios needed to establish a new casting procedure. The AMPP was not so much concerned with ameliorating the plight of extras as with addressing the ways in which the troubles impacted Hollywood's public image.

It was Beetson's job to find a solution. The AMPP needed to develop a gatekeeping mechanism that would help vet potential extras and impose some kind of bureaucratic organizational system that the studios could administer. In his letter to the AMPP membership, he offered two choices: 1) each studio could maintain a single list of extras for casting, or 2) studios could do all of their casting through a centralized agency apart from any individual studio's control.[59] The producers chose the latter option and cooperated through the AMPP to develop the Central Casting Bureau, or Central Casting. The AMPP, funded by fees from each of the major studios, paid for Central Casting's staff and overhead, and in exchange Central Casting handled all the casting and payroll for extras and maintained personnel files. Beetson was tasked with hiring staff and overseeing general operations. He subsequently divided Central Casting into men's and women's sections—each of which had a team of telephone operators to field casting requests and administer placements. Central Casting effectively functioned in the same way as many of the exploitative agencies, but with direct studio oversight and significantly more publicity related to its procedures. The similarities between previous casting agencies and Central Casting were underscored by the overlapping personnel in the case of Dave Allen, the men's section manager, who had previously run Screen Talent, one of the casting agencies that the Motion Picture Players Union was trying to shut down in 1919. In contrast, the women's section was led by someone with greater moral authority. Marian Mel came to Central Casting from the California Industrial Welfare Commission, which was one of the organizations that investigated labor conditions in the film industry.[60] Central Casting not only resolved Hollywood's image problem but also shifted oversight for extras casting to the studios. In one decisive move, Central Casting resolved decades of issues with casting agencies and acting schools by effectively putting these agencies out of business and simultaneously staving off unionization.

Central Casting could monitor labor conditions for the extras, but it would do so as an arm for the studio system, and without empowering extras to improve their own working conditions or to advocate for themselves independently of management. In Will Hays's announcement of the bureau's opening in the *Los Angeles Times*, he celebrated Central Casting for "do[ing] away with the evils of the employment bureaus, which have extracted more than $500,000 a year from extras," and proudly announced, "This [Central Casting] will cause the elimination of all make-up and screen-acting schools."[61] Hays's denouncement of employment bureaus is of course evasive—he addressed various financial transgressions, but placed the blame squarely on the shoulders of the ancillary businesses. Studios, however, were either explicitly supporting these businesses by using their check-cashing services, or implicitly supporting them by mistreating their own noncontract actors. Employment bureaus (claiming they could aid with job placement), makeup schools (which promised to teach aspiring actors everything they needed to know about acting and enhancing their appearances), and acting schools took advantage of aspiring actors trying to break into the film business, but they would have gone out of business long before without the cooperation of the major Hollywood studios.[62]

Despite the misleading nature of the official industry narrative, Central Casting was a significant improvement for extras. Prior to Central Casting in 1925, extras had to physically traverse significant distances between studios (in Hollywood or Burbank) and employment bureaus (downtown) to check for work. The Central Casting offices had only two locations where extras could check in, one on the corner of Hollywood Boulevard and Western (centrally located for the studios), and another downtown on First Street (affiliated with the California Free Employment Bureau). Central Casting also used a call-in system to place extras for studio work, which was an additional improvement on background casting procedures. Studios called in to make requests for extras, and Central Casting employees would match the demand with the extras who called a special phone number to find out if there was any work. The call-in system eliminated the need for extras to walk between studios (as Leo Rosencrans had done less than ten years earlier), keeping would-be stars and starlets off the Hollywood streets and (theoretically) inside their respectable residences. Heidi Kenaga concludes that the move toward rationalized casting was especially important for the image of women in Hollywood, arguing, "In trade and popular discourse, the focus on the body of the extras as not, in fact, extraneous but rather as a disciplined, desexualized effect of modern

Original location of Central Casting office on Hollywood and Western. Photograph taken by author in 2017.

Administrative workers busy casting extras at the Central Casting office in 1929. Photograph licensed under a CC-Attribution ShareAlike 4.0 license.

corporate organization was designed to deflect suspicions that sexual availability was a determining factor in whether a female extra would be hired."[63] Thus, if the casting process could be described as a process of exchanging information and data about actors rather than an imagined job interview in which women, desperate for work, performed for men in intimate settings, then Hollywood could start to transform its image from rampant immorality to organized, rational objectivity.

Central Casting was a top-down system to monitor extras and regulate wages and payroll in Hollywood. For extras and the public, Central Casting's bureaucratic systems made extras' casting appear more professionalized than it had been in the past. The new organization also paralleled many of the broader shifts in the industry's bureaucratic processes. As Tom Kemper argues, data collection and maintenance of data for casting became essential for Hollywood agents in the next decade and represented a significant development as the film industry industrialized.[64] From the perspective of studio management and producers, the phone-in system made extras easier to control. For extras looking for work, this system often posed problems. If an extra finished up at a studio or was not selected for work that day, he would have to find a phone to pursue the next lead. While the use of the telephone for casting kept extras out of the street, it required them to have access to a phone. Industrialization in this case required access to technology and created a new barrier to entry for film industry aspirants who would not have had easy access to telephones, which were not ubiquitous in the 1920s.[65] Wealthy families were more likely than blue-collar families to have telephones, and many working-class individuals relied on pay phones to place calls.[66] Central Casting contributed to the bureaucratization of the film business with new protocols designed to create fairer hiring practices for extras, but the result was simply that new procedures created new barriers and gave Hollywood a means to understand the demographics of this workforce more clearly.

Central Casting gave studios and the general public a somewhat clearer picture of the general population of extras and their income. General manager Campbell MacCulloch claimed that there were twenty thousand registered extras in 1925 (when Central Casting formed).[67] These numbers vary widely between sources and do not reveal what percentage of extras was using this work as their primary source of income. What these numbers do indicate, though, is that there was a significant pool of extras that far outnumbered the available jobs. This benefited the studios because they had a diverse casting pool, but there was not sufficient work for all registered extras. In the late 1920s the various jobs staffed by Central Casting were divided into six rate categories: $3, $5, $7.50, $10, $12, and $15 per day. To put these wages in perspective, in 1920 a waitress in Los Angeles made $12 per week.[68] Thus while these categories suggest the potential to earn a great deal of money compared to other unskilled jobs, the reality of extra work was that very few people made a comfortable living working as extras because there were so many aspirants.

The casting process was designed to manage the availability of extras for the studios, but in doing so extras had to put a tremendous amount of faith in Central Casting to distribute the roles appropriately and without bias. Central Casting regulated wages and payroll procedures across the industry, but many extras were still unable to work sufficient days to make a living. Although the organization interfaced with struggling and aspiring on the margins of the film industry, Central Casting was established to address the bureaucratic and structural problems that faced the studios. This effectively created a conflict of interest—although Central Casting was helping extras, it was a service that worked for the studios.

Changes to the casting procedures solved the studios' public image problem, but most of the actual labor problems facing extras and marginalized actors remained. The new organization reduced the worker pool of registered members, but still could not promise extras reliable work. Central Casting was also unable to eliminate some of the key problems in casting, such as nepotism. Central Casting workers supposedly searched their files to assign extras at random, but there was no mechanism to intervene if assistants or producers bypassed their casting system and called specific extras to the set. In subsequent decades, extras would continue to make allegations against Central Casting, which would be a constant source of trouble for the unions. Ultimately, Central Casting was an imperfect solution for extras, but a model for casting efficiency that was indicative of larger changes that would follow in subsequent decades as agents, new businesses, and eventually the unions all played a role in vetting and managing Hollywood's labor pool.

(DIS)UNITY AMONG ACTORS

"There are applicants for extra work," as former extra Leo Rosencrans observed, "who skip school to go to the studios, and old men and women who can scarcely stagger into the offices and all ages in between."[69] Rosencrans's description of extras sums up some of the complications of organizing actors. As a group, extras and actors are not only demographically different but also experience their work and career trajectories in individualized ways that make it difficult for them to coalesce around shared experiences. Although the nature of these differences made it challenging for existing unions or union leaders to unite screen performers around common grievances, it was also the nature and the will of Hollywood as an industry that successfully staved off unionization for the first decades of filmmaking.

By the 1930s the national culture around labor and unionization was changing, and the US government implemented protections for organizers. Like many unions in the United States, organization and the formation of unions became more feasible with the 1933 passage of Title 1, Section 7(a), of the National Industrial Recovery Act (NIRA), which guaranteed workers the right to unionize and collectively bargain on their own behalf without repercussions from management. Although it was still difficult for workers to organize, and the Screen Actors Guild certainly faced opposition from management as well as jurisdictional challenges, the presence of legal protections could, at the very least, mitigate some of the past efforts to block unionization in the film industry. Changes in government policy, the unifying crisis of the Depression, which brought together all actors (from stars to freelancers to extras), and a more clearly defined sense of film acting as a specific performance style and career trajectory separate from theatrical acting all collided to provide the cultural foundation for SAG to form in 1934.

In the late 1920s the Actors Equity Association leaders, who represented New York theater actors, aggressively tried to incorporate film actors into their union. Extras had been incorporated into AEA in 1920, but in an effort to boost their prestige and expand their geographic reach, AEA wanted character actors and film stars as well. Performers in all venues experienced difficult and exploitative working conditions in the early twentieth century, but the working conditions in Hollywood differed tremendously from those of the New York theater, and the conditions that led New York theatrical actors to unionize in 1913 under AEA were quite different from those that inspired film actors to unionize. Kerry Segrave explains that from 1880 to 1900, stage actors were often engaged for performances that were never compensated, especially in the case of so-called "additional" performances, such as Sunday shows.[70] In addition, even though many stage actors were based in New York, the necessity of touring companies created an obstacle to labor organization with actors who were continually required to travel around the country.[71] Although AEA had been unsuccessful at organizing film actors in the past, the union saw an opportunity in 1929 after thousands of New York-based theater actors (and AEA members) moved across the country to work in film. AEA's new president, Frank Gillmore, and the rest of AEA's leadership thought that conditions in Hollywood had changed and film actors would be more receptive to their approach.

The nature of filmmaking meant that film actors experienced different hardships than theater actors experienced. While theater actors negotiated issues such as long rehearsal times and uncompensated performances, film actors had different sets of grievances, including studios hiring them for multiple pictures under a single day-rate and long shooting days often in heavy makeup and on multiple locations. Remembering his earliest films in the 1930s at Warner Bros., actor Charles Lane recounted: "When I started in pictures my salary was $35 per day. I'd go over on Stage 26 at 11 o'clock and play an elevator operator with four lines, and at 3 o'clock another one. Then I'd go over to Stage 13 and do a taxi driver with four lines. I'd often do three pictures in one day. That was before we had the Screen Actors Guild."[72] Other actors complained about the uniquely harsh on-set conditions, including Boris Karloff who recounted that he spent 25 hours in his makeup while shooting *Frankenstein* (1931).[73] Karloff's story points out that the specificity of nonlinear film production lent (and continues to lend) itself to longer workdays than are possible in the theater. What film actors wanted their unions to address were the specific working conditions of screen-acting labor.

When Equity finally tried to organize a strike on behalf of screen actors in June 1929, Gillmore and AEA learned how different film actors were from those working on stage in New York. Although AEA maintained a small office in Los Angeles, many in Hollywood still perceived it as an East Coast union. According to journalist Morton Thompson, "Equity [AEA] wasn't daring enough."[74] Los Angeles labor historians Richard Perry and Louis Perry attribute AEA's lack of success in 1929 to four reasons. First, many of the silent-screen actors remembered being ridiculed by theater actors (who devalued screen acting) about their profession and could not accept AEA's claim over their profession. Second, AEA made incorrect assumptions about the working conditions for screen actors, falsely equating them with the conditions that theater actors fought against. Third, unlike stage actors who had support from other New York unions, film actors could not rely on sympathetic strikes from other unions to help shut down productions.[75] Finally, AEA severely underestimated the desperate Hollywood actors' willingness to accept low wages.[76] AEA's strike and negotiations ultimately failed, which convinced film actors that it could not improve their working conditions.

While AEA failed to bring film actors into the union, many of the founders of the Screen Actors Guild began as theater actors with an understanding of the value of a union of performers. The theater and film actors who began organizing SAG were members of Hollywood actors' clubs, including the Masquers Club (male), the Dominos (female), and the Hollywood Cricket Club. These clubs were largely social organizations that had clubhouses for meals and gatherings. However, since these were professional clubs, they provided the first spaces away from the supervision of producers where actors began to organize. In 1934, after AEA relinquished any claim to screen actors, SAG officially became the sole representative of film actors.

An effective union had to represent all actors, not just the most disenfranchised Hollywood workers. AEA's efforts initiated actors' unionizing activity, but what finally united them were the studios' proposed

Depression-era salary cuts that helped stars see the value of a union. Facing financial troubles in 1933 and prompted by President Roosevelt's New Deal policies, the MPPDA assembled a document called the Code of Fair Competition. This document not only placed restrictions on contracts but also looked to cap the highest earnings, claiming that overpaid actors were causing studios to struggle. This studio document specifically targeted stars, who constituted a minority of actors—a SAG brief on yearly (gross) salaries indicated that in 1933, one quarter of all actors made less than $1,000, and approximately three quarters made less than $5,000.[77] Even though many actors below the level of star had struggled for years under the existing studio leadership, it was only when stars' salaries were threatened that actors across the hierarchy of labor power united against the producers.

While actors were attempting to protect their jobs against Depression-era belt-tightening, the situation for extras remained dire because the problems that Central Casting was designed to address persisted. In 1933 the Academy of Motion Picture Arts and Sciences initiated its own investigation into extras and confirmed that there was still a wide disparity between the number of registered extras and available jobs. The AMPAS findings were used to help establish the National Industrial Recovery Act's Standing Committee on Extras (a committee of five extras and five producers), which sought to regulate work distribution for extras and hours worked per day. In 1934, Central Casting reported that there were approximately seventeen thousand registered extras.[78] On any given day, Central Casting received an average of approximately seven hundred job openings per day, which meant they were only able to find work for about 4 percent of registered extras, and even within that group only a smaller percentage was able to live off their wages as extras.[79] In 1938, Central Casting reported that seven hundred people were able to earn seventeen dollars per week, and seventy-four people were able to earn thirty-eight dollars per week (most of them dress extras who were required to maintain their own wardrobes).[80] Despite the demand for extras, Central Casting was very explicit that extras work "should NOT be depended on for a livelihood."[81] Central Casting provided institutional oversight and monitored how jobs were distributed, but its role was simply to maintain this large number of semi-employed workers.

Despite all the studies on extras and their grievances, none of this data was incorporated into SAG's mission upon its unionization. According to David Prindle, SAG's mythology was that they formed in part to help fight for the underemployed actors and extras, even if there is little truth to this rhetoric. Prindle explains, "[working actors] didn't know if the extras had problems because they didn't know any extras."[82] As evidence, Prindle draws on an interview with Lyle Talbot, a Warner Bros. B-actor, TV actor, and later the star of several Ed Wood films. Talbot claimed that he never heard any mention of extras at the early SAG meetings; addressing the relationship between on-screen labor contingents, he stated, "There was this star, who doesn't speak to the supporting player, and the supporting player who doesn't speak to the bit player, and the bit player, who will have nothing to do with extras."[83] In their founding conversations the SAG board of directors stated that the Guild was "founded for actors only."[84] Indeed, if there was any doubt about who the union was meant to represent, by 2004, when the SAG Foundation started work on a documentary about the union's history, the extra was entirely written out of its founding mythology. According to the SAG Foundation's documentary, the union grew as actors talked to their friends whom they knew and trusted.[85] As Leo Rosten's study of actors would later indicate, only 1.9 percent of the actors he surveyed ever worked as an extra.[86] Not only did few actors know any extras, but few actually experienced the hardship and exploitation of extra labor firsthand. Throughout history extras faced the most documented problems in terms of exploitation and underemployment, and they had been the object of several unionization attempts, but when SAG formed, the concerns of extras were largely marginalized.

SAG continued to lobby on behalf of extras, but its interest in representing them was determined primarily by material concerns and the realization that including extras was necessary for the union to remain financially viable. Although much of the history of the screen actors' unions and of screen acting more generally positioned extras as marginal or even nonactors, the vast population of extras provided an easy solution for the nascent union's funding problem. The risk, however, was that SAG leadership did not want extras to usurp power in the union based on their outsized population. SAG's solution was to admit extras as members in a Junior Guild for extras and bit players who would have limited voting rights. The Junior Guild was affiliated with SAG, but votes were subject to vetoes by SAG members, and junior members were not allowed to vote in SAG elections. However, as part of the union, extras could rely on SAG to help mediate labor disputes. In 1936 when African American extras went on strike for a raise on *Too Hot to Handle* (Conway, 1936), SAG council member Jesse Graves and Audry Blair, executive secretary of the Junior Guild, successfully negotiated higher pay for a small number of them, 35 out of the 285 extras in the film.[87] Even though SAG had some successes working on behalf of extras, extras' lack of agency in the union was an extremely undesirable position. Writers in the black press expressed concern that SAG was specifically not looking out for its African American extras.[88] As such, J. Buckley Russell, a member of SAG and the founder of the Hollywood Picture Players Association, continued to try to organize extras to split from SAG. SAG did not want another union coaxing members away, and in 1937 it fined Russell $1,000 and suspended him from the union for one year.[89] This incident suggests that many extras were not satisfied with SAG's representation, but more importantly it indicates that sharing the screen and even sharing some labor conditions was not enough to bring all performers together in a unified position.

The concept of "freelance" or "freelancer" as it applies to actors and the film industry dates to the silent era, but the terms and conditions of freelance work only began to take shape in a way that was broadly and consistently applied across the industry in the 1930s, after the actors had unionized. In the 1930s there were approximately five hundred actors under contract (a number that would briefly increase in the 1940s and take a downturn after 1948) across the major studios.[90] Those who were not under long-term contracts fell into two categories: extras or freelance. Although both extras and freelance actors worked sporadically, the industry leaders and workers drew very stark distinctions between each type of work. From an aesthetic and narrative standpoint, extras are background to speaking characters. From a labor perspective, Campbell MacCulloch of Central Casting explained, "They are casual workers on a daily wage basis, running from $5.50 up to as high as $16.50 a day."[91] These were not only material distinctions, but ones that also accounted for job prospects. Unlike speaking roles, Central Casting believed that extras work should not be a substitute for full-time employment. Extra work was not the first rung on the ladder to stardom; as MacCulloch explained, "Broadly speaking, extra work has no future."[92] By drawing attention to extras' bleak prospects, MacCulloch created somewhat of a false distinction between the career prospects of extras and freelance actors.

Freelance, in contrast, was a designation that applied to actors contracted for roles on a weekly or daily basis, but contractually did not include extras.[93] The minimum compensation for a freelance actor, however, might be less than for a well-paid extra who was doing some kind of specialty or stunt work. In a March 1935 freelance agreement, AMPAS president Frank Lloyd explained that the new agreement covers "actors receiving between $15.00 a day and $40,000 a picture," a salary range that was inclusive of the earnings for extras as well as well-paid actors.[94] As these pay scales indicate, actors across a wide array of incomes had the shared experience of sporadic employment. In 1935 the freelance rates were determined by AMPAS, a studio-run organization, and, as such, these rates represent what was agreeable to the studio rather than rates that emerged through collective bargaining. When SAG negotiated its first agreement two years later, they won a higher minimum rate of twenty-five dollars, but many of the terms and conditions were carried over from the earlier AMPAS agreement for freelance actors. Even though the union made great strides, they were building off AMPAS's previous norms and practices. Actors were able to form a union, but they were only able to negotiate based on the existing terms determined by the studios.

The freelance designation encompassed an array of actors, including those who chose to work freelance and leverage their previous success as well as those who did freelance work because they were not perceived as meriting a long-term contract. In the 1930s there were around forty freelance stars, such as Fredric March, Jean Arthur, Adolphe Menjou, and Constance Bennett, who were in high demand and were able to strike their own deals with studios on a film-by-film basis.[95] Stars in the 1930s pursued freelance contracts for a variety of reasons, including better financial terms, more creative opportunities, and greater control over their star images.[96] The freelance terms differed by star and contract. For those actors who had proven value within the Hollywood market, working freelance offered opportunities not afforded by restrictive contracts. As Emily Carman explains in her insightful study of independent stardom in Hollywood, "Freelancing provided a means to attain creative control, more jurisdiction over their screen image, higher salaries, and increased visibility in the industry."[97] For those in powerful positions able to leverage their fame, compensation could also come in the form of profit sharing—an option that was particularly desirable after the United States increased tax rates for annual incomes over $70,000.[98]

Unlike the stars who chose freelance work to attain leverage, choice over roles was not a viable option for most freelance actors. As Carman observes, "for other talent in Hollywood, . . . binding contracts—providing secure, stable employment—were a coveted commodity."[99] For the most part, a freelance actor without a studio contract was in this position because she was not recognizable or marketable. The best-case scenario for many character actors was being typecast. For actor Fritz Feld, typecasting generated a substantial amount of work (approximately thirty-six film appearances between 1925 and 1940). Feld explained: "Each studio had a different way of typing me: at Universal, I played only butlers;

at Paramount, mostly counts with monocles; at MGM, conductors of symphony orchestras; at RKO, gamblers and strange individuals; at Fox, train conductors, postmen, and ministers."[100] As Feld's examples point out, versatility was essential for freelancers, but to be typecast, actors needed to have an appearance that lent itself to a particular kind of casting and versatility for nonessential roles.

Instability was imposed not only upon those who filled smaller roles, but also on people of color who had star status but fewer opportunities for roles. As Carman explains, minority actors, who were regarded as "types," experienced a kind of "forced freelancing."[101] Chinese American actress Anna May Wong was one who suffered from racism and the limited roles offered to people of color. "Freelancing," Carman explains, "did not give Wong the freedom to shape her star image, only the ability to find work. And if she wanted to work, she had to play roles that continued to stereotype her and limit her creative opportunities."[102] Although freelance work benefited a select few, for many stars and featured players the inconsistency was a hindrance to career growth.

Freelance actors who were able to make a living in character roles often found that their financial stability came at the expense of creative fulfillment. John Qualen, an actor in the 1930s, remembered, "Fox put you in one after another; many of them were just two or three days work. I was ashamed of some of the pictures I did, but you didn't have any choice. Later, when I could afford to—when I didn't have to act in order to eat—I studied the scripts."[103] Although contract players often found themselves in the same position, the work and paychecks were more consistent. For most actors, freelance work was an unwelcome necessity born out of Hollywood's structural inequity, which tended to push out older actors and actors of color. In a letter to SAG executive secretary Kenneth Thomson, Bela Lugosi voiced his frustration with the existing casting structures in Hollywood. Lugosi lamented: "Studios cast their pictures with their contract players regardless of whether they fit the part . . . until conditions are adjusted it would be my salvation if *I could have my turn*—after ten years of freelancing and studios could have me on a term contract for 30% of my freelance salary."[104] Lugosi's frustrations mirror much of what actors experienced as they were pushed out by sound technologies. As technologies changed and audience demands evolved, many were left to piece together a living with a willingness to work for less than other actors.

For actors of color it was even more difficult to drum up any type of work, with some actors requiring more established stars to advocate on their behalf. These struggles persisted after World War II, when actors and unions had explicit conversations about how industry structures disenfranchised actors of color. Gregory Peck reached out to several prominent producers, including Dore Shary at Selznick and Walter Wagner at Universal, on behalf of Arnett Williams, an African American actor who Peck worked with on Zoltan Korda's *The Macomber Affair* (1947). Peck wrote: "He now has a . . . card in the Screen Actors Guild, but, as you know, parts are few and far between for colored actors and he needs extra work to keep him going. The only way that he can get an SEG card is through a letter from a producer or a director, stating that they plan to use him in extra work in a forthcoming picture."[105] Despite regular correspondence with Peck throughout 1946 and 1947, Williams eventually gave up his dream to work as an actor. In his final letter to Peck, Williams lamented: "I want to re-pay you for the kindness you have shown to me. I thought I could make this proposition of mine pay, but I can't buck the SAG, the State, the City, and County—SEG all in one united front against me. I did not mean to sponge on you—I honestly thought it would work, and at times it did look good. But it did not."[106]

Williams's inability to find work, despite Peck's lobbying on his behalf, negates many of the conclusions that the SAG board reached with respect to black actors in Hollywood. In 1947 the board discussed the possibility of reestablishing the Committee Against Negro Discrimination, but decided unanimously that there *was* sufficient work for black actors. The minutes read, "Statistics show that more Negroes are working now than last year, and almost all scripts have parts in them now for Negroes. . . . It was felt that it might hurt the Negro rather than help him if the Guild were to continue to go to the producers with repetitions of our plea on behalf of the Negroes, particularly in view of the fact that cooperation is being given."[107] Efforts to improve conditions for actors of color were always met with a bit of trepidation, in part because all actors faced underemployment. The industrial desire for a large labor pool left many actors un- or underemployed, a fact that made it difficult for some to recognize how structural racism exacerbated labor conditions for minority actors.

The freelance designation offered stars more flexibility and power than it did to nonfeatured actors. Whereas stars could use past box office numbers to point to their value, the extras and actors who moved between projects did not have the same documented success to fall back on and could not individually negotiate. For those below the level of star, the best bet for establishing fair and equitable conditions was to rely on the strength of collective bargaining. Although the work of freelance actors and extras shared certain characteristics, the cultural distinctions and material differences between the types of work contributed to a persistent rift in SAG.

Extras' grievances continued to mount, and SAG recognized the growing tension. In 1940 SAG's board of directors tasked the executive staff and the legal department to develop a plan to grant extras complete autonomy from SAG. Change did not come quickly enough, however, for Harry Mayo, the chairman of SAG's Extras Advisory Committee, who filed a complaint against SAG with the American Federation of Labor (AFL) on May 13, 1941.[108] Mayo was also part of a new union, the Screen Players Union (SPU), which was attempting to win jurisdiction over extras. Mayo argued that SAG did not look after extras' interests, thus extras needed their own union. One of his chief allegations against SAG was that when they negotiated rate increases, the rates for extras remained stable.[109] In December 1944, the AFL decided to put the question of representation of extras to a vote. In the election, 76 percent of extras voted to split from SAG in favor of representation by SPU.[110] But SPU's jurisdiction over extras was short-lived. Even though the National Labor Review Board granted SPU the right to bargain for extras, the Associated Actors and Artistes of America (the parent union for nine branches of performer unions, including SAG, SEG, and AEA) did not. The 4As claimed that SPU did not effectively or democratically represent extras and decided to recognize a new union called the Screen Extras Guild (SEG) instead of SPU.[111]

With the question of jurisdiction over extras seemingly resolved, the Screen Extras Guild was tasked with implementing systems to best serve their historically underserved and mistreated population. Although extras had always navigated the industry differently than those with freelance speaking roles, the institutional separation of the unions had distinct ramifications for extras' bargaining power. In 1945, SEG leadership began meeting and sending out applications for members. They were faced with a familiar problem: how to minimize the labor pool and reduce competition for roles. In an early meeting, the board instructed the administrative staff to "accept applications for membership only from those actively employed in the motion picture industry, or former employees in the industry whose absence from the industry in the past year or so was for good cause, e.g., Members of the armed forces, etc."[112] While this was one method of keeping membership numbers low, this approach kept out actors of color, such as Arnett Williams, who struggled to find work as an African American actor in Hollywood.

Although extras worked on screen, their working conditions and grievances differed from those who spoke on camera, and separating from SAG allowed extras to foreground their own issues. Unlike bit roles, actors viewed work as an extra not as a first step in an on-screen career, but as a different form of labor altogether. SEG meetings offered extras a place to voice their labor complaints, many of which stemmed from two core issues: underemployment and poor compensation. The issue of steady employment was hard to address because filmmakers often used a variety of background actors (to avoid repeating familiar faces), which made it difficult to be continuously employed in the industry. Although the unions would be able to bargain for increased compensation, ultimately this was moot if actors were only able to scrape together a few days of work per year. Without the power to transform how extras were cast, SEG union leadership would never truly be able to address the needs of its membership.

CONCLUSION

As actors all competed for work, they likely concurred that their labor conditions could be improved, whether that was in the form of more workdays, more money, or more screen time. However, striving for a better life did not necessarily lead to a coherent bargaining position for extras or actors. The men and women who had opportunities for roles often had a wide array of financial interests, and the people of color who were unable to find roles because of structural racism were faced with an additional set of challenges beyond their white colleagues.

Looking at Hollywood from the perspective of actors shows how labor insecurity was central to the development of long-standing industrial structures and practices. The history of the studio system is often painted as rational and efficient, but beneath this image of organization was a narrative of chaotic union representation, unpredictable labor conditions, and hierarchical divisions within the large and unwieldy population of actors. Many Hollywood actors were simultaneously excluded from and exploited by the studio system. The marginalized position of many actors allowed for the emergence of new gatekeepers operating outside of the studio walls, as well as the emergence of Hollywood unions.

TWO

ACTORS AND THE MAKING OF TELEVISION'S FIRST GOLDEN AGE

*We should not overlook the possibility of radio and television
absorbing the picture industry a few years from now.*

SAG BOARD MEMBER BRADLEY PAGE IN A NOTE TO
SAG PRESIDENT RALPH MORGAN, JULY 20, 1933

After many years and millions of dollars in research, television arrived in public view at the 1939 World's Fair. In its earliest version television drew a large audience, as well as numerous critical comparisons to existing media forms. Billed as "hear-and-see radio,"[1] RCA's first broadcasts attracted fifty thousand curious visitors in the first week.[2] The image quality of late 1930s television programs was poor in comparison to the film images of the day, with critics noting the minimal range of gray and a lack of details in the shadows.[3] The content of this first broadcast was also disparaged by critics—*New York Times* columnist Orrin Dunlap noted that announcers needed to talk less and highlight the visuals rather than describing everything happening on screen.

Despite these shortcomings and critiques, early viewers were intrigued by the new technology. Television's appeal did not lie strictly in its technological novelty, nor was it viewed entirely as an extension of motion pictures, but rather it was immediately seen for its ability to foreground human action. In identifying New York mayor Fiorello La Guardia as "the most telegenic man," a word quickly coined to describe the visual appeal of people on television, Dunlap argued that the most engaging figures on television punctuated speech with movement (a toss of the head or a wave of the hand). Even as a nonactor, La Guardia's movements underscored the importance of action to engage viewers, as well as television's unique ability to highlight human gestures. It appeared that television's strengths resided closer to these visual qualities, rather than to its similarities to radio. Yet television also possessed its own unique characteristics. Dunlap summarized his observations, commenting, "It becomes increasingly evident that television is a new art; it cannot follow a fixed formula developed by stage and screen."[4] If television seemed to possess inherent qualities that were not present in film, radio, or theater, what would this mean for actors who were already working in these established media forms? How would television impact acting as a profession? These questions about television were not solely taking place on the pages of newspapers, but were part of conversations that fueled debates around performance labor and preoccupied acting unions for the next decade.

One year before television's successful debut in 1939, various actors' unions—the five unions headquartered on the East Coast, Actors Equity Association (AEA or Equity), Chorus Equity Association (CEA), American Federation of Radio Artists (AFRA), American Guild of Musical Artists (AGMA), and American Guild of Variety Artists (AGVA), as well as Hollywood's SAG—began to discuss the impending arrival of television in earnest. Television's status for screen labor was a contested space, with many different professional identities seeing television as a potentially lucrative (and disruptive) transformation of their fields. In addition to film, radio, and theater actors, film extras and variety and chorus performers all contributed to discussions about the future of television that would shape broader assumptions about its specificity as a medium for decades. The unions considered a diverse range of issues, including the nature of television's qualities as an art form, the on-set norms and compensation structures, whether television production would ultimately be on the East or West Coast, the acting styles best suited for this new medium, and, perhaps most pressing from a union perspective, the kinds of job opportunities in this new medium. The results of these debates among the screen actors' unions ultimately determined who could bargain on behalf of television actors and, by extension, which union would dramatically increase its membership and expand its influence.

The unions, all of which had their own interests and aspirations in this changing media landscape, struggled to work together as they competed for jurisdiction over television jobs. Hollywood unions had a number of jurisdictional disputes in their formative years as various unions jostled for power over film workers. Ida Jeter's case study of the jurisdictional dispute between the short-lived Federated Motion Picture Crafts (FMPC) and IATSE was only one of several craft disputes in the 1930s and 1940s. As Jeter explains, these jurisdictional battles frequently work in favor of producers because they delay contract negotiations.[5] The infighting among the actors had a similar effect around the issue of television, eventually becoming so heated that it necessitated mediation from the Associated Actors and Artistes of America (4As) and the National Labor Review Board (NLRB). These jurisdictional disputes typically shape labor relations, but the television dispute was unique in its contributions to shaping the industrial and cultural understanding of the new medium.

As the East Coast performers' unions debated jurisdiction with SAG, the newly formed Screen Extras Guild (SEG) became increasingly marginal to industry conversations and public concern about labor. Further, television programs had no use for extras who could not fit into the small-screen frame, so the decision to form a new union consisting solely of extras was unfortunately timed. SEG members identified as screen actors, and as such, they aligned themselves with SAG in all television jurisdictional disputes and negotiations. However, SEG's core bargaining interests, which continued to focus on set conditions and daily compensation rates, diverged from those of SAG and the interests of actors. Actors and extras may have shared space on the screen, but they did not share the same professional priorities.

Although the issue of television jurisdiction was important for the development of boundaries around specific media forms, these jurisdictional rulings were not considered landmark cases in the history of labor and therefore were not archived with the NLRB. Newspapers and industry trade papers took an occasional interest in the debates among actors throughout the 1940s and 1950s, but many conversations about acting and compensation took place strictly in union correspondence and hotel conference meeting spaces as union leaders and membership debated their problems and strategized their position in the expanding technological landscape. To illuminate these conversations, I draw heavily on internal union documents from the New York Public Library for the Performing Arts, the SAG-AFTRA Archive, the Tamiment Library and Wagner Labor Archives at New York University, and the collections at the Wisconsin Center for Film and Theater Research. These documents rarely contain discussions of acting as a creative endeavor, instead foregrounding concerns about the financial value of performers, particularly in film or theater. Yet at times, individual actors express a commitment to specific forms of performance or media, stressing the importance of maintaining the artistic integrity of acting, and often enacting cultural distinctions between different acting venues. These passages belie their concerns about the importance of art rather than commerce, while also showing how financial concerns were intertwined within the community's conversations. These primary documents, which are rich resources for understanding acting as a profession, offer insights into professional values, hierarchies, concerns, and labor conditions during a moment of shifting discourse around screen acting and popular culture.

The debates over television jurisdiction offer a worker's perspective on a significant moment in media history. Scholarship on the development of television has explored the medium's technological, infrastructural, and audience histories, but there has been minimal focus on the experience and influence of creative workers. Writing about the contexts that shaped television's programming, cultural status, and position in the home, Jonathan Sterne enumerates various forces, including "struggles in the industry around proprietary technology and transmission rights; dispositions in the regulatory apparatus; the ideology and practice of corporate liberalism; postwar commercial culture; and the relations between federal, state, and local jurisdictions."[6] The cultural and industrial forces Sterne identifies were also at the root of the intra-industry conflicts between film, radio, and the nascent television industry that Michele Hilmes details in *Hollywood and Broadcast.*[7] Absent from these histories, however, is the role of labor in television's development amid these intra-industry disputes. Characterizations of television that focus on technology and infrastructure privilege a top-down model of media's development and elide the influence of creative labor, erasing key contributions to the production of television. While technology and regulatory structures were central to the development of industry, so were interpersonal relationships and cultural hierarchies. Focusing solely on how television was programmed and received by audiences generates a limited perspective, one that assumes television's primary impact was on consumers and omits the experience of those working in television. Without worker perspectives, we only have a partial picture of television's arrival, and one that fails to fully account for the ways in which various changes were enacted and acculturated into existing entertainment cultures and the cities where media work was clustered. From the perspective of actors, television necessitated the restructuring of work, professional norms, and identities. Denying creative workers a place in the histories of industry development undermines their agency and influence on media history and diminishes the importance of how major industrial changes affected those making media.

Television's arrival encouraged unions, especially the Screen Actors Guild, to reorient their priorities and to consider how the creative and professional career of an actor could span media. As the studio system shifted its business model toward more independent productions in the late 1940s, many screen actors were released from their contracts, thus increasing the ranks of freelance actors. As this chapter shows, the unions tacitly accepted that television would create more lucrative freelance opportunities and support a model of media work that was shifting away from stable long-term contracts. Thus the arrival of television ushered in a new way to understand the definition of a professional actor, a status that could have been previously defined by whether or not an actor was under a studio contract. In an increasingly freelance era, the definition of "professional" began to transform into one that more and more required organizational initiation, self-categorization (defined either through unions or producers), and self-definition. Conversations over television jurisdiction and television acting as a profession were not working toward long-term contracts, greater stability, or even creative development, but rather offered a consensus that a career was composed of a series of different projects.

Actors had limited power over policy decisions, but through their unions they were able to help shape the terrain of production and the cultural value of television more broadly. Whereas the practices and norms for the film actor largely developed in response to the demands of Hollywood producers and directors, internal disputes within unions and their members played an active role in creating the conditions for television actors. Rather than reacting to labor conditions and advocating for changes, the professional norms and practices of television performers developed as producers experimented with different television programming formats. What complicated the process of standardizing terms for television were the territorial disputes between union leaders and the conflicting desires of memberships exacerbated by the cultural distinctions between actors. As television assimilated into the existing media landscape, its reliance on nonstar actors and its differentiation from theater as a form of performance helped shape its identity as a medium.

UNDERSTANDING TELEVISION

As early as 1933, six years before the World's Fair demonstration, actor Bradley Page urged Screen Actors Guild president Ralph Morgan to begin strategizing for the future of television. Television's introduction immediately reminded Page of the arrival of sound film and the theater union Actors' Equity Association's failure to prepare for that previous technological shift. He wrote, "When Equity was organized, the talking picture was only dreamed of—so we could not be blamed for not looking ahead to its potentialities and doing something about it; which resulted in that organizations [sic] failure in California some years ago and our work of organizing the Actor's Guild at the present time."[8] The excitement and possibility surrounding the new media form, as well as the desire to avoid repeating mistakes made at the introduction of a previous media technology development, led the performers' unions to ask questions about the nature of television work before actors were even working on television and well before television had a mass audience. Although unions had no specific information about programming or early working conditions, they recognized the need to anticipate what television would be and how it might align with existing types of performance and performers' unions.

During the initial jurisdictional debates between 1938 and 1940, union leadership was considering the future of the medium, but was also ostensibly engaged in debates about the medium-specific aesthetics of television. They recognized that television shared characteristics with film as a screen-based visual medium, but its mode of transmission was over broadcast signals like radio. Whereas histories of television focus on its infrastructural specificity, development as a commercial system, and service for the public good, union discourse, though rooted in material conversations about labor, sheds light on the artistic *possibilities* envisioned in this new media. Television had the potential to capture daily viewers and to enable dissemination of staged events, including live music, variety shows, and dramatic performances. As a live medium, many assumed TV would favor comedians or vaudeville performers who were adept at improvisation.[9] Amid all this speculation about television's form and affinities with other media, one thing was clear: unions were determined to get ahead of television negotiations.

Television's shared qualities with multiple performance fields piqued the interest of several unions' leadership, but members and leadership were unsure of what television was or which of the unions would be the most equipped to bargain for television actors. The 4As, which was a leadership body designed specifically to mediate disputes between the member unions over issues like jurisdiction, took charge of these initial conversations about television. Between 1938 and 1939, the 4As met with the member unions on several occasions to discuss television and its working conditions in the hopes of coming up with a collective bargaining agreement to negotiate with the networks and television producers. The two main adversaries in these debates were AEA, which represented stage performers (although not the variety performers), and SAG, which represented film actors and extras at the time. Although each union had members on both coasts, the geographic divide between the theater business and the film industry caused this debate to devolve into a coastal battle between New York-based and Los Angeles-based unions.

Challenges over who would obtain television bargaining rights began when SAG's executive secretary Kenneth Thomson fired off a private letter in response to an editorial in AEA's internal publication, *Equity*. Thomson's letter to Frank Gillmore, president of the 4As, pointed out that television's identity and function was not totally clear, explaining: "It was then and is now entirely impossible to determine which organization will be best qualified to serve those Four A's members who will perform in television."[10] Thomson's position functioned as a stalling tactic aimed to galvanize support from Gillmore and to make sure that television jurisdiction did not fall to Equity, the oldest of the performer's unions, without due consideration. The uncertainty Thomson observed in television's jurisdiction was related to what he saw as fundamental differences between types of performance. In this letter, Thomson enumerated these differences between performance types by setting up a comparison between theater, motion pictures, and radio: "If television broadcasts are centered around legitimate theater, unquestionably Equity would be in the best position to give service to the artists. If, on the other hand television should center in the motion picture field, there is no doubt that the Guild would be better equipped to perform necessary duties. If, as is more likely, television remains primarily a radio problem, then the rights of the membership of AFRA must be considered very carefully."[11] The language in this statement demonstrates a core belief in medium specificity as a driving force for understanding the structures and needs of a performer's labor. While not all actors looking for work distinguished between media, the aesthetic and cultural differences were essential for unions and producers who relied on these characteristics to create administrative distinctions with real material consequences.

Medium specificity as a theoretical concern has been an essential topic among artists, critics, and theorists working to elevate their craft and develop evaluative criteria for art. In labor debates such as those that took place during television's formative years, these theoretical concerns become material, as they influence compensation and working conditions. While many characteristics of TV production labor emerged from filmmaking, differences in program duration and method of distribution raised new sets of questions around medium specificity. With respect to television, the key questions revolved around distribution methods and their relationship to content: what were the qualities of live broadcast television, and what were the characteristics of filmed programs? It is possible to answer these questions theoretically by considering formal qualities, but the aesthetic is also determined by labor and industrial infrastructure. Within the television jurisdictional debates, it is evident that notions of medium specificity had practical ramifications for work on set and compensation. Rather than solely considering the technologies and the differences between the final products, actors and unions had to think about process and practice. Thus their conversations were about developing an understanding of *performance* specificity and how the distinctions between different media performances would translate into medium-specific structures of remuneration.

The media unions were ostensibly delineated by media type, but the oscillating power dynamics determining union memberships resulted in continued ambiguity. The actors' unions were not always distinguished based on media jurisdictions; in fact, AEA's charter claimed the right to bargain for all entertainers. As explained in the previous chapter, despite Equity's claims over all performers, it did not necessarily have the organizational capacity to understand the needs of all performers. AEA ceded jurisdiction to SAG, AFRA, and AGMA but still attempted to maintain an umbrella of responsibility over all performers—in their rhetoric, they *permitted* other unions to claim jurisdiction over various media industries (rather than admitting they lost it on their own). One memo read at a meeting of 4As members proclaimed that each of these unions "secured it [jurisdiction] by requesting a release of that jurisdiction from AEA."[12]

Given their charter and status as the first and oldest performer's union, AEA leaders felt that bargaining rights to television naturally belonged to them. The problem with this assumption was that they had already established a precedent of ceding bargaining rights to organizers who could better serve and negotiate for new media industries such as film and radio. As the mediating body for all performers' unions, the 4As had to intervene. Writing to AEA's president Paul Dullzell, 4As president Gillmore challenged AEA's claims over television actors, reminding him, "There is no doubt that Equity has given up its jurisdiction over motion pictures and of radio, so it is possible that some might consider that jurisdiction over television is not as unarguable as it was before."[13] Central to AEA's claim over all media was that all performance professions shared qualities. However, by giving up their claims to film and radio, AEA had weakened its entitlement to television. The division of the unions was another way medium specificity was made material, although AEA leadership was not thinking precisely in terms of medium specificity splitting jurisdictions and putting them at a disadvantage.

With the arrival of yet another media form, AEA looked not only to assert its right to bargain for television actors, but to determine if there was any jurisdictional overlap between the performers' unions. In May 1939, AEA proposed a resolution that maintained its claim over television bargaining while also requesting that the 4As form a committee to investigate the complexities of television. The conversation about television provided an opportunity for the unions to address a long-standing issue for their membership, namely the fact that many actors, even in the 1930s, worked across performance venues and media and as a result were forced to join and be represented by multiple unions.

On the surface, it seems that Equity was attempting a multipronged approach to align television work with theater work, but its request opened a dialogue about the connections between what audiences perceived as distinctly separate industries. In a letter to all the member unions in the 4As, Gillmore explained, "The question of television jurisdiction is only part of a larger problem of reconstructing the Four A's, with a view to eliminating multiple branch memberships and dues."[14] The issue of multiple memberships inspired discussion about potential mergers between performers' unions. The logic for uniting actors' unions was that a larger union encompassing more actors across theater, film, radio, and television would eliminate in-fighting, and that a single merged union would have greater unified strike power and strength at the bargaining table. Gillmore's proposal did not prevail during the 1939–1940 negotiations. The merger plan resurfaced in the late 1940s, only to be met with significant resistance from SAG leadership, who had no interest in giving theater actors (or their union leadership) a stake in the business of film acting.

Even though the unions had not yet reached an agreement over television, they realized that they needed to create at least a temporary plan outlining terms and minimum compensation in order to avoid producers setting an undesirable standard for television screen labor. Throughout November 1939, various union attorneys circulated preliminary plans to establish workplace protocols for television performances while they sorted out internal conflicts. These drafts provided guidelines for producers that the unions hoped would influence future agreements. First, early plans accounted for variable lengths of television shows and accompanying minimum pay rates. The need for varying minimums reflects the instability of early television programming: programs were not necessarily slotted into a predetermined schedule. Second, the plans laid out detailed payment plans for rehearsals, which were essential for live broadcasts. Finally, attorneys outlined terms for replay of material and/or second performances. The elements contained in this collaborative and preliminary endeavor guided the terms of later contracts.

The initial demands combined several different specializations of the various unions. Terms for rehearsal and reuse were more consistent with theater and radio contracts than film-acting contracts, which did not account for the value of replay or rereleases before television. Working in a medium that profited tremendously from reuse in different markets, leaders and workers in radio saw this as an essential term. The groundwork for discussions was laid by musicians, who had suffered significant financial and job losses to both the recording industry and the film industry's conversion to sound. The American Society of Composers, Authors and Publishers (ASCAP) was already actively fighting and negotiating with television networks over replay terms as early as 1940. The American Federation of Musicians (AFM), who represented live performers rather than musicians' publishing rights, had to take a different tack, which included advocating for a ban first on live music in television in 1949 and a year later on recorded music on television.[15] With the topic of reuse already under discussion in relation to music, it inevitably became a point of contention among the actors' unions. For actors the challenge was that the jurisdictional split by medium meant that each union had a different experience discussing residuals, with theater and radio leadership expressing concern that SAG was not doing enough to benefit its membership for the reuse of filmed material.

Letters shot back and forth, debating AEA's "rightful" claim over television, and thus demonstrating sustained tension between East and West Coast unions. Whether union animosity was a continuation of concerns that emerged during AEA's ill-fated venture into Los Angeles in the early '20s or its failure to anticipate the studio adoption of sound, or a combination of the two, many of the problems preventing a smooth resolution to television jurisdiction bore a striking resemblance to those of the past. For the next seven years, encompassing Hollywood's adjustments to World War II, television conversations paused, but when the war ended, the topic of television was even more urgent and the jurisdictional battles reemerged.

Union discussions around television's medium specificity were part of larger industrial conversations about the relationship between media forms and whether they were in competition or could coexist as collaborative forms. Although television was often considered a threat to box office revenues, film studios were interested in television as a potential revenue stream from an early stage. Christopher Anderson explains that "throughout the early 1950s, the industry trade press debated whether television would reveal itself to be friend or foe of the movie studio."[16] The relationship between film and television was in flux, and the struggles between actors' unions added an extra dimension of conflict to television's cultural development. Television became more ubiquitous just as many film actors were released from their contracts, and many found themselves in need of this new work. These social and industrial factors made it all the more pressing for the unions to establish bargaining terms and to begin negotiations with networks and television producers—as soon as they could resolve their internal debates.

AN UNCERTAIN PROFESSION FROM COAST TO COAST

Television was envisioned as a national medium at every stage of its development; as Jonathan Sterne explains, "National planning, national advertising and a national infrastructure were to characterize the structure of American television."[17] Although the medium was oriented toward a mass audience between the coasts, the political economy of television production was not evenly disbursed across the United States. Programs were typically produced in one of the major cities (primarily New York, but occasionally Los Angeles), and in the late 1940s studios, networks, and various competing parties were battling to decide where this would continue to happen. Allen J. Scott describes television's move to Los Angeles in the 1950s in simple terms: "The studios now set about establishing specialized television programming divisions in order to capitalize on their own creative capabilities. . . . television program production and motion picture production became irrevocably intertwined, and a major shift of the former from New York to Hollywood occurred."[18] Although Scott's book is about how and why regional clusters of labor are so successful, he presents a summary of this history that emphasizes top-down decision-making. But labor disputes are not executive decisions; they are collaborations between workers and across hierarchies that identify how industries work, often even before an industry is fully established, and determine terms and parameters. In the case of television jurisdiction, conversations among the actors contributed to television's shift to become a bicoastal medium.

If the performers' unions seemed excessively preoccupied with television's potential to offer more jobs, this was largely a result of changes to the labor markets for actors in Los Angeles and New York. By the late 1940s, the opportunities for professional acting were entrenched and regionally concentrated, with film production predominantly in Los Angeles, live theater in New York, and radio split between the coasts. To obtain full-time work in film or theater, actors needed to live in either New York or Los Angeles. As Scott points out, regional industry clusters tend to form around industries "where relations between firms cannot be planned over extended periods of time so that useful inter-firm contacts need to be constantly programmed and reprogrammed."[19] In essence, the regional concentration of creative industries formed in order to accommodate the nature of creative productions. For example: aspiring actors needed to be in cities where talent scouts might see their work, and working actors needed to be able to get to and from auditions easily and be available for performances or shooting. With respect to film, the importance of being near centers of production, which also included film studios as well as agents and talent scouts, accounts for the waves of Hollywood hopefuls who began flooding into Los Angeles beginning in the 1910s.[20] As work began to diminish in both of these cities, television offered a way to fuel these cultural hubs and present a solution to labor's woes.

Although the basic struggles facing actors in New York and Los Angeles were the same, the reasons that actors faced a scarcity of roles differed. The contrasting industrial conditions facing performers on each coast, as well as the uncertainty regarding whether or not television production would be centered in New York or Los Angeles, laid the foundation for heated debates over television and who would benefit from the opportunities generated by this mass media form. Wherever television production resided would help reshape the labor market for actors. If television production was going to be centered in New York, this would create tremendous opportunities for AEA and AGVA members, but if it moved to Los Angeles, SAG members would be closer to auditions and casting opportunities. The history of television's industrial location is a significant part of television's development and identity as a medium, but the story of actors and unions shows why location mattered and how actors contributed to broader decisions about where television would be made.

New York

Like Hollywood film actors, New York theater and radio actors faced an overcrowded workforce—too many job seekers and not enough jobs, making it difficult for actors to earn a living from acting work alone. The immediate history of theater actors experiencing the constriction of available jobs over several decades provides a parallel for the experience of the studio-era film actor. In the nineteenth century, theaters maintained stock companies that kept actors under contract and working consistently for a particular theater, but the centrality of the stock company began to diminish in the 1870s. As Sean Holmes explains: "American theatergoers had grown progressively less willing to patronize shows that did not offer the promise of a star, leaving theater managers with little alternative other than to cut the size of their companies in order to meet the salary demands of big-name performers."[21] By 1880 there were only eight remaining stock companies in the United States.[22]

In the mid-twentieth century, the outlook for theater actors was equally grim. According to a survey of theater actors working between 1941 and 1942, only about a third of all Equity members were employed within a given month.[23] Both the senior and junior members of Equity were struggling to make their minimum workweeks, as the number of new theater actors joining Equity was steadily growing and the number of productions continued to shrink.[24] In the years after WWII the number of new Equity members was more than double the amount at the beginning of the 1940s.[25] With an expanded labor market and many unemployed actors, Equity leadership was looking for other ways to find performance work for those within the New York market. By 1940, theater actors could already see what television could offer. That year Robert Henderson, a theatrical producer, asked AEA about the possibility of filming "When We Are Married" at the Lyceum Theatre to air on NBC. AEA and the actors agreed to do this in addition to their regular salaries on the condition that the show was not commercially sponsored.[26] This agreement demonstrated that television could offer an additional revenue stream, but at this time only with the caveat that the artistic integrity of the performance was not compromised. Although the arrangements for televised theatrical performances had to be made on a case-by-case basis, this presented badly needed income opportunities for theater actors.

When actors were not consistently working on stage, many found other paid performance opportunities, a process that involved bouncing between jobs and performance venues represented by different unions. AEA represented principal performers, Chorus Equity Association (CEA) represented performers in the chorus (until CEA merged into AEA in 1955), the American Federation of Radio Artists (AFRA) represented announcers and voice actors on radio broadcasts, the American Guild of Variety Artists (AGVA) represented performers in nonbook shows (which could include variety shows, nightclub performances, cabarets, circus performances, etc.), and the American Guild of Musical Artists (AGMA) represented singers and dancers. For New York actors, this setup was logistically complicated and financially onerous, requiring them to pay union dues to up to five unions. Thus, when television and the prospect of yet another union arrived, some New York actors, though comfortable navigating multiple unions, dues, and memberships, were eager to simplify this process with a merger.

Discussions about television forced everyone to confront one of the key complications associated with the performers' unions: namely, that journeymen actors and extras did not necessarily distinguish between jobs and types of performances as cleanly as the unions did. As theater, film, and television actor Norman Lloyd explained, "I never thought of it [TV] in terms of its impact, I just thought it was another place to get a job."[27] Lloyd's pragmatic comment underscores that for him the priority was acting, and distinctions between performance venues were largely irrelevant. While Lloyd may have looked at TV as another place to work and get paid, as his credits indicate, once he started taking television roles in the 1950s he would not act in another film for more than twenty years.

Embracing fluidity across venues did not always work in favor of the working actor. When Hollywood stars, who had greater visibility than other actors, decided to perform in new venues, this could disrupt opportunities for stage actors. For example, stars might make appearances at New York clubs, but if they were not paying members of the AGVA, they would be performing in violation of the AGVA collective bargaining agreement. In 1948, AGVA sent letters warning Jane Russell, Milton Berle, Judy Garland, Betty Hutton, and Harry Ritz that their surprise appearances at New York clubs were "inconveniencing" New York performers and, most importantly, that they were not paying the appropriate union dues.[28] Thus the increased movement of stars outside of Hollywood films in the late 1940s not only pushed working actors out of paying gigs but also impeded other unions' jurisdictions.

Stars did not initially disrupt opportunities for actors on television because the Motion Picture Producers Association (MPPA) banned film stars from appearing on television from 1950 to 1953.[29] The result of this ban was that in the early years of television, producers adapted many radio programs, and frequently took those stars and actors along with the programs. Even after the official ban ended, as Susan Murray explains, this had a lasting impact on who appeared on television: "In part because of the reluctance of Hollywood stars and the desire for format continuity on behalf of sponsors, the talent lineup for early television would contain many familiar radio names. It also included a number of vaudevillians who failed on radio and in film but eventually found success in television."[30] Hollywood stars did not need the money from television shows and often avoided it because of its lower cultural prestige. But even if Hollywood stars had the desire, they were simply not allowed to be on TV. This ban on stars in television demonstrates another aspect of infrastructure and division between mediums. Eventually this would create cultural expectations and influence hiring pipelines for broadcast work that would accompany the development of each industry over subsequent decades.

Los Angeles

For many film actors, especially stars, the studio system offered a degree of income stability. As I explained in the previous chapter, approximately five hundred actors were under contract in the 1940s, but the Paramount Decrees in 1948 set in motion changes in production financing, Hollywood profits, and, for many actors, the stability of contract work. In the late 1940s, more actors lost their contracts and joined the ranks of underemployed actors. The studio transformation from a system that balanced contracted actors with freelance actors to a primarily freelance labor system was gradual. The transition began when character actors, who did not serve as a marketing draw for films, were released from their contracts. This resulted in moving a group of actors who were previously consistently employed into the same precarious position that other actors and all extras had occupied for the past two decades. In 1947 there were 742 actors working under contract; only one year later that number dropped to 463, and by 1956 to 229.[31] Some, like Lucille Ball, were dropped from their contracts only to find greater fame in television, but others weaved between media forms as they pieced together a career.

As studios considered how to reorganize their business models for film production, they were simultaneously trying to negotiate and assimilate the popularization of television. Film studios hoped to expand their influence into television and eventually produce for both media forms, but there were some significant barriers to the film studios achieving this goal.[32] First, an interventionist FCC prevented the film studios, which had recently been forced to divest their theatrical exhibition wings, from acquiring television stations as a new mode of exhibition. Second, the radio broadcast networks, CBS and NBC, had a competitive interest in keeping film studios out of television production.[33] From a network perspective,

TABLE 2.1. ACTORS UNDER CONTRACT AT THEATRICAL STUDIOS

Year	1947	1948	1949	1950	1951	1952	1953	1954	1955	1956
Actors under contract	742	463	360	315	318	344	304	232	236	229

Source: From Irving Bernstein, *Hollywood at the Crossroads: An Economic Study of the Motion Picture Industry* (Hollywood, CA: Hollywood AF of L Film Council, December 1957), 23.

liveness, as Michele Hilmes argues, "helped the networks hold onto their primary reason for being and to their industry dominance."[34] Immediacy had its benefits, but the problem for the networks was that live recordings could only air once (unless they were kinescoped, which meant the broadcast was recorded on film).[35]

In contrast to the studios' fear of television and obstacles to its business, actors never looked at television as a threat—its arrival was only seen as a blessing. With no FCC interference or established television unions or actors to compete with, the existing acting community saw only increased opportunity. By the 1940s the sporadic and competitive nature of acting was accepted as a given, and television offered some immediate financial and creative benefits for actors seeking work. Thus while media producers attempted to form the infrastructural boundaries and connections between film and television, many actors were already on the ground trying to navigate the similarities and differences between television and other modes of performance.

For SAG actors, television was important not only to ameliorate the loss of contracts, but also because they hoped it could provide a solution for jobs lost to runaway productions. Speaking just prior to his departure as counsel for SAG, Laurence Beilenson explained to the board that the main concerns facing the industry were the establishment of SAG jurisdiction over television and unemployment—concerns that were clearly interconnected in the eyes of union leadership.[36] Rather than identifying unemployment as a fundamental attribute for film-acting careers since the beginning of the motion picture industry, Beilenson blamed postwar runaway productions for the rampant unemployment in the 1950s. After World War II, film industries worldwide designed policies and established tax incentives to attract foreign investment and bolster their own domestic film industries in the process. Suffering from diminished profits after divesting their exhibition wings alongside new competition from television, US studios took advantage of global financing opportunities and sent US filmmakers and stars to foreign locales in the postwar period, shooting 563 films abroad between 1948 and 1962.[37] The shift toward location shooting did not significantly impact the stars who headlined foreign productions and jetted around the world to shoots in England, Spain, Italy, and any country that courted Hollywood. In fact, stars experienced additional financial advantages in the postwar period in the form of income tax breaks.[38] However, this production shift toward international productions had a demonstrable negative impact on the availability of work for US character actors and extras who were not worth transporting to foreign locations or were forced out of films due to quotas and conditions requiring US films to cast non-US actors in order to qualify for foreign funding or incentives.[39] There were myriad financial benefits that sent studios abroad, and location shooting also facilitated opulent yet inexpensive productions that were conducive to the new widescreen and color formats designed to compete with small black-and-white television screens. As runaway film productions were becoming a concern for Los Angeles film workers and their unions, television would, at least rhetorically, become important as a substitute venue for domestic production jobs and help keep acting work in Los Angeles.[40]

While television provided a significant number of job opportunities, these jobs differed from those lost and contributed to the growth of freelance acting roles. Between 1947 and 1950, 427 people were released from studio contracts, all employees previously receiving weekly salaries who now (presumably) joined the ranks of actors seeking work.[41] Left without steady contracts, actors had two options for comparable on-screen work: freelance film contracts or television. But in 1950 these two avenues did not provide sufficient work to make up for the lost contracts. A SAG survey of employment records from March 20 through April 3, 1950, of television producers shooting on film revealed that television employed 266 actors in this two-week period working at SAG minimums (fifty-five dollars per day for films and forty-five dollars per day for commercials).[42] Television provided a welcome source of income for actors looking for work, but it did not cover all the people released from contracts, even assuming the work went solely to former film actors.[43]

While some of these character actors turned to television for work, most remained in the film industry. In 1954 actors on the low end of the earning scale ($7,500 per year and under) still worked primarily in film, with only 38 percent of workdays spent on television shows. A year later, television had become significantly more important, constituting 46 percent of workdays for SAG members.[44] As Christine Becker notes, television was less important for the successful actors who earned over $7,500.[45] However, this data indicates that in the 1950s television was growing and becoming essential for performers in an increasingly freelance economy. To a certain extent, television was fulfilling its potential for actors as a new source of job opportunities, even if it was not a clear replacement for lost income.

While union leaders were attempting to figure out the best way to advocate for actors, they also realized that they were under tremendous pressure to speed up their internal debates and draft a contract. This was extremely important for unions looking to maintain their power within the industry, because, as demonstrated in the previous chapter, unions that are unable to establish a contract or agreements with producers lose membership and eventually the ability to continue representing actors. But more importantly for individual actors, working without a collectively bargained contract can often create wildly variable and often poor or unsafe working conditions. Nevertheless, amid all the uncertainty over contracts, actors looking to dive into the new medium or simply earn enough to pay rent began working in television without representation and protections.

LOCATION, LOCATION, LOCATION

In 1948, *New York Times* television critic Jack Gould reported on a town meeting on the future of television, observing that "television combines the close-up of the motion picture, the spontaneity of the living stage and the instantaneousness of radio."[46] As this comment indicates, critics (as well as directors like Rouben Mamoulian, who was quoted in Gould's article) were interested in understanding and defining the essential stylistic properties of television. For actors, this was not merely an issue of aesthetics and creative possibilities—formal elements such as the close-up and liveness informed contract negotiations and impacted television's compensation and labor conditions. In these earliest days of television, union leadership and actors were navigating tricky terrain; television was not ubiquitous, the narrative form was uncertain, and there was not yet an established star system that guaranteed work for anyone. In such an environment, all actors were replaceable. The most effective way for actors to position themselves as viable TV actors was to work to define a TV form and style that most benefited them.

Although the unions were territorial and fought with each other over television, the approach that actors adopted throughout their negotiations with producers could be characterized as collaborative rather than antagonistic. Sociologist Stanley Aronowitz criticizes this kind of negotiation as "class collaboration" between the union and producers.[47] Although many performers in the actors' unions made little money, they did not identify with the working-class consciousness; actors instead focused on how to be better working television professionals by understanding the core elements of television and its potential as a creative medium. These central concerns were visible in the way that actors approached their inquiry into television.

In 1947 the 4As created a Television Committee and tasked it with surveying and standardizing television work. The primary objective of the committee was to craft a contract for television, but its first step was to gather actors' experiences and try to reach a consensus on the existing practices and abuses of a nascent industry.[48] Given the state of the television industry, drafting a contract required both a study of the industry and a healthy degree of speculation. Focusing on the concrete issue of establishing wages, committee chair George Heller explained the broader challenges facing the unions:

> So long as there is not a television audience as yet we cannot expect to arrive at anywhere near the standard wage AFRA has arrived at in radio. . . . We have to make certain that we provide work for the members of the branches. It is a serious problem between trying to establish a high scale and at the same time see that we are not depriving our people of work . . . if they cannot get professions [*sic*] they will use amateurs except possibly for important parts.[49]

Although he is speaking about television, Heller identifies some of the general problems unions face with new technologies. New technologies take time to realize their mature form and full profit potential. As such, media producers often require workers to accept low wages as they figure out how to maximize profit from media content. Asking for too much at an early stage could jeopardize the ability of actors to reach an agreement with producers and potentially drive them into working with nonunion actors. Thus with any major technological development, the unions are positioned in a reactive stance, forced to figure out how to craft a strong contract for workers that does not drive networks and producers away from the negotiating table.

Part of the difficulty for committee members trying to get a handle on television working conditions was that there was such a wide array of television programs in 1947. Television in the late 1940s featured popular children's shows, including *Howdy Doody* (1947–1960) and *Kukla, Fran and Ollie* (originally titled *Junior Jamboree*, 1947–1957), shows that achieved long-running success, and in the case of *Howdy Doody* generated significant additional revenue through merchandising.[50] However, for the most part the television landscape was eclectic and featured respected anthology series such as *Kraft Television Theatre* (1947–1958), live and recorded plays (featured in shows such as *Television Playhouse* [1947–1948]), variety shows, films made for television, and educational and public service programs, some of which were commercially funded while others were network-funded. Networks were also in the process of figuring out how to program and schedule television, which had an impact on the shows they ordered. The independently produced *Public Prosecutor* was shot in 1947 and set to air one year later, but was pulled from NBC because the network decided that shows needed to be thirty minutes rather than twenty minutes.[51] Although some of these shows were lauded and lasted throughout the "Golden Age of Television," others were stiff, exceedingly similar to radio programs, and short-lived.

Public Prosecutor is punctuated by Steven Allen's (John Howard's) account of the case. Howard appears like a newscaster, sitting in the center of the screen as he directly addresses the camera. Thomas Schatz comments, "Actors appear distracted, if not anguished, as they try to hit their marks consistently in the first take."[52] Although filmed programs should have been able to carry over performance practices from film, the reality was that programs filmed for television had a much smaller budget and shows were shot on shorter schedules, leaving little room for actors to improve performances. For actors like Howard, who had previously worked in film, it is likely that they were stressed about nailing everything on the first take, and the effect is also often quite stiff.

Live television necessitated distinctive performance demands and offered different challenges for actors. For example, performers working as hosts had to engage directly with the camera, something film actors were discouraged from doing.[53] These particular performance styles, which privileged spontaneity and direct engagement with audiences, developed over several decades and were characteristic of theater and variety performances rather than film performances.[54] Actors in live engagements only had one chance to hit marks and lines, which required different competencies and rehearsal strategies than those familiar to film actors (who could take advantage of multiple takes). Knowing lines and blocking required extensive rehearsal time and improvisational skills to produce a professional and engaging performance. Television actors likewise were concerned with the large variation in compensation for rehearsal times, as well as the amount of time they were required to work under harsh lights, a physically taxing job that frequently generated pay bumps for actors working in other performance fields. The lighting was a function of close-ups, which were necessary for audiences to see actors on the small screen. All these components constructed the uniquely televisual performance, which combined aspects of both film and theater work.

Attempts to account for these factors contributed to uncertainty about the monetary value of different kinds of television roles. Comparisons between different experiences on television sets tended to be purely functional, focusing on hours worked and pay; they also revealed that the wide array of programs and their unpredictable rehearsal and recording times created inequity in compensation. Actor Ben Lackland, who worked in television throughout the 1950s, explained that he was paid $100 for twelve hours of rehearsal and performance in a three-act play (one hour and fifteen minutes).[55] In contrast, Vinton Hayworth (later known for his role on *I Dream of Jeannie*) described rehearsing forty-four hours for a play of the same length for a fee of $200. Translated into an hourly wage, the difference was significant; Lackland earned about $7.50 per hour, while Hayworth received approximately $4.50 per hour. Within the programs, pay also varied wildly. Hayworth reported earning $200 for his work in a televised play, but noted that some featured players only received $50 or $75. In this information-gathering conversation among union members, Hayworth did not discuss performance specifics such as artistic quality or even whether or not those being paid more had greater star power based on previous performances; thus, it is difficult to assess the logic of these comparisons. In essence, these comparisons simply highlighted the vast compensation differences that seemingly had no discernible rhyme or reason.

Conversations between union members about their own pay attempted to account for big-picture financial and labor considerations. For example, Hayworth explained that the networks established the budget to be divvied up among the workers: "Directors are victims of the higher up men; . . . actors salaries are a matter of individual bargaining and . . . most of the directors are for the actors but NBC sets up a budget for television and tells them what they can spend."[56] In this explanation, Hayworth imagines a degree of camaraderie as actors and directors are similarly disenfranchised by the new and chaotic system of budgeting and individual negotiation. Actors experienced fewer problems in the beginnings of television than in the early days of the film industry, but it was clear there was little transparency in production or minimum pay scales for television. This mode of information-gathering was somewhat haphazard, as actors had incomplete information and little means of obtaining more from others on set. Without union representation facilitating conversations with networks and producers, there was no way to gain a holistic understanding of television's budgets, practices, and payment system.

Some network producers were more consistent in payments and labor practices than others. One actor reported that NBC paid daily rates of $35 for speaking-bit roles, which was consistent with SAG minimums, and $10 for nonspeaking background roles.[57] NBC's rates were reportedly higher than other television studios, but still lagged behind the rates SAG and SEG negotiated for comparable parts; in the same year, background work in film began at $15.56 per day.[58] The networks, such as NBC, that were paying close to union rates likely did so because they expected to eventually reach an agreement over standardized rates and terms and wanted to remain in the good graces of the union leadership. But during this nascent stage, networks seemed to capitalize on uncertainty by setting low bars for compensation.[59]

Union leadership was tasked with surveying and assessing television work in order to create minimum terms. In these discussions, working conditions were described and defined via analogies to theater and radio practices much more so than to film practices. There were elements of live television work that resembled theater practices, such as long rehearsal times, work under harsh lights, and, perhaps most importantly, geography—like theater, early television production was based in New York. As several committee members, including Vinton Hayworth, pointed out, some directors and networks had already communicated that if the unions set rates that were too high, they would abandon live TV for filmed programming.[60] Although these comments were anecdotal, they indicate that actors in New York were nervous about demanding too much from producers and sending television production to Los Angeles. Filmed television had a different set of conditions and could be shot anywhere, which was undoubtedly at the heart of some concerns in these meetings.

In the late '40s, the East Coast unions proposed two strategies for handling jurisdiction over television. The first, which all the unions supported except for SAG and SEG, was to merge all of the performers' unions. Expressing his pro-merger position, AGVA representative George Price stated, "I belong to four branches and I don't like it."[61] Pro-merger advocates typically identified multiple memberships as an essential reason for merger, while others cited administrative efficiency and a larger (and therefore stronger) union. As a 1948 merger proposal document explained, "the merged union, with one office in each city instead of four offices, with branch offices throughout the country, and with interchangeable executives and personnel, can be more efficiently administered than the four separate unions, each with separate offices and personnel . . . unification of the memberships of the four unions involved will strengthen the performers' ranks against inroads by anti-union legislation."[62] The desire to consolidate resources was part of the unions' attempt to manage the inevitable geographic expansion that was part of the burgeoning national broadcast form. What is also significant about the merger discussions was that they were concurrent with committee investigations into television's labor conditions. Some performers felt a merger would answer the question of who should bargain for actors, but this position was controversial. Throughout the merger discussions, actors had to determine if they believed it was possible to administrate a union on a national scale, as well as grapple with the prickly subject of whether all performance work was essentially similar. Even though the merger made administrative sense, it could not eliminate the actors' feelings about cultural distinctions between types of performance.

While those in favor of the merger emphasized the streamlining of resources and the elimination of multiple sets of union dues, those opposed expressed concerns that the merger was shortsighted. In a lengthy and well-reasoned memo delivered to the AEA council, Margaret Webster, both a longtime theater actress and daughter of generations of theater actors, explained: "the interest of AFRA and SAG . . . have always been, and in the nature of things cannot help but be, competitive with and in many respects injurious to the interests of the theatre. . . . If it were not so, we should not now be having meetings and discussions re chronic unemployment in the theatre. Their representatives cannot possibly be expected to guard, promote or cherish the interests of the theatre as such."[63] As these comments make clear, Webster is not operating from an assumption that all types of performance are equal; instead she positions these forms as in competition. With respect to union politics, Webster's argument was that a large union with diffuse interests would fail to serve the interests of all members appropriately. Of further concern to actors like Webster, who "cherish" the theater and had no interest in working in film or television, the merger would cause their dues to increase and would fail to solve the issue of un- or underemployment in the theater.

The strength of Margaret Webster's letter seemed to reside in its specific point of view. Webster wrote as a theater actor, invested in the interest of other theater actors, and responded with confidence in the strength of Equity as a union. As Webster observed, Equity would shoulder significant financial costs in order to support the development of television agreements. From this observation, Webster concluded: "I do not believe that this proposed merger is for the good of the theatre or the theatre actor."[64] Although this merger would theoretically create more jobs, there was no guarantee as to where these jobs would be, and, as she explicitly stated, it was unlikely that the benefit would be to theater actors. Webster's memo circulated among SAG leadership, and although many were previously in favor of the merger, it helped galvanize opposition to the merger and provided language to solidify their own anti-merger arguments. As an actor and longtime member of Equity, SAG, and AFRA, merger supporter Alan Hewitt lamented, "Miss Webster gave crystallization to . . . [others'] misgivings and doubts."[65] For Webster and those who supported her position, strength came from a clearly defined identity, and attempts to collapse an array of types of acting would ultimately weaken the union's identity and solidarity.

Those in favor of the merger maintained that it would increase leverage for all actors, and it would allow actors to focus on performances across venues rather than on medium. In essence, the merger encouraged a model of acting that emphasized individual creative work rather than the ways performances contributed to a larger creative piece. One of the AEA merger committee members argued, "this arrangement is dedicated to the fellow who works across craft lines."[66] In response to Webster's fears that AFRA and SAG had competing interests with Equity, Hewitt wrote, "1098, call it 1100 members of AFRA are also members of Equity, that's 20% of our membership. . . . These other people are not a race apart; they are made of the same stuff as we and dream the same dreams our lives are made on, of success and acclaim in the theatre. . . . These people from other unions are sitting next to you now as fellow Equity-members."[67] By drawing on Equity's membership numbers, Hewitt indicated the importance of radio to a significant number (although not the majority) of union members. As the dual-membership total indicates, one-fifth of

New York's theater actors relied upon radio jobs to earn a living. The organizational boundaries between the unions ultimately made it more difficult for performers to move between unions, which was a problem for actors and the reason why many of them supported a merger. However, Hewitt did not rely simply on the membership numbers to make his case for the merger—he made a point to stress the class and prestige similarities between theater and radio.

The specificities of the arguments for and against the merger indicate the importance of cultural capital, often at the expense of material benefits, in the actors' decision-making process. Rejecting the merger did not change the reality of making a living for many actors, but it did maintain the preexisting boundaries between stage, film, and radio. Historically, success in artistic fields has been measured by cultural rather than economic capital. Pierre Bourdieu offers the theoretical construct for how cultural capital in production fields shapes the stakes of an art form's cultural status. Bourdieu explains that in the field of cultural production, "what is at stake is the power to impose the dominant definition of the writer and therefore to delimit the population of those entitled to take part in the struggle to define the writer."[68] Artists (whether they are writers or actors) attempt to sustain cultural and creative capital. In the media industries, the unions are powerful official bodies that have, as Bourdieu describes, "the monopoly of the power to consecrate producers or products."[69] Margaret Webster's and Alan Hewitt's statements about the merger seem to indicate that they both implicitly understood the monopoly power of the union, but they addressed this cultural reality in different ways. Webster linked the importance of union autonomy to the maintenance of performance specificity, whereas Hewitt attempted to appeal to logic about the realities of performance labor and the potential for acclaim in contemporary media such as radio. In both cases the actors attempted to shift the conversation to define the cultural values of performers. Webster's position won, and Equity remained autonomous.

The merger was positioned as a solution that allowed all actors and all union leadership to share in the opportunities television presented. However, the cultural, administrative, and geographic differences all proved to be too much to overcome. Although there was much debate among theater and radio actors in New York, ultimately the most resistance to the merger came from the West Coast. SAG and SEG flatly refused to merge with the other performers' unions, and the remaining unions rejected a partial merger. When the merger strategy failed in 1949, AEA, CEA, AFRA, AGMA, and AGVA proposed a separate unit to bargain for television, which would eventually be called the Television Authority (TVA).

The proposal of the TVA did little to resolve the issue of television jurisdiction, which continued to be a source of conflict between the unions. The mood was tense during the various meetings and negotiations among performers' unions in 1949. There was much to discuss regarding who should bargain for television, but the geographic distance between unions and the complicated logistics of scheduling meetings to accommodate all the voices bred anger among the members of the 4As. The unions shot telegraphs and letters back and forth across the country lamenting the hardship of cross-country travel and the high cost of scheduling meetings. Leaders grew fearful that further delays would make it more difficult for them to establish the contract terms. As AEA member and TVA founding member Philip Loeb explained in a February 1949 statement to union leadership, "The need for organization is pressing and should not be delayed. Abuses and exploitation abound."[70] Television's mercurial form created challenges for the battling unions. As Loeb continued in his statement, "The future of television is unknown. It looks as if its effect might be cataclysmic. Right now, no one can foresee if it will remain half film, half live or not, whether the center of production will be East, West, or National, whether radio, the screen, the theatre will survive as they now exist."[71] Technology and distribution were central to Loeb's concerns, but all the issues he listed, particularly location and the continued existence of the unions, were of direct importance for actors looking for work.

The West Coast unions, SAG and SEG, rejected the formation of the TVA, claiming that there was no need to create a new bargaining entity, as it might create additional jurisdiction conflicts in the future. They claimed that supporting a new union was tantamount to "committing organizational suicide."[72] Instead, SAG and SEG favored a strategy that divided television production between filmed and live and assigned its jurisdiction to existing unions (SAG and AFRA respectively). However, as they explained in a 1949 meeting of the unions, they were willing to accept a position in which they jointly negotiated for television alongside the TVA. Thus the conclusion of the union meetings was to retain their regional cultural control over their discrete art forms, and to affirm the distinctions between unions as a function of geography.

The specter of geographical divides shaped cultural differences and actively hampered negotiations. In July and August 1949, representatives from the 4As met at the Roosevelt Hotel in Los Angeles at SAG and SEG's invitation. In his opening remarks, AEA executive secretary Paul

Dullzell attempted to soothe some of the tension, declaring, "If there is prejudice about the 3000 miles between us and that is the only objection to the Guild becoming a part of TVA, that can be overcome."[73] Without offering any concrete solutions, this statement ostensibly downplays the significance of location, but it clearly raised an important issue that had percolated in conversations about union governance since 1920. Although the meeting opened with many representatives explaining their plan to keep an open mind during negotiations, the tone of the meeting quickly became strained. SAG leadership was willing to grant the TVA control over live television as long as SAG retained the rights to filmed television. This did not satisfy the East Coast unions, which still wanted a single television union that included SAG representatives.

The East Coast unions were never able to address SAG's concerns over how the East Coast could represent and understand the needs of the West Coast membership. Speaking to union leadership, SAG executive secretary Jack Dales asked, "How would we work on the situation so that the 8000 actors on this [west] coast could be represented if TVA were the sole authority?"[74] If union leadership moved to the East Coast, SAG also had to grapple with the issue of who among the membership could represent the union in New York. SAG attorney William Berger explained, "the TVA plan would have the governing body meet in New York. The Guild could not be represented by working members and therefore could not accept [the TVA proposal]."[75] Even though SAG represented numerous high-powered stars, location was still of paramount importance to protect its workers.

Despite the initial resistance from SAG and SEG, by the end of 1949 the unions had all accepted the TVA proposal. This was not the solution that everyone wanted, but the jurisdictional debates had gone on long enough. The East Coast unions were unhappy that SAG and SEG retained their autonomy and did not join the TVA. SAG and SEG were also on the defensive, proclaiming in an announcement to the membership, "If in spite of the reasonable approach of the Guilds the sponsors of the proposed Television Authority insist upon invading the Guilds' motion picture field, then they will be solely responsible for forcing an unwarranted and unjustifiable jurisdictional war upon actors and the public."[76] SAG and SEG's righteousness in their claim over television seemed to echo Equity's sentiments about their natural right over actors almost a decade earlier. Between the first conversations in 1938 and the renewed debates in the 1940s, the cultural import of film had grown, giving screen actors and their union more power and weight in these conversations. Although many leaders in the 4As believed that television's affinities with other forms of performance could serve as a bridge between the unions, West Coast unions were focused on securing television work in Los Angeles.

By 1950 the TVA was an active unit working to organize television actors, which meant that the unions had laid the groundwork for helping actors establish their working conditions. But this was only the first step. The TVA (and, separately, SAG) still needed to negotiate contracts for television actors. This tumultuous struggle among the unions and their slowness to organize served to benefit television producers, as they could continue to coast on lower production costs while the unions negotiated terms. Even though the TVA was instrumental in eventually determining conditions for actors working in live television, this hard-fought internal battle could not resolve the existing problems of exploitation and under-employment that many actors faced, as was especially apparent for those on the lowest rung of the performance hierarchy: the extras.

THE MARGINS OF TELEVISION

As stage, screen, and radio performers all vied for control and influence over television, extras struggled to figure out how they fit into this new media landscape. In the early twentieth century the labor conditions of extras had contributed to new casting procedures and the creation of labor structures that developed a broad ecosystem around actors. The culture around extras changed, but they continued to struggle with sporadic and temporary film work. At the time of the jurisdictional debates, most work for extras was in the film industry, as films had more on-screen space, longer run times, larger budgets, and well-established aesthetic and narrative conventions that necessitated and justified spending money on extras. The primary challenge for extras was to make themselves relevant to television as a media form and an industry, a task that would prove very challenging for a group of workers with minimal leverage and no apparent value in early television.

Formed in 1947, one year before the television jurisdiction conversations heated up, the members of the Los Angeles–based Screen Extras Guild (SEG) found themselves in the midst of interunion conflict before they could fully develop their own union identity. As a screen performers' group located in Los Angeles, SEG primarily associated itself with SAG in debates between the unions and aligned itself accordingly against the New York–based TVA. As SEG president Richard Gordon explained to the membership in 1951, the screen guilds battled against "the selfish and short-sighted program by the promoters of the so-called Television Authority to force a new union upon motion-picture extras and actors merely because a new market had been developed for motion-picture film in television."[77] Even if television was not a significant battleground for extras, Gordon made this statement to affirm the union's solidarity with SAG on this issue.

Historically, extras were a vulnerable group of performers who elicited a great deal of sympathy, but never acquired any leverage. As performers who remained in the background, they were inherently tangential to narrative action, not part of a film's marketing, and could be easily replaced. As I discuss in the previous chapter, SEG formed because extras felt neglected by SAG. Members' feelings of marginalization and neglect persisted through the struggles over television, in part because SEG was still a new union with minimal resources. Generally, unions maintain a treasury surplus to defray potential costs during a strike, but SEG members earned less per project than SAG members, and their dues were also lower, which meant that the union had limited resources available in the late 1940s and 1950s.

SEG's relatively weak bargaining position contributed to the anxiety union leaders felt upon the arrival of television. For most performers' guilds, television presented an opportunity for new roles, but its small screen, reduced budgets, and more intimate domestic narratives left few opportunities for extras. Speaking candidly at a conference of the performers' unions in 1949, SEG president Edd Russell declared, "We fear television taking away the extra's livelihood as it cannot take away yours. We are fearful of a new union."[78] In addition to the uncertainty of what television could offer for extras, Russell was speaking to a table of union representatives who only a few years earlier had attempted to deny SEG a seat at the table to discuss the issue of television jurisdiction at all.

Since extras could not directly influence television negotiations, they focused on strategies such as expanding the geographic reach of each union, which could provide SEG with long-term benefits. SEG's role in the jurisdiction conversations was minimal, but in the interest of maintaining control over its membership and keeping the West Coast film unions autonomous, the union submitted a proposal to help negotiate on behalf of television actors to establish several regional television councils in key cities (New York, Chicago, and Los Angeles). Each of the member unions of the 4As would have representatives on each regional board, and within each region. AEA, CEA, AFRA, AGMA, and AGVA would be tasked with establishing bargaining terms for live television, and SAG and SEG would bargain for filmed television.[79] This plan benefited SEG by administratively aligning them with SAG. SAG leadership opposed the plan, in part because they felt that it gave too much control to the East Coast unions.[80] Members from AGVA supported the plan, but it was widely rejected by the other members of the 4As.[81] Even though the plan was rejected, the focus on regional control illustrates some of the key concerns for below-the-line workers. In order to monitor and improve working conditions on sets, the union staff needed to be able to visit sets and check up on members. However, SEG's interests were increasingly not aligned with SAG, which made it difficult for them to participate in larger conversations about work.

Simply staying present in television conversations was a significant financial hardship for SEG, and the union's frustration peaked in November 1949 when President Gordon sent an angry telegraph to the 4As declaring:

> The Screen Extras Guild wishes to protest the fact that it has been completely ignored and bypassed in the establishment of arrangements and procedures for forthcoming meeting. While the income of our members may be less than that of other Four A's performers, SEG expects to be accorded the same consideration and courtesy as any of its sister branches. Because of the flagrant disregard of SEG in laying plans for these meetings . . . the Screen Extras Guild will not participate in such proposed debates.[82]

Although SEG leadership, most notably Edd Russell, recognized that extras were not central to the television conversation, there is no acknowledgment of this in the telegraph tantrum. Gordon's resolve on this issue was weak, however; between 1950 and 1951, SEG spent $12,000 flying leadership back and forth to New York for meetings about the TVA, a sum that was approximately three times more than what they spent annually on rent.[83] But for a union with no real bargaining power or cultural clout, maintaining presence at the 4As meetings was important for SEG lest they find themselves further marginalized from the unions that could support them.

In a 1951 SEG membership meeting supposedly devoted to the new television representation, the issue of television was virtually ignored beyond a simple report about the current status of the TVA. Instead, the extras focused on their more immediate concerns: getting work and qualifying for unemployment insurance. Chief among their concerns (still) was the role of Central Casting in their livelihood. The problem of finding work plagued all members equally, including SEG president Richard Gordon, who summed up the issue describing his own under-employment. Gordon lamented:

> As of last Tuesday there were 850 people cleared through Central Casting Corporation, not counting what went through Allied and Independent, and the 200 people on location. Now Mr. Philbrick [the head of Central Casting] will tell you that when they have used a thousand extra people in the industry they have scraped the bottom of the barrel, yet I was home, I didn't work. . . . This isn't something that just happens. It happens all the time. It's a worry to me.[84]

Gordon was in a leadership position, but his concerns and the evidence for his claims about casting problems were fundamentally rooted in his own personal experience. Rather than reflecting on the fact that, by his estimate, over a thousand people had worked the previous Tuesday, he worried that if he was not working it was a sign of, or at the very least a perception of, his inadequacy. The amount of time and thoughtful reflection devoted to Central Casting at this television meeting demonstrates how extras themselves were struggling to see themselves in these broader conversations about television.

As the debates around television developed, it became clear that SEG had different demands than those of actors working in SAG. In subsequent decades, the gulf between SAG and SEG's interests grew wider, but the bifurcation of interests became particularly clear in the television jurisdiction conversations. As the lowest members of the actors' hierarchy, extras, who were never under contract with the studios, continued to struggle with the core issues that transcended technological development and medium-specific properties: too few jobs to accommodate the supply of the workforce and poor working conditions. When they did try to combat the loss of roles, they were largely unsuccessful because they had no leverage. In 1952, SEG lobbied for the thirty-mile zone to extend to the entire state of California and for extras around the United States to earn SEG scale.[85] The Association of Motion Picture Producers felt this request was "excessive," and SEG did not have enough bargaining power to win this battle.[86] Even though SEG members might have been on screen with SAG members, their bargaining position was as marginal as their position within the frame.

The vast differences between SAG and SEG meant that they made for an unlikely alliance in the battle for control over television, but together they thwarted the plan to merge all the performers' unions and managed to retain control over film work in Los Angeles. The unions saw this as a victory for screen actors, specifically as it created more opportunities for freelance work. In the face of a new medium, screen actors were able to retain their control over the Los Angeles labor market and carve out a space for the specificity of film acting. Although the battle over television was seemingly coming to an end, SAG still felt it should have jurisdiction over content filmed on celluloid. Just as one jurisdictional battle ended, SAG was gearing up to advocate for bargaining rights for actors on television films.

A NEW MODE OF PRODUCTION OR DISTRIBUTION?

The TVA initially challenged SAG's jurisdiction, but SAG escalated the debates and attempted to settle their differences once and for all. In 1950, with SEG's blessing, SAG finally sought outside arbitration and went to the National Labor Review Board (NLRB) over the issue of films made for television. In sorting out these jurisdictional issues, the ensuing investigation came to embody a legal attempt to conclusively determine the similarities and differences between an actor's work in film versus television. Finally, a governing body would have to clarify some of the key issues of medium specificity that had haunted debates for over a decade.

The TVA was designed to be a temporary solution, in part because the New York unions were still holding out for a merger of all the performers' unions. Union leaders announced in 1950 that "television cuts across all existing craft lines—the stage, films, radio, vaudeville and night clubs. Thus . . . television should be covered by a separate 'authority' representing artists in all acting fields."[87] Conceptualizing television as a medium that crossed all performance venues takes a distinctive view of television as a mode of distribution rather than production. Yet the unions were unable to adopt a bargaining solution that treated television as technology of distribution; their solutions instead emphasized differences in production.

Just because the unions had worked out the administrative jurisdiction did not mean it was clear how the TVA would work for actors. The creation of the TVA initially seemed to mean that the jurisdictional issues were momentarily resolved: TVA would negotiate for actors working in live television, SAG and SEG would cover negotiations for actors working in filmed television, and anything shot on a closed-circuit kinescope (which resembled film production) would be resolved on a case-by-case basis by the 4As. But even with these clear boundaries, confusion persisted among the membership over which union to join. The TVA would also need to forge relationships with television producers to function as an effective bargaining agent for actors. As a new union, the TVA also faced some significant financial barriers and needed operating costs and resources to sustain themselves in the event of a strike. To generate revenue for basic operations, they set their membership fees slightly higher than those of SAG, surely an undesirable rate for a union that still had to prove its value. The administrative tasks were important for the TVA's ability to perform its duties, but it was still unclear precisely who the TVA was going to be working for.

Clarifying some of the nuances of jurisdiction between SAG and the TVA did not completely assuage interunion tensions. The neat division of television jurisdiction between live and filmed programs created the impression that these were organic divisions between types of performance. In December 1950 the TVA complicated the division between film and television by claiming that establishing the TVA never truly resolved who would have jurisdiction over films for television. From the SAG board's perspective, the TVA's offer violated their previous agreement. In an internal intelligence report, SAG claimed it "was a retrogression from previous peace proposals by both TVA and SAG, which contemplated either a clear cut division of jurisdiction between live television shows and televised motion pictures, or limited partnership in a small portion of the television film field known as the fringe or 'gray' area."[88] As these comments illustrate, SAG was working from the assumption that the recording medium was the primary determinant for how contracts would be divided, whereas the TVA was adopting an understanding of medium specificity based on method of distribution.

The TVA's attempt to negotiate more telefilm contracts spiraled into a full jurisdictional debate and rehash of the specificity of types of filmed performance. The unions brought the case to the National Labor Review Board, where they had to present their respective cases about the specific actions of workers. The TVA made the case that television closely resembled radio production, while representatives from SAG explained the similarities between film and television production.[89] SAG's argument before the NLRB rested on the technological specificity of film stock and cameras. Beloved comedies like *I Love Lucy* (1951–1957), popular presold properties like *Amos 'n' Andy* (1951–1953), and numerous feature-length programs were shot on film. The primary benefit of recorded programs was that film produced a program of higher-quality images than was possible with recorded kinescopes of live programs, and they could be replayed. "Telefilms" were shorter than feature films and made to air on television rather than be released in theaters. Although these were frequently low-budget productions, the fact that they were shot on film allowed for larger casts and higher production values.[90] Even critics who preferred the "spontaneity" of live television admitted that the filmed programs "provide a smooth performance."[91] In addition to better image quality, producer Hal Roach Jr. cited the flexibility of locations, ability to replay films, and ability to edit a program in advance as three benefits to shooting on film rather than broadcasting live.[92] Many of these telefilms were on par with B-movies and frequently shot on the dwindling "poverty row" lots as B-film production declined. Given the higher image quality, telefilms had the potential for additional air dates on television and possibly (though less commonly) theatrical release. Not all telefilms were sold to networks, as Christopher Anderson has explained—prior to 1952, eight hundred telefilm producers shot two thousand unsold pilots.[93] William Boddy puts this in perspective relative to the film industry, noting that by 1954, Hal Roach Jr.'s telefilm company was "consuming more film stock than MGM, Twentieth Century-Fox, and Warner Brothers studios combined."[94] Rather than being a unique mode of production, telefilm production resembled and even replaced some of the B-film production economy. Given the overlap of space and personnel in B-film and telefilm production, there was a clear case to be made about the similarities in these types of productions.

At its core, the dispute over telefilms had the same stakes as the earlier debates over the right to bargain for television: availability of jobs as a determinant of union power. Earning the right to claim programming shot on film, in whatever form, would boost the number of available jobs for either SAG or TVA members, and, looking ahead, would increase the membership rosters of dues-paying actors for the winning union bid—something the TVA desperately needed in its early days as a union. When SAG filed its petition asking the NLRB to rule once and for all over who should bargain for telefilms, it was not fighting for control over a lucrative media venture. By filing the petition over filmed television, SAG staked a position on the future rather than the present of television production. Although SAG's investment in telefilms was forward-looking in terms of production opportunities, this perspective was still limited in comparison to what the East Coast unions saw in television's potential as a mode of distribution.

The purpose of this NLRB investigation was to arbitrate the debate between SAG and the TVA by collecting data on the nature of film production and filmed and live television work. Although the terms of these conversations resembled those of theoretical discussions about medium specificity, the unions tried to make these determinations based more in empirical evidence. Chester Migden, who would later go on to work for SAG, collected the testimony for the hearings and investigated the working conditions on filmed television sets to determine the validity of SAG's claim that "if an actor were employed to act at Hal Roach [a studio that shot on film] he would not know, unless he were told, whether he had worked in theatrical film or television film."[95] The problem, from Migden's perspective, was that in 1950 it was difficult to find people to testify and describe filmed television. Most productions were live, so the scope of the NLRB testimony from filmed programming was primarily based on interviews with actors who worked on *Amos 'n' Andy* (1951–1953) along with hand-selected representatives to speak about the nature of filmed television.[96]

The testimony for this case consisted of expert opinions and detailed descriptions of production methods. As part of the investigation, both SAG and the TVA identified a set of witnesses who would support their respective cases about the nature and future of television production. SAG's witnesses included television industry leaders and actors who had worked in both film and television, such as Charles Boren, the vice president of the Association for Motion Picture Producers, television producer Hal Roach Jr., Dixie Fuller, who worked as a casting director, stuntman David Sharpe, and numerous actors who transitioned from film to television, such as Duncan Renaldo, a western actor turned star of *The Cisco Kid*. The TVA called Sid Cassyd, the founder of the Television Academy, and John H. Brown, a radio actor who transitioned to television (and was blacklisted in 1952). The TVA's primary argument was that the process of making a TV film requires "identification with a product, emphasis on delivering a commercial message, [and] greater strain, tension, etc."[97]

Their argument was ineffective because the TVA legal team overemphasized live programming broadcasts and the work of voice actors and announcers such as Thurl Ravenscroft and Kenneth L. Carpenter rather than directly focusing on telefilms, which were the subject of the hearing. The TVA representatives focused on challenges of acting on television such as: "Low wage rates; longer working hours; increased nervous tension because of shorter shooting schedules."[98] The TVA representatives, however, primarily highlighted the commercial nature of television in their argument, explaining that actors had "to memorize lines in advance of production; [and] commercial advertising limits employment by identifying performers with product."[99] The TVA presented the various ways television differed from film *in general*, but in reality, the TVA did not have a strong case as to how telefilm production differed from film production.

The NLRB agreed with SAG's logic, adding that telefilms and films often relied upon the "same" pool of actors (even if these telefilms were not necessarily using the top Hollywood stars). The NLRB ruled: "the same technical processes are involved in the production of motion pictures whether the film is produced for the theatre, television, or other type of market. . . . acting abilities required of motion picture performers are the same for all types of productions and that there is no separate 'pool' of actors which is drawn upon for the making of television pictures."[100] From the perspective of the NLRB, SAG had a much stronger case and was able to point to the similarities in production, which was in part evidenced by much of the overlap in terms of personnel. Speaking to the case the TVA attempted to make about differences, the ruling read: "most of these alleged differences do not in fact exist [and] many of these conditions are present in the production of all low-budget films, whatever the medium of release."[101] The NLRB emphasized the inherent similarities in acting labor despite the technical differences in the delivery of the filmed content. This ruling helped codify different programming tiers and further separated the actors working under SAG contracts from those working under TVA contracts. Unsurprisingly, perhaps, neither SAG nor the TVA saw this conclusion as a justification to merge interests. The hearing resulted in a victory for SAG and SEG and their attempt to expand their membership and jurisdiction into television.

In addition to settling the issue of who would bargain for television actors, the NLRB ruling helped to cool the tension among union leaders. Reporting on the mood of the 4As meeting, SAG and SEG attorney Robert Gilbert explained, "For the first time in the long series of 4As meetings, the bitterness and personal accusations and bad tactics were missing."[102] The results of the NLRB ruling and SAG and SEG's newly defined jurisdiction over filmed television meant that the other unions had no incentive or leverage to lure SAG and SEG into their merger. As a result, representatives from the 4As had to try their plan B, which was to roll the TVA into the American Federation of Radio Artists (AFRA) and thus create the American Federation of Television and Radio Artists (AFTRA). With both unions in charge of bargaining for different types of live broadcasts, they were amenable to a merger that they felt would improve their positions at the bargaining table. The 1952 merger of AFRA and the TVA was not a momentous occasion, but it marked the first time that entertainment unions merged to face the growing strength of Hollywood management.[103] The NLRB hearings, all of these debates over medium specificity, and finally the AFRA and TVA merger established long-lasting boundaries between film and television actors and their unions.

Interunion disputes such as those between the East Coast unions and the TVA and the West Coast unions and SAG and SEG shed light on the relative strength of each industry and union. In the case of the dispute over telefilms, unions waged battles over television jurisdiction to maximize membership and dues, but the rulings had long-term effects that helped establish distinctions between live and filmed television as a mode of production. The hard-fought battles and divisions created between SAG and the TVA (and later AFTRA) helped define the union identities for decades to come, with SAG as the prestigious film union and AFTRA as the less prestigious union with fewer barriers to entry.

CONCLUSION

Throughout the 1940s and 1950s studios, producers, sponsors, writers, actors, and directors were actively experimenting with and creating the foundations of US television. The destabilizing force of a new media form offers tremendous potential rewards to executives and producers, but in a new technology's development, the high costs associated with these experiments often mean that talent is undercompensated. The arrival of television was effectively a moment of crisis for industry management, producers, unions, and laborers. In this moment of crisis, each of these sets of social actors had to clarify its values in relation to the media economy. Producers typically have a financial imperative and know to make arguments that benefit their bottom line. In contrast, unions and actors frequently find themselves collectively and individually debating and redefining the relationship between craft and commerce.

Within the tumultuous arrival of television, unions found themselves with an increase in out-of-work members. Many actors worked under freelance contracts in the studio era that preceded television, but from the 1950s onward the media landscape can be characterized by an expansion of short-term contracts and an accompanying increase in financial instability. Between 1950 and 1960, SAG and AFTRA union membership nearly doubled, creating even more internal competition as actors vied for work across media platforms. Unions, like other powerful figures and organizations in Hollywood, also fought to maintain power and influence. For unions, power comes from retaining and providing for their members, so television was a critical development in the media industries that seemed to offer the potential to help unions thrive and grow.

While the arrival of television weighed heavily on the union organizers, these concerns ultimately had little impact on the struggling freelance actors and extras who were trying to break in or make a living. Actors working with sporadic contracts who need to find their next job, hone their craft, and cultivate a continuously employable persona all had to follow individual paths. Television added another set of possibilities for short-term contracts, further fragmenting the labor force and allowing for different paths into the industry—yet the number of jobs did not significantly change. Bargaining interests, as indicated by SEG's split into its own distinct union, also demonstrated that as the industry changed, screen performers had a wide array of interests they needed to balance. Television had effectively made it more difficult for actors to find pathways into the profession and forced them to consider a wider array of entry points than ever before. This moment of industrial transition brings into relief a number of tensions between individual creativity and collective interest, the influence of workers on industrial practice, and the nature of performance not only as an artistic endeavor, but as a job. As the unions demonstrated during the jurisdictional disputes, unions would take a leadership role in establishing professional norms for actors and reimagining the cultural and monetary value of screen performances.

THREE

REUSE AND REPLACE?

Actors, Reruns, and the Cable Era

> *Even as few years ago as 1960, TV was a syndication market for motion pictures. The possibility that they might be played in prime time—and on network exhibition—was unthinkable. But the unthinkable of yesterday is the fact of today.*

SAG EXECUTIVE SECRETARY JACK DALES'S OPENING REMARKS IN THE 1965 THEATRICAL FILM NEGOTIATIONS

As SAG geared up to renegotiate its theatrical contract in 1965, Jack Dales took the moment to reflect on some of the rapid changes that had occurred. In the first half of the twentieth century, many of the changes to screen media had stemmed from new technologies such as the coming of sound, widespread use of color, the addition of new cameras offering widescreen vistas, and, of course, the arrival of television. Television, as suggested by Dales's comments, was uniquely influential because of its profound influence on distribution. Despite initial fears that television would be broadcast in movie theaters and replace film, film and television distribution remained largely separate after the integration of television into the media landscape. When the two industries eventually became more intertwined, it was film that was broadcast on television. Theatrical films did not appear on television until 1955, but by 1965 films were a profitable piece of the television economy, and the film and television industries were reliant on each other for profit.

As Dales noted, television was becoming a source of film distribution (rather than solely a vehicle for replay) and thus a necessary topic for discussion in *film* negotiations. Dales's comments point to the role of distribution methods in frequently troubling the line between film and television—media that remain culturally apart, but whose intersections are essential for determining union jurisdictions and worker compensation. The development of new methods of distribution and the increasingly blurred boundaries between media forms influenced professional concerns as actors' unions tried to navigate the media landscape throughout the twentieth and twenty-first centuries.

The regulation of broadcast networks and the increased deregulation of other segments of the media industry in the 1970s established a new climate for media ownership and profits. During the period in which cable networks were finding their footing, broadcast networks were searching for ways to navigate policy changes such as the Prime Time Access Rule (PTAR) to maintain the same level of profit. One solution was to rely more heavily on reruns and theatrical movies to fill the programming time at a lower cost. Content increasingly could move from film to television, broadcast network to local broadcast affiliate or cable, and later to VHS for home rental and purchase, making the profit life of media content one of the primary focal points for above-the-line unions. By recycling old media, the broadcast networks found themselves at odds with the unions at the same moment that industrial power was beginning to shift away from the big three networks—leaving all these key industry actors on tenuous footing at the beginning of the cable era.

Scholarship on the rise of cable has taken a predominantly industrial focus, emphasizing policy, infrastructure and technology, programming strategies, and breaking down the industrial and financial relationships between film, broadcast, and video on television.[1] Regulatory policy has historically mediated the relationship between subsets of the media industries, but as Jennifer Holt explains, "This nexus of regulatory practice, politics, and media ownership . . . is the foundation for the media industries' decades-long winning streak."[2] The connections between government policy and the consolidated media industries' financial success has, as Holt points out, generated politicized research and calls to action to reform media, cultural policy, and degrees of regulation. The responses of communication and media researchers frequently focus on how consolidated ownership limits a diversity of viewpoints. These interventionist approaches could benefit workers, but the research tends to focus on how ownership limits the availability and diversity of content and viewpoints while leaving out the ways that media workers negotiate industrial changes on the ground.

Cable provided the foundation for significant changes in production and remuneration, but in the context of the contracts they negotiated, the influence of cable on the unions was cultural rather than simply structural. Actors had a considerable task in taking on negotiations during the early cable era, to collectively reorient their thinking beyond the production of new programming and to consider the life cycle of films, programs, and previous screen performances. In the past, more distribution avenues created the illusion of more opportunities for work. Cable, and later home video, did not so much offer more work as more opportunities to profit (or recoup expenses) from existing content. To address the new model of content distribution, actors and their unions returned to some of the conversations initiated during the television jurisdiction debates (including the topic of a merger) and began to advocate more seriously for residuals.

Residuals have a longer history in the media industries, but they became more significant for the actors beginning with the strike in 1960.[3] The concept of residuals, a form of payment for the reuse of material, emerged from a 1930s radio practice in which performers were paid when their recordings aired. Managers were concerned about airing recorded programs, so they asked performers to be on hand during broadcast recordings in case there was a problem with the tape and the performance needed to be re-created live.[4] The standard of residual payments remained long after the practice of keeping performers on hand stopped and was so well-established that unions began to consider this precedent in early discussions about television. Over two decades, SAG and AFTRA laid the foundation for residuals through collective bargaining and strikes. In the 1950s, payments for reuse were inconsistently applied, but after a strike during the 1960 contract negotiations, the actors achieved a workable system for residuals. The importance of second-run syndication, commonly known as reruns, continued to expand in the coming decades with a series of negotiations, threatened strikes, and actual strikes over residual payments in newly emerging venues for the redistribution of material for profit. As these continuing strikes across more than thirty years indicate, the right to residuals was something that had to be continually renegotiated with each new technological development. Despite the importance of residuals in negotiations and as a sticking point that resulted in numerous labor strikes, residuals could not solve all of the issues that faced actors as media content and platforms proliferated—they were only effective as a supplement, not as a replacement for income.

While some union benefits such as health care and retirement benefits are accessible to all consistently working actors, residuals are connected to above-the-line status within a film or television program and its continued reuse. Residuals construct a divide between the perpetually unemployed, extras, and even consistently working below-the-line actors. Even though SEG partnered with SAG in most of the battles over television, SEG representatives were not able to join forces with SAG over residuals.

The significance of residuals is in the way that they underlie the material reality of media content. Residuals do not help us to understand how *The F.B.I.* (one of the shows mentioned in this chapter) was made, but they do help us to understand the conditions under which actors might be incentivized to take bit roles in *The F.B.I.*, how they are compensated for their work, and how they are supported through periods of unemployment. As was the case in previous decades, cultural distinctions between actors continued to influence not only decision-making in the union, but also compensatory changes that further exacerbated them.

Residuals rest on an understanding that just because actors are not working does not mean that they are not generating revenue. All motion picture media have a necessary gap between performance and the post-production process of preparing the final product for release. For actors, freelance contracts mean work on discrete projects, often with significant breaks between projects. As the work of screen actors became increasingly untethered from long-term contracts, stars such as James Stewart gained the power to negotiate percentage deals on their films as a form of profit participation. As television became a more significant venue for exhibition, actors waited or auditioned for new projects and watched as their previous work on film and television continued to generate revenue through rebroadcasting or syndication. Thus the existence of residuals helped to redefine the professional terms of screen acting and served as a financial acknowledgment of the continued value of performances.

This chapter is about the afterlives of media from the perspective of media workers, and as such it is a history of percentages, dollars, and administrative detail. As in previous chapters, I rely heavily on union correspondence from the SAG-AFTRA Archive, the Tamiment Library, and the Wisconsin Center for Film and Theater Research. However, this chapter draws more heavily from periodicals and the industry trades, which took a special interest in the 1970s union strikes and the campaign against reruns. Charles Acland identifies the 1980s as the period that "expanded the circulation and salience of industry information [and] a newly invigorated industry of film-consumption statistics," but it is clear that by the '60s and '70s there was already a growing interest in how industry labor and politics shaped media.[5] Whereas labor disputes of previous eras did not merit attention in more mainstream publications, information on work stoppages and actors lobbying to eliminate tired reruns appeared not only in *Variety* but also in *TV Guide* and the *New York Times*.

In the 1970s SAG, AFTRA, and their memberships were rethinking their institutional and professional priorities. The impetus to reflect and regroup around new goals grew out of a struggling economy as well as a complex network of social, cultural, and economic changes stemming from deregulation that influenced many industries beyond media. Around the United States, people were fighting for social justice, protesting the Vietnam War, and striking more in the 1960s and 1970s than at any other time in the nation's history.[6] Speaking about labor unions across the United States, historian Alyssa Ribeiro argues that throughout the 1970s workers were agitating for more progressive changes and priorities within trade unions.[7] This trend within trade unions is consistent with the work that happened within the performers' unions, as well as the Writers Guild of America (WGA) and the Directors Guild of America (DGA).[8] During the 1970s, many unions examined membership diversity and the limited job opportunities available to women and people of color. However, in the case of SAG and AFTRA these efforts were funneled through the Women's Committee and the Ethnic Minority Committee (both founded in 1972). Concerns about the availability of roles for women and people of color never became the focus of bargaining platforms, even though SAG was concerned about the amount of new workdays in the early '70s.

As evidenced by the "Anti-Rerun" Campaign, unions and membership did not immediately land on residuals as the way to address changes in programming strategy. Between 1971 and 1975, actors were concerned with diminished television seasons and the increase in reruns because these changes would reduce the number of working days (even as they created more opportunities for residuals). The anti-rerun position was indicative of previous union priorities that focused on workdays, but the new focus on residuals reflected a significant change in how an actor's work was valued over time. Increasing opportunities for new productions, for example by challenging runaway productions, became less of a bargaining focus. As residuals became more central to actors' demands, they also added a new dimension to the profession, one that necessitated more focus on finances and administrative business. Unions bargained for residuals, but also took on the administrative work of processing and distributing residuals in cooperation with studios. On the surface, this would appear to affirm observations from historians and sociologists that over time unions become more committed to the maintenance of contracts and union bureaucracies.[9] As Stanley Aronowitz argues, management and workers become so invested in stability and the status quo that contracts are not enforced by law, but instead "by the joint efforts of corporate and trade union bureaucracies."[10] In contrast to this argument, focusing on residuals, which seem to be more of an administrative right, effectively ensured that the unions were prioritizing those who consistently worked in the face of significant changes to media distribution. However, for some actors, particularly women and people of color who typically faced longer periods of underemployment, residuals failed to solve fundamental employment concerns. While residuals signify an important part of union negotiations, for many actors paying SAG-AFTRA dues they were merely aspirational.

REPLAY-ABILITY AND THE SPECIFICITY OF SCREEN PERFORMANCE

In the 1950s, it became apparent that the nature of media content was increasingly at odds with the nature of performance. An actor's performance takes place at a specific moment, but recording technologies remove the performance from its specificity of time and place and complicate the monetary value of an actor's work through its reproducibility. For the workers who lend their faces and voices to media properties, much of the work is completed after recording wraps. This has always been a core challenge for compensating a screen actor's performance, as films have the capacity to garner profit long after the performance is complete. What emerged with new technologies in the 1970s, particularly cable and home video, was an increased emphasis in the deployment of technology toward the replay-ability of content. For producers and media owners, these technologies meant that content offered more potential for profit at each opportunity for replay.

Until the arrival of television, residuals were seen as largely irrelevant for screen workers for two reasons: first, there were not additional sources of revenue for films beyond ticket sales; films could only replay in theaters, which only happened for very successful films, and rarely with much fanfare. The second reason reflects class divisions among actors. Given the prevalence of long-term contracts in the studio era, the most visible and established actors had consistent income even when they were not actively working on set. As the industrial structure changed and television became a more important mode of content delivery, labor struggled to adapt. When actors were released from their long-term contracts, it became increasingly important for them to be able to sustain a living from sporadic work. The arrival of television and its potential as a new distribution channel posed a threat to existing compensation structures. Residuals are a form of payment, but they do not imply or signify any proprietary rights over media properties. The fact that residuals do not grant any ownership is significant because it means that labor's claims to media properties, even for those who receive residuals, is tenuous (based solely on bargaining agreements). This also explains why these rights need to be constantly renegotiated as technologies and distribution methods change. Unlike benefits, pensions, or even wages and working conditions, residuals are extremely sensitive to changes in technology and the addition of new media outlets.

In the 1960s, film and television contracts were more or less divided between SAG and AFTRA, and the unions diverged on their philosophies and negotiation goals for replay and reuse of material. Filmed content, regardless of when it was made, could be broadcast and rebroadcast in perpetuity. Live broadcasts could likewise be kinescoped and rebroadcast on television, but the quality was not good enough for projection on a large screen, which meant that different types of exhibition were not an issue in the earliest days of television. Realistically, only shows shot on film stock could hold up to multiple replays in the 1950s. The other difference between film and television replay was that the broadcast unions, such as AFTRA, already had policies in place from radio for dealing with rebroadcasting material. Since this was new terrain for film, the film unions, such as SAG, were largely unprepared for television's demand for existing content to fill programming time.

Film studios and labor were collectively concerned with the various ways that airing films on television might upset the distribution status quo. Actors and their unions were afraid of studios reaping huge profits from existing media content with no remuneration extended to those who appeared in it. The technological capacity was certainly in place: television was capable of rebroadcasting old films. Film and television were also increasingly synergistic in their business practices. Despite growing cooperation, however, film studios were initially unwilling to license their films to television networks, seeing it as fueling their competition. Maintaining a distinction between film and television was also useful, as it sustained the cultural divide between them. The importance of distinguishing between these two media help account for Eric Hoyt's observation that if studios were going to air films on television, they preferred a pay television model rather than television's advertiser-supported model.[11] Studios were fearful of disrupting other existing business practices. As Frederick Wasser points out, resistance to offering residuals was a key factor that prevented studios from licensing films for television. Notably, from a labor perspective, film distributors were afraid of alienating labor, as the unions were already raising the issue of residuals in the 1940s. In 1948, SAG first began mentioning residuals and threatened to strike (although this did not come to fruition) in order to get a remuneration formula in place for film on television. For studios to begin profiting from films on television, they were well aware that they would have to implement a plan with the unions. As such, even into the early 1950s, the major studios were not interested in beginning these conversations that selling their old films to television would demand.[12]

With the major studios temporarily out of the picture, television networks found a way to bring film content to television by fostering professional relationships with smaller studios. In a letter regarding the possibility of a cooperative effort between NBC and film studios, production executive E. A. Hungerford Jr. noted: "I think I would prefer to work with Republic and Monogram [rather than the big studios] since they are smaller concerns and could grow with us on a more or less even basis."[13] The small studios, unlike the majors, needed to make money more than they needed to worry about the prestige of their studio image. For the smaller studios, it was advantageous to generate any money from their existing content that was otherwise sitting dormant. The influence of labor unions was also an important factor in the decision to partner with smaller studios. As Frederick Wasser explains, in the early 1950s, the only studios willing to license for television were foreign and bankrupt studios who were not worried about relationships with the US labor unions.[14] Major studios were unwilling to sour their relationship with the unions for a quick buck; thus the turn toward smaller studios indicates both the prominence of unions by the 1950s as well as their role in the development of and influence over the quality of postwar television programming.

SAG's failure to engage with major studio producers on the residual issue created tension in the late 1940s television jurisdiction meetings. In a July 1949 meeting, George Heller lamented SAG's inability to reach an agreement about residuals for existing films, stating:

> You have a historical problem here on the question of theatrical rights. The producer can do whatever he wants with pictures made for theaters. You have done nothing about it. We feel that people in television now are accustomed to the limitation of use of whatever work they are doing. In other words, they are used to the theory of repayment for reuse. We feel the most important thing in television is to establish that Kinescope cannot be used for anything except television; is not for motion picture use. Also, if there is any reuse, payment should be made for that reuse.[15]

As this was in the midst of the jurisdictional disputes, Heller was positioning AFRA as the appropriate negotiator for television, and his point, that television's terms would help facilitate negotiations for repayment for reuse, was correct. The similarities between the kinescope replays and radio practices undoubtedly made these residual conversations easier for the East Coast unions. Actors began receiving residuals for kinescope reruns (live shows recorded on the East Coast and replayed on the West Coast) in 1952. It is possible that SAG did not actively concede this, lest it give AFRA a strategic advantage in their jurisdictional debates. However, beginning in 1951 the Guild decided in its meetings that "[the] Guild Board should announce publicly, as soon as possible, the basic minimum wage demands which the Guild plans to seek in the forthcoming negotiations, in addition to the specific demand for repayment for reuse of pictures made for television."[16] It was clear by 1951 that SAG needed to prepare for eventual changes to the landscape of film distribution and the role of residuals in future negotiations.

Receiving residuals is one sign of professionalism in a career marked by uncertainty. Establishing residuals, however, had significance beyond the supplemental income they provided. In 1958, SAG and SEG attorney Robert Gilbert outlined the legal and contractual details that gave actors a legitimate right to residuals in 1952, explaining, "actors who have acquired residual rights under these collective bargaining agreements range from lesser performers to stars," but extras were (and are) excluded from SAG and AFTRA contracts.[17] In this case, professional actors could be distinguished from background actors based on their rights to residuals. Residuals are not unique to acting guilds, but in the case of SAG and AFTRA, they provided a mark of distinction within the guilds. Residuals have been and continue to be one of the key material distinctions that separates different tiers of actors—those working on projects that are successful and have long lives on television as compared to those collecting short-term credits on programs without the same level of success. This is significant because it creates different bargaining stakes for different guild members and exacerbates long-standing tensions between union membership groups: those who get residuals (working actors with speaking roles) versus those who continue to struggle to get sufficient roles in the competitive climate.

As was the case with other technological advancements in the past, actors had strong opinions as to how the unions should organize their priorities. Writing to the AFTRA board in 1958, Grant Code (who had a variety of small television roles in the late 1950s) pleaded: "In my view [of] the situation, the problem of video tape has to be solved immediately and no other problem should be permitted to interfere with the discussion and solution of that problem."[18] With residuals established for some of the work airing on television, the unions had to take the next steps to contend with the use of film on television and establish a baseline for how actors would receive compensation for their existing work. The strike for residuals in 1960 marked a significant turning point for actors and their union, one which clarified the priorities of the union shifting from a focus on insufficient workdays to residuals as a means to offset underemployment.

ACTING GOES (MORE) COMMERCIAL

Unions had always been overtly concerned with the financial value of an actor's performance, but these conversations were traditionally balanced, at least rhetorically, with concerns over the artistic merit and cultural value of performance. But this rhetoric shifted beginning with SAG's first strike in 1952 over filmed commercials and later in the 1960s when television commercials emerged as an increasingly important part of the work and income for actors. Commercials, in combination with reruns, tipped the balance of these conversations explicitly toward financial concerns and the commodity value of a performance.

The increased importance of the commercial landscape was particularly important for SAG as it navigated many of the changes to the film landscape and its relationship to AFTRA. There was no precedent for residuals in the film industry, which meant that one of the main changes to film acting in 1960 and beyond was to acculturate actors to the idea and importance of strikes to gain leverage. When television networks aired old films, the networks profited from advertising, but actors received nothing. Moreover, from the perspective of actors, the airing of old movies on television represented a loss of new work during time slots that could potentially feature new programming (even if this was not necessarily true). Producers, however, took a hard position against residuals. During the 1959 WGA strike, the executive vice president of the Association of Motion Picture Producers declared that the AMPP "cannot make any agreement for such payment with the Writers Guild or any other guild or union."[19] Producers and actors had opposing perspectives on this issue: producers felt that actors were asking to be paid twice for one job, while actors were asking to receive a piece of the continued profits of their creative work.[20]

Beyond replaying films, the climate of television production and programming began to shift dramatically in the late 1950s to favor the terms of the big three networks. The model of a single advertiser sponsoring a show and time slot was replaced by advertisers buying "independent slots across several different programs and time periods."[21] Mike Mashon explains that this allowed advertisers to spread their money and influence across several shows, thus minimizing their investment risk. The new development also gave networks greater control over television programs as they were no longer beholden to sponsor demands.[22] The transition from sponsorship to stand-alone advertisements also changed the format of television programs. Independent television producers in the late 1950s had the ability to produce shows that could be sold to networks as first-run syndicated programs. As television shows were packaged for replay on other networks, and as Cynthia Meyers explains, television became untethered from the single sponsorship model.[23]

The shift toward stand-alone advertisements as interruptions within or between television episodes also meant greater opportunities for nonstar actors to find commercial work. Actors could now find work not only in programs, but also in the commercials that would be interspersed across multiple time slots. In the late 1950s the unions recognized the value of this growing market and began to advocate for substantial raises in commercial rates (reportedly from 15 to 100 percent rate increases depending on the type and regional scope of the advertisement).[24] By the mid-1960s (when SAG started tracking total actor earnings by contract), commercials were consistently outpacing both film and television as the most lucrative contract. In previous eras, new forms of content typically failed to pull more actors above a salary threshold that allowed them to live off their earnings. The addition of television commercials was no different. Even though commercials offered a new way for actors to make money, in the 1960s approximately 85 to 90 percent of actors still made under $10,000 per year through their work as actors—this work was now just spread across more diverse work opportunities that each carried its own respective work culture and compensatory arrangements.

The beginning of the 1960s also saw another troubling trend for the competitive work environment among actors—a tremendous jump in membership that began in 1960. In 1950, SAG had 7,338 members, but by 1960 membership had ballooned to 13,685.[25] This significant spike in membership marked the beginning of a sustained upsurge as SAG's membership continued to increase throughout the remaining decades of the twentieth century. The primary reason for this change in the number of

TABLE 3.1. TOTAL DOLLARS EARNED BY SAG
CONTRACT, 1965–1970 (IN MILLIONS)

Year	1965	1966	1967	1968	1969	1970
Theatrical film	$25.7	$23.7	$26.6	$25.0	$27.6	$17.9
Television	$33.9	$40.5	$35.9	$36.0	$35.9	$34.4
Commercials	$38.6	$40.6	$46.3	$51.6	$57.1	$61.4

Source: From Summary of Contract Earnings, SAG-AFTRA Archive, Los Angeles, CA.

members is tied to the expansion of contract jurisdictions throughout the 1950s.[26] In 1950, SAG solely represented actors making theatrical motion pictures. By 1960 it had successfully expanded and negotiated contracts in theatrical motion pictures, television entertainment films, television commercials, and industrial and educational motion pictures. Adding more contracts created a greater array of options for actors to become eligible for and find union work, but the growth in opportunities did not keep pace with the number of aspiring or working actors seeking roles. The reality for actors was increased competition for work, as well as a union of more disparate parts and an unwieldy professional definition of "actor" that included a greater percentage of explicitly commercial work.

The expansion of SAG contracts, which now covered an array of different content produced for television, seemed to further confuse the boundaries between the unions. In the late 1950s, actors struggled with the fact that SAG and AFTRA existed as separate unions even though they shared many members. As discussed in the previous chapter, actors who opposed the performers' union merger, as voiced by Margaret Webster, demonstrated a strong preference for one mode of performance over another. Other actors moved more fluidly between media, but often out of necessity rather than a general feeling of nonchalance about how their work was exhibited. Grant Code, an actor with a list of small television roles, adopted a perspective that barely differentiated between modes of production. On the issue of the difference between performances in film and television, Code explained in a letter to the AFTRA board:

It is really of no interest to the members of either union what technical process is used in recording or projecting their performance nor whether the performance is shown in theaters or on TV sets. It is true

99

that there is a certain technical difference in acting for movie cameras and in acting in live shows, whether they are on stage or in a studio. But most members, if not all members, of both unions are perfectly capable of adjusting their performances to these differences.[27]

Although it is unlikely that Code spoke for all members, his letter indicates a growing frustration with the addition of new technologies and the insistence that the unions remain separate. A merger was no longer on the unions' agenda in the late 1950s, but as Code's comments indicate, the topic had not been forgotten. For actors like Code, the changing media culture, in which methods of distribution were converging, only affirmed the importance of a union merger. Code was not in the majority, but the desire for more streamlined union administration in an increasingly busy world of distribution continued to percolate.

By 1960 the contract era of acting had firmly ended, and unions focused their attention on negotiating points that the leadership believed would create more stability for working actors. In addition to asking for residuals for past televised films (made pre-1948) and films made after 1960, the union wanted the AMPP to establish a 5 percent contribution to a health and pension fund for actors.[28] Combined, these terms allowed for a more financially sustainable career. The union was adamant that these three concerns were linked, and thus could only be resolved as a package. Residuals, health, and pensions also added new administrative functions to the unions, which enhanced their role in actors' professional lives beyond collective bargaining, as well as having the benefit for the union itself in establishing its presence in the day-to-day livelihoods of its members.

When actors went on strike over residuals for films on television in 1960, they did so alongside the screenwriters and the WGA, whose membership required similar compensatory adaptions to reflect the new media economy and concomitant professional instability. The 1960 strike was successful in part because SAG joined the existing WGA strike, which meant that the unions were more effective at shutting down production. The SAG, AFTRA, WGA, and DGA contracts all expired at different times but in relatively rapid succession, thus a long-running strike could easily bleed into the next set of negotiations (as it did in 1960). Scheduling created clear opportunities for joint strikes, and in this case maximized effectiveness. The collaboration across these four unions also demonstrated an alignment of interests for the unions composed of above-the-line workers.

Even though actors had gained the legal right to residuals, the unions needed to expand these rights and standardize rates through a new agreement as the studios reaped increased profits from the reuse of media content. During the 1960 contract negotiations, SAG negotiators requested residual payments for all televised films from 1960 forward, a lump sum credit to the pension fund for films made between 1948 and the date of the new contract, and a 5 percent contribution (based on earnings) to the SAG pension, health, and welfare program.[29] When studios refused (based on the logic that actors should not be paid twice for one job), 83 percent of SAG members voted to strike. Eventually, after a thirty-three-day stand-off, they reached a compromise: residuals would be paid on films from 1960 forward, with an additional $2.5 million paid toward the SAG pension and health care fund. Even though the strike did not turn Hollywood upside-down—the studios only had to pause production on eight projects—it did successfully establish a more robust residual payment structure and lay the groundwork for one of the most important financial changes for actors, writers, and directors in the history of Hollywood.[30]

In an industry where unions could never seem to find a means to help actors make a consistent living and offset the sporadic pay of project-based employment, residuals from the churn of reruns and legacy films seemed to offer a potential solution to this problem. Actors already received residuals for kinescope replays of East Coast broadcasts on the West Coast, but the 1960 strike marked the first SAG victory for residuals. It is important to note the limitations of the agreement, though: it was a contract only with the film studios, and only for select films that were rebroadcast on television, thus encompassing only one method of replay. In subsequent decades, unions grappled with other technologies of rebroadcast to integrate residuals into the fabric of television and, several decades later, VHS. Despite this major victory, the rate for residuals assumed a particular production landscape and a set number of television episodes per season, standards that limited the impact of these particular negotiations over time.

By the end of the 1960s, actors seemed to have a clearer, but not complete, picture of the challenges reruns posed to their profession. For many decades SAG, AFTRA, and the other performers' unions had been preoccupied with the importance of workdays. If a film moved production overseas, or if a union gained jurisdiction over a new area of the industry, these developments represented either the loss (in the case of overseas production) or addition (in the case of new contracts) of workdays for actors.

Although residuals offered some relief to this problem, SAG in particular continued to take the loss of workdays seriously in the next decade.

THE BRIEF TROUBLE WITH RERUNS

In March 1971, film and television editor Bernard Balmuth was excited to watch a new episode of *The F.B.I.* (1965–1974), but he was irritated to discover that the rerun season had arrived a bit early (in spring rather than summer). This frustration inspired Balmuth to file a complaint with the FCC claiming there were simply too many reruns on television. Although Balmuth was an editor who had worked on episodes of *The Monkees* (1966–1968), *I Dream of Jeannie* (1965–1970), and *The Partridge Family* (1970–1974), his concern was not that of a worker making his living in the industry, but of a loyal fan and television viewer. His story and the subsequent conversations, arguments, and efforts that followed were of interest to a broad audience of professionals and television viewers and were reported in the trades as well as more populist publications such as *TV Guide*.[31] What began as an audience member's problem with television content quickly spiraled into a significant industry labor campaign against reruns involving multiple unions, the Office of Telecommunications Policy, and extending as far as the White House. Audience members and industry workers both identified reruns as a problem, but for different reasons. For viewers, the problem was repetition and not enough new content from their beloved shows. Industry workers, however, argued that this was a problem because reruns represented lost workdays. According to the union surveys of television programming, reruns constituted over half of all prime-time programming in 1972.[32] From the union's perspective, each half-hour rerun represented a day of lost work across all the unions. As a result, the unions joined forces to investigate the issue in a Film and Television Coordinating Committee (FTCC), and SAG had its own committee to boot.[33] Reruns in essence became the focus of SAG's efforts, even though they were only one of many union concerns about the television programming landscape.

Prime-time reruns were one of several concerns for the unions, but they provided the galvanizing point that led SAG president John Gavin to set up a meeting with US government representatives in the early 1970s. Gavin and the unions advocated for the government to intercede with regulations and force the powerful broadcast networks to boost employment opportunities for actors. In addition to making a case for government assistance against the networks to reduce the number of reruns, Gavin had two other petitions relating to the availability of work: first, elimination (or a loosening of restrictions) of the Prime Time Access Rule, which restricted the amount of network programming that local stations could air during prime time; and second, a requirement that government films and training aids hire union actors. Neither of these issues received the same amount of attention as reruns, though: discussions about government training films stagnated, and the Prime Time Access Rule remained in place for two more decades, but reruns, which were an understandable annoyance for viewers and a fundamental problem for workers, were a much more practicable problem to resolve.

Conversations about reruns coincided with a growing perception that broadcast networks controlled the airwaves and had grown too powerful within the television landscape. Beginning in 1970, the broadcast networks were restricted by the Financial Interest and Syndication Rules (Fin-Syn). These rules dictated that the broadcast networks were not allowed to produce or own their prime-time programming or to profit from the syndication of anything they aired. As Jennifer Holt explains, this policy effectively separated production and distribution and functioned comparably to the Paramount Decrees as applied to the broadcast networks.[34] Broadcast networks were no longer being protected as the privileged source of television. This transition was part of a general loosening of regulations designed to increase the number of independent producers, but it instead led to the expansion and growth of the cable networks. Actors' experience of this shift in the balance of power more closely resembled the way audiences were experiencing this change, as one of increased television channels and more frequent reruns.

Government officials took a noninterventionist response to the pleas for regulation of reruns. Although President Nixon was willing to regulate networks, as he had done with the Fin-Syn regulations, this was not consistent with broader media policy trends, which in the early 1970s were already tending toward deregulation. After John Gavin's meeting in Washington, DC, Nixon expressed his sympathies for the plight of actors in the culture of television reruns. In a 1972 letter Nixon wrote, "I agree with your view that the increasing number of re-runs on the networks in prime time constitutes an economic threat to the talented men and women of the American film industry."[35] Nixon tasked director of telecommunications policy Tom Whitehead with monitoring and helping the unions and networks reach a reasonable agreement, but, barring that, Nixon promised to "explore whatever regulatory recommendations are in order."[36] The conversation about regulating reruns ultimately ended with this sentiment, and the unions were left to work out terms through bargaining.

SAG member efforts coalesced around an anti-rerun committee and a campaign titled Save Television Original Programming, or STOP. Those within SAG who led some of these efforts had careers that seemed to exemplify that of the modern actor, with consistent credits across film and television: Don Dubbins (an actor with short runs on shows such as *Dragnet, I Dream of Jeannie*, and *The F.B.I.*, among other films and shows), Jack Kruschen (an actor who appeared in *Cape Fear* [1962], *Columbo, Bonanza, Freebie and the Bean* [1974], and many other roles across film and television), and Kathleen Nolan (an actor who worked most prominently on *The Real McCoys* and *Broadside*). The committee leadership worked in conjunction with the FTCC's position to get the membership to sign the petition against reruns and to garner widespread support among the base. The committee's goal was to convince the government to put a cap on reruns or to obtain residuals equal to 100 percent of an actor's salary for each replay.[37] Emboldened by both the support of other unions and a public that was tired of reruns, SAG took a hard-line position against the networks.

Support from the government was limited, but there was broad-based promotion of this cause from other unions. Each union bargains separately with AMPTP, but they support each other, knowing that their respective demands are relational. In August 1972, the president of the AFL-CIO, the federation of US trade unions, announced his support in the anti-rerun campaign.[38] This broad showing of national support for the cause gave the FTCC greater strength. Although the issue of reruns was a central concern in the 1970s, it is important to note that this was not the only threat to US media jobs that concerned the FTCC. In addition to campaigning against reruns, they were also tracking location shooting and criticizing film shoots that went overseas.[39] Reruns were one important and visible way that actors were losing work, but they were only part of a broader culture of diminishing opportunities for US actors. This general concern about keeping work in the United States was enough for other unions to rally around.

The US government took a softer approach toward the issue of reruns, opting for an investigation into the impact of reruns rather than intervention. FCC analysts sought to explain in economic terms *why* networks had been increasing the number of reruns on television, and in early 1973 the FCC released its "Preliminary Analysis of the Causes and Effects of

Rerun Programming and Related Issues in Prime Time Network Television," which looked at the cost of television production between 1962 and
1971. Essential to their analysis was data on the increase in production
costs as well as changes in labor costs. According to the FCC, the production cost of an original episode of television rose 89 percent from 1962 to
1971.[40] Within these cost increases, the greatest change for labor was the
cost of above-the-line talent. Using *Bonanza* as an indicative example, the
study explained that above-the-line costs increased 174 percent between
the 1962/1963 season and the 1971/1972 season. Salaries for actors increased
4.5 times faster than SAG scale, thus the higher salaries were not union-
driven, but the result of individual negotiations between talent, representation, and networks.[41] In conclusion the FCC explained, "there exists a
cycle of rivalry behavior, which has the effect of driving down the quan-
tity of original programming and the maintenance of high profits."[42] The
FCC concluded that although reruns helped to reduce the expenditures
for networks, the need for reducing costs came more from the competition
between the networks than undue pressure from talent or their unions.

The problem of the 1970s for television screen labor was that even as
production costs increased, industry practice and government policy combined to create a production climate that diminished the availability of
jobs. Reruns received more public attention, but the issue was less reruns
than the implementation of the Prime Time Access Rule, which gave
more time over to reruns in the programming schedule. In theory, the
PTAR was supposed to create more diverse programming. The Department of Justice ruling that created it restricted the number of hours of
prime-time programming that networks could produce for local affiliates
and gave the affiliates guaranteed time for syndicated programs or local
programming. According to Megan Mullen, one of the unintended effects of this rule, however, was that networks began to focus on increasing
their syndication libraries—a trend that created ample resources for new
cable networks when they began to license old shows to fill programming
time and recover costs for original program development in the future.[43]

Under the auspices of creating more space for diversity in programming, the Department of Justice had effectively created a financial wind-
fall for networks. For actors, the impact of this was very clear. At the
end of his annual address to membership, SAG president Dennis Weaver
enumerated a series of problems for actors:

The frustration of seeing our profession become a seasonal occupation. The frustration of knowing that while profits continue to swell

the number of jobs for actors continue to dwindle. The frustration of knowing that we are competing with ourselves and undercutting our own salaries for we are saddled with the continuing, ever expanding, intolerable rerun policy. And worst of all, the frustration of knowing that we are not receiving fair and equitable payment for those reruns.[44]

Weaver's list of grievances emphasizes a kind of downward spiral of diminishing opportunities for creative work. Yet many of the core issues Weaver identified, that acting was becoming more inconsistent and actors were making less money, were not specific to the 1970s. These were the same problems that actors faced throughout the previous decades with the arrival of new technological forms—but his diagnosis of the source of the problems in television reruns was unique. In the 1970s, changes to programming practices and new methods of distribution posed new challenges for actors, but offered tremendous benefits to the networks. In a comparative study between 1959–1961 and 1970–1973, the FCC noted that average annual network profits tripled when reruns increased.[45] By diagnosing the source of the problem as reruns rather than the age-old problem of too many actors and not enough work, unions offered a kernel of hope for change and perhaps some new solutions to old problems.

Networks had discovered an effective way to reduce expenses and raise profits. The fact that this strategy frustrated audiences and angered labor was of little concern for the networks, as they were able to deploy it without significant legal or financial repercussions. Without any leverage to change network practices, unions looked to their best strategy for participating in these newfound profits, which was, as Weaver identified at the end of his speech, to prioritize residuals. Weaver concluded, "The correcting of the existing structure for residual payment will be the number one priority in our upcoming negotiations. . . . If the networks feel that it is necessary to flood the airwaves with rerun after rerun, let us at least get our fair share of the pie."[46] Weaver framed this discussion in terms of fairness, but the stakes were more about keeping acting a viable profession for as much of the union membership as possible. In his speech one year later, Weaver demonstrated a revised understanding of how to make the case for fewer reruns. As he articulated his new strategy, Weaver implored: "Please stress the public-interest aspect of limiting reruns—the fact that viewers are poorly served when the networks flood public airwaves with second-hand programming six months out of the year. We all know reruns take jobs away from us and seriously reduce our income, but the FCC is not interested in our economic plight."[47] Whereas union speeches and discourse often engage with actors about their profession and advocating for rights and terms as workers, this comment is a reminder that audience preferences can be used as leverage in negotiations. However, Weaver does not remind actors that they are also members of the audience who could apply pressure to the FCC from their position as viewers. This absence is curious given that much of the anti-rerun sentiment of the early 1970s was initiated by a worker in the media industries. The key to Weaver's comment is the broad realization that despite the union's power and the recent memory of a strike, SAG could not wield leverage solely based on an argument around work and compensation. Changing the culture of reruns had to come from a more sustained movement focused on widespread audience dissatisfaction.

The period of economic recession in the 1970s and 1980s and the culture of deregulation restricted broadcast network influence and helped to expand the number and influence of cable networks. Derek Kompare characterizes this as a sweeping industrial impact that influenced profits, programming, and labor.[48] In essence, the business and policy landscape changed, as did the television programming landscape. Not every policy and change affected workers equally, but some, such as the Prime Time Access Rule and reruns, were felt more acutely by actors and became the focus of their lobbying efforts. Although actors were initially focused on the loss of jobs that accompanied increased reliance on reruns, the campaign for more new productions lost steam as SAG won better television residual rates in the mid-1970s. Unions continued to see the importance of residuals, especially as networks continued to rely on reruns to keep down the costs of programming a television schedule. Although residuals remained a mere substitute for more work, they would also provide an important point of connection between SAG and AFTRA and further alienated SEG from the concerns of the actors' unions.

Extras were absent from this strike and conversation about residuals. The changing media climate of the 1960s made extras work increasingly difficult to find, and their union was deteriorating. SEG attempted to gain momentum to negotiate for residuals in 1966, but without the support of other guilds they were unsuccessful.[49] After failing to gain traction in negotiations such as this one, members became more frustrated with their leadership, and the union's budget looked grim. By 1968, rather than increasing membership numbers to fill their financial reserves, SEG attempted to raise its membership fees in order to alleviate some of its budgetary troubles.[50] The increase in dues and fees did not accompany better support from union officials or more union work, which did little to endear the membership to their leadership. The union's problems continued in 1972 when five hundred members dropped out of SEG. The mass exodus not only diminished the amount of money coming into the union, but also signaled that the union no longer effectively served its base. Behind closed doors the union was plagued by infighting and power struggles, and the leadership fought over expenses and how best to support extras. Although extras are tangential to the story of residuals, shifting priorities among unions and changes to the industry are essential to understanding how extras became more marginalized from the significant conversations about labor in Hollywood.

RERUNS OF RACISM AND SEXISM

Residuals were an important gain for many creative personnel in the media industry, but working actors continued to be plagued by structural inequities that impacted who was hired to tell stories in film and television, and of course who could make a living working in Hollywood. In 1972, alongside similar actions from the WGA and the DGA, both SAG and AFTRA formed National Women's Committees and Ethnic Minority Committees to address these glaring disparities in pay and work opportunities. Social activism to combat race, gender, and other inequalities contributed to Hollywood's increased awareness of the quality of representations on screen and of how their hiring practices contributed to a homogenous on-screen world.

The Women's Committee and the Ethnic Minority Committee were specifically tasked with assessing current problems and finding constructive and pragmatic solutions for the systemic discrimination that women and people of color faced in casting. Discrimination and system-wide injustice was a persistent problem for actors, and the unions had not been a source of sustained progressive action on hiring parity. Much of the political action came from outside groups, such as the NAACP, which had been raising awareness of racism in Hollywood hiring and addressing poor representations of African Americans over many decades. Historically, women and other minority groups did not have the same level of organized or consistent backing. What was noteworthy about the union committees in the early 1970s was that they represented organized efforts to change Hollywood culture from within.

The committees for women and minorities took the lead on collecting data to quantitatively demonstrate inequity in Hollywood.[51] As expected, the number of roles for white men outpaced those for women and people of color. In particular, commercials continued to be the primary source of income for actors, and there was a tremendous gender disparity in commercial hiring. The SAG survey of 1973 commercials found that there were two times as many men starring in commercials as women.[52] The proportion of men for voice-over work was even greater—93 percent of all commercial voice-over in 1973 was done by men.[53] The conclusion was clear: given the importance of commercials for actors' incomes, privileging men clearly harmed the financial bottom line for women. However, the quantitative data in this article, like many surveys from this period, was positioned as purely informational.[54] The article concludes with a brief statement: "The study will be made available to the advertising community as a guide to constructive reexamination of current practices."[55] Even though this was a significant issue for women in the union, it was framed as a topic for industry self-reflection rather than an issue for collective bargaining or industry activism. Notably, the data on commercials was printed in an issue of *Screen Actor Magazine* that featured a number of different articles about many pressing issues for actors, such as viewer preferences on television, data on representations of race and gender on television, and articles about future negotiation issues such as rates for pay cable and the FCC investigation into television reruns. Although these issues were all concurrent and shared space on the pages of *Screen Actor*, issues of representation were written about separately from new technological developments, even though they worked symbiotically to produce disparities and inequalities.

Strategizing ways for the committees to influence and transform hiring practices posed challenges, since the unions do not have a direct role in hiring. At a 1971 meeting, members of the SAG Ethnic Minorities Committee met with actors from the Actors Equity Association (AEA) to discuss and consider several approaches to improving hiring. One option, as actor and Equity representative Vincent Beck pointed out, was to mirror what AEA had recently implemented by forming a committee to read scripts and look for roles that might work for minority actors.[56] In response to this suggestion, committee president Robert DoQui noted that he was familiar with this approach because the NAACP had a group that read scripts for this purpose.[57] This approach would of course only be in an advisory capacity with respect to casting. What became apparent over the course of the meeting was that without any direct power to influence hiring policies, the most effective method for diversifying casting was to provide broader media education regarding representations.

The importance of enhancing understanding of representations came up several times in the meeting minutes as a solution to many different problems; for example, "Mr. Robert Ito presented his thoughts on whether it is the actors' problem or the problem of the writers, producer or directors. He sighted [*sic*] the example of "Sanford & Son." To him this program is merely a new twist on the "Amos & Andy" syndrome. Mr. Migden agreed. However, he pointed out that by using the attack of speaking to young people in schools and not worrying about specifics on TV at this time, the committee's work would be started at least."[58] Particularly noteworthy in Chester Migden's comments is the emphasis on educating "young people in schools." Efforts to improve media literacy around representations of race and gender are incredibly important, but for professional organizations these are not the only tools, nor are they necessarily the ones that will help change the current culture. Educating young people stresses an emphasis on the future rather than the present. With every point of discussion regarding race on television, the conclusion was that the issues were large and there were no concrete steps that could be taken to transform the industry for minorities.

Both the Women's Committees and Ethnic Minority Committees sought to improve on-screen representation as a means to create greater employment opportunities for women and minority actors, but this would only be possible with new opportunities in programming. In this way, reruns worked against many of the goals of these committees—limiting new original programming means limiting the casting opportunities for more diverse groups of actors. In a 1974 survey about attitudes toward television, viewers expressed what they wanted out of the medium. Their desires included fewer reruns and better depictions of women and minorities on television.[59] The lack of effort to link these trends demonstrates a failure to recognize their connectedness: reruns of existing shows that failed to offer diversity in casting only perpetuated the existing homogenous media landscape.

RESIDUALS REVISITED

Between the 1970s and 1980s actors navigated a new terrain of filmed entertainment that often excluded them. The state of television programming in the 1970s featured a heavy slate of reruns, and there were a number of substantive industrial changes that ensured that television was not simply a performer's medium. Television was a mode of distribution for a wide array of entertainment forms that brought together performers, broadcasters, and occasionally everyday people. On network television, actors continued to lose opportunities as production companies returned to the quiz show format (now rebranded as "game shows") and increased the number of game shows for broadcast. Olaf Hoershelmann observes that the formal aesthetics of game shows create "an impression of liveness and immediacy: using a proscenium stage, using direct address, and creating presence in time."[60] Shows that emphasize liveness generically place a premium on new episodes rather than reruns, presenting one opportunity for fresh content in an era of reruns. The difference with game shows, as with other nonnarrative genres, is that they can be produced and shot inexpensively and rely largely on contestants rather than performers, thus allowing producers to minimize the use of (and cost of) union talent. Cable networks, which would not become competitive players in the production of new scripted shows for several decades, also embraced many of these cost-cutting strategies. Early cable programming during the late 1970s and early 1980s often fell into the news, unscripted content, or talk-show formats. The earliest successes of original cable programming catered to what niche audiences were unable to find on broadcast networks, such as Christian shows like *The 700 Club* and *The PTL Club*, but still fit into the talk-show format. In the 1930s and 1940s actors optimistically looked at television as a venue for new types of performances, but television's reliance on old programs and live formats meant that the medium seemed to leave less room for actors to craft new characters and push boundaries of small-screen storytelling.

If actors struggled to find roles in these live formats, extras found even fewer opportunities for work in this media landscape. Extras continued to struggle during this period, choosing to focus on the loss of film roles rather than trying to develop their presence in television. In contract negotiations in 1976, SEG leadership allowed television productions to lower the cap on union extras while raising the cap for union extras in film productions.[61] Although SEG leadership felt that the gain in film productions was advantageous because film often used more extras, the concession indicates that SEG was unable to hold onto its previous contract gains in the 1970s. While many unions try to increase their membership base in order to boost union revenue and bargaining strength, a larger membership would have had a deleterious effect on extras, since they were already struggling to find sufficient work for members—who often had low morale as a result of their marginalized position on screen and on set. As Edie Lynch explained in 1970, "You're a thing being used. You don't expect kindness when you work as an extra."[62] In addition to this marginal position, there was also frustration with the union, which often made greater concessions than gains in its bargaining.

While SAG and AFTRA continued to work out their relationship to each other in the constantly shifting landscape, SEG was becoming increasingly irrelevant to the conversations among actors' unions. Many of SEG's troubles in the 1960s and 1970s stemmed from the union's weak bargaining position. The function of many unions, especially SEG, is to protect workers from exploitative workplace conditions, but strength at the bargaining table and a continued relationship between studios and unions requires workers to have some degree of leverage. The studios needed to believe that the union members were irreplaceable workers, which meant that SEG's viability as an effective union depended on the perception that its workers were professional and worth the higher wages. Many directors, such as Robert Altman, disagreed with the need for a union for extras. Referring to unionized extras, he proclaimed: "They're not necessary. . . . I see no point in hiring or signing contracts with un-skilled people."[63] Altman was concerned with the cost of his productions and seemingly understood the function of a union contract as an indicator of craft and skill rather than a protection against worker exploitation. As this statement indicates, extras were not always perceived as an underclass that merited concern or that needed to be protected to mitigate bad publicity for the industry (as they did in earlier decades); the understanding of an extra's value had diminished from the studio era. Altman's quote was indicative of an attitude that sent the union searching for some new solutions for its members.

While the two actors' unions were thinking about residuals, SEG began to reach out to SAG to talk about a potential merger. SEG's position in Hollywood was growing weaker—by the mid-1970s, SEG producers had started to refuse to use union extras in their productions. Between 1975 and 1976, SEG members picketed film productions—much to the frustration of producers—but they gained little traction, and it was clear that they had no leverage without additional support from the more powerful unions. SEG entered into active merger talks with SAG in 1977, and in 1980 SAG's executive secretary, Chester Migden (formerly of the NLRB) announced that SAG and SEG were discussing a potential merger. However, this merger did not come to fruition in the 1980s, possibly because the actors' unions were occupied with larger concerns about residuals and their looming strike. Extras were again marginal to the broader conversations and conflicts in Hollywood.

With regard to television, actors needed to think more about the life of a screen performance in addition to the creative process on set. Given the state of television throughout the 1970s, it should be unsurprising that when SAG and AFTRA's contracts came up for renegotiation in 1980, the unions had a number of substantial contract demands. As the unions entered into conversations with producers, SAG and AFTRA's many issues could not be contained in a single *Variety* article; instead they spanned three, with the titles "SAG Wants Big Pension and Welfare Contribution Hike," "Higher Ceilings Sought on P'time Show Re-Runs," and "SAG-AFTRA Offer No Concessions On Supplemental-Market Product," each identifying the main points of contention as pension and welfare funds, television reruns, and supplemental markets.[64] The unions had significant demands related to television and the afterlife of media forms. They were unwilling to waver on these demands and were prepared to play hardball in their negotiations. Although actors went to the bargaining table with an array of requests, the agreement on supplemental markets, which at the time was characterized as "pay-tv, videodisks, [and] cassettes," would be the key legacy of this strike. During these early negotiations in 1980, the actors' unions knew that videocassettes would be an important new technology, but failed to anticipate the scale of the profits from this new technology. This was a failure with significant ripple effect because it established a baseline for future negotiations regarding future home video technology negotiations.

When the VCR arrived in the US market in the late 1970s, it offered viewers another way to rewatch old media and generate new sources of revenue for owners of media licenses from the sale of cassettes. Scholarship on the rise of video and the VHS format in the United States examines this phenomenon predominantly from an industrial perspective, shedding light on competing formats, technological innovators, and Hollywood's response to VHS as a home recording device.[65] Within these industrial histories of VHS, though, is another story of struggle over compensation of media workers and control over a new industrial sector. In the earliest days of VHS, Paul McDonald explains that Hollywood had two basic concerns about the technology: how to control it and how to monetize it.[66] For the actors' unions, these interests trickled down: their concerns were how to participate in the control and how to share in the potential profits. Frederick Wasser observes that "while video revenues have contributed to media concentration, we should not assume that power flows have been one way."[67] For Wasser, these checks on the power and development of VHS included corporate battles, the brief success of independent distributors, and changing audience demands that shaped business practices. In 1980, actors attempted to assert their own power over this new replay technology.

As the union geared up for the 1980 negotiations, the VHS and video-disk market in the United States was still largely speculative, but it was not uncommon for the unions to discuss the potential uses and profit avenues of these new technologies. In 1980, less than 2 percent of households owned a VCR.[68] Throughout the negotiations, industry news still actively conjectured whether the market would favor VCRs or videodisk technology, which at the time was priced much lower.[69] Thus actors were betting on one of these technologies to be profitable in the future. As union correspondence and meeting minutes illustrate, union members frequently expressed concerns about how new forms of distribution might impact the industry and how their ability to anticipate change could translate into stronger contracts. From labor's perspective, the problem they have predicting and anticipating technologies is that they do not have unfettered access to data on the financial success or failure of new media. Furthermore, in the initial negotiations, new technologies are seldom at their full profit potential. When new technologies are still finding an audience and consumer base, producers rely on the unions to present lower or flexible terms, which then become locked in during an early moment when the new technology only yields a small profit. As *Variety* reported in 1980, "Producers . . . have been pleading hardship on the grounds that these are markets with limited short-run revenue potential."[70]

In the 1980 negotiations, SAG and AFTRA decided to draw a hard line with VHS and other supplemental market agreements, refusing to believe that these technologies would not generate significant profits for the industry. Negotiations stalled, and on July 21, 1980, SAG and AFTRA both went on strike. One of the complicating factors in the strike was that the unions were negotiating jointly, but the issues on the table did not affect them equally. For example, the issue of prime-time reruns was more significant for AFTRA (the television union) than for SAG. To bargain successfully, the negotiators had to make sure that improvements in one area, such as supplemental markets, did not come at the expense of other contract terms. As the strike stretched on into September, *Variety* reported that the main sticking points for SAG and AFTRA were related to specifics about *when* (after how many airings or units sold) residuals would kick in for pay TV, videodisks, and videocassettes.[71]

During the strikes of the 1980s, most of the unions had shared demands, but SEG attempted to bargain from a completely different vantage point. SEG struck to maintain jobs and wages at the same time that DGA, WGA, AFTRA, and SAG were on strike for residuals. Unfortunately for SEG, the other guilds did not support its positions (and SAG had already refused to merge with SEG). This left SEG in a precarious position, operating alone, without backing or support from any of the other Hollywood guilds. Left without the benefit of cross-union support, extras' wages were reduced by 25 percent, the studios negotiated a higher number of nonunion extras on productions, and overtime regulations loosened.[72]

By the end of September the negotiating team reached what they felt was a reasonable agreement, with new minimums and residuals, but this resolution was met by vocal dissenters who resisted ratifying it. Over the next month SAG leadership battled with members who were critical of the plan led by spokesman Michael Swan, as well as Ed Asner, Bob Ferro, Brit Lind, Jack Lindine, Thomas Logan, and Bruce Stidham. On October 10, 1980, the SAG board and the anti-ratification group paid for dueling open letters in *Variety* to summarize their respective positions. The open letter supporting the agreement emphasized the substantial (over 30 percent) gains in minimums and residuals, along with the addition of a dental plan, a new affirmative action program that would encourage more diverse hiring, and wider application of California child actor laws to wherever minors work.[73] The oppositional stance hinged solely on the terms for pay TV, which also applied to videocassettes and videodisks.[74] Early in the strike, producers offered actors 3.6 percent of producers' gross on supplemental markets—a number that reflected the terms of the 1960 strike.[75]

Of particular concern for those advocating for a longer strike was the fact that producers had unlimited airings of a film on pay TV for ten days before triggering profit for actors. At the core of these concerns was that a weak foundation for pay TV would establish a poor position in future negotiations, a point that did not worry the pro-ratification group, who said, "we are confident that it can and will be improved in future negotiations."[76] The problem with the oppositional camp's position was that it relied on SAG members to agree with their interpretation of what would happen in future negotiations around a technology that was still speculative in 1980. Despite the controversy among a minority of actors, the ten-week strike resulted in substantial negotiating gains for SAG and AFTRA actors. The gains and the desire to return to work all contributed to an overwhelming number of actors (83.4 percent) ratifying the new contract.[77] The final contract was almost 1 percent higher than the producers' initial offer, with actors receiving 4.5 percent of the producers' gross after the sale of 100,000 units (videocassettes and videodisks). This percentage increase was hard-fought and represented incremental victories over the course of the strike.

Early in the strike, the two unions had to work together to make sure that each one benefited from the negotiations, but ultimately the strike underscored the many shared interests between SAG and AFTRA and demonstrated the effectiveness of joint bargaining. The success of the strike thus led SAG and AFTRA to reconsider a merger. Resolving to take this process slowly, the unions established a three-phase agreement: Phase 1 would combine negotiations, Phase 2 was to combine union governance, and Phase 3 was to finally merge SAG's and AFTRA's memberships. Despite the goodwill between the unions in 1980, the merger remained in Phase 1 until 2008, when joint negotiations imploded and temporarily soured the relationship. However, at this juncture SAG and AFTRA had, for the first time, developed an agreement that seemed to be bringing them closer to the oft-disputed merger.

In the aftermath of the VHS strike, SAG members had to figure out what their relationship was to the other screen performers' union: SEG. Prominent actors split on this issue. Charlton Heston and others (such as Frank Sinatra, James Stewart, and Clint Eastwood) formed Actors Working for an Actors Guild (AWAG) to vocally oppose the merger.[78] Others, such as Ed Asner, who had recently been part of the vocal opposition to the VHS agreement, and Alan Alda, supported the merger between SAG and SEG and positioned it as a form of solidarity with extras—who they viewed, perhaps in some cases incorrectly, as struggling actors.[79] The vote over the merger was delayed until 1982 (well after the strike had ended). With 60 percent majority of SAG members needed to approve the merger, in both 1982 and 1984 the membership narrowly rejected a merger with SEG. In 1982, 57 percent of members voted "yes," and in 1984, 52 percent.[80] Both merger attempts failed because SAG would have been required to take on SEG's assets and liabilities, which would have been a burden to SAG given SEG's financial state in the 1970s. The alliance between AFTRA and SAG and the rejection of the merger with SEG were both a function of what actors saw as their best interests at this historical moment and offer a picture of how actors envisioned themselves as professionals.

After these two failed merger proposals, SEG opened conversations with the International Brotherhood of the Teamsters in 1986. The Teamsters had 1.6 million members across various industries, including three thousand studio drivers.[81] Had SEG been able to successfully merge with the Teamsters, this would have created a fundamentally different labor identity for extras that situated them alongside blue-collar labor histories. Rather than being aligned as a point of entry into the creative work of acting, extras would have been explicitly associated with other below-the-line production workers. Given many of their members' ambitions as above-the-line performers, extras worked against their own self-interest and continued to look to SAG rather than the Teamsters (who were willing to incorporate SEG).

In the 1980s, SAG and AFTRA had rallied around residuals, and SAG had narrowly rejected two separate attempts to merge with SEG. On the one hand, bringing extras into SAG meant that all types of screen performers were again contained within a single union. But on the other hand, from the perspective of many working actors, folding extras into the Screen Actors Guild created an unwieldy union with disparate interests. At this point in the 1980s, it seemed that the actors' unions were forging complementary identities. These unions seemed to be prioritizing advocacy that was on behalf of a middle tier of actor that worked regularly or semiregularly, but had not (for any number of reasons) achieved significant fame. In previous decades the division of film versus television weighed on many of the decisions, but in the 1980s the cultural and economic tiers of various actors weighed more heavily than the technological differences between media.

CONCLUSION

The practices of recording and replaying media content, whether on kinescope, videotape, or VHS, were all part of the cycles of technological development within a concentrated amount of time. By the end of 1980, the technological landscape was beginning to take a clearer shape. VHS was emerging as the preferred home technology, and the two-year videodisk experiment was already beginning to fail after selling an estimated eighteen thousand players in the United States.[82] Over time these technologies transitioned from industrial to home use, and, as is the case with the transition to digital technology, the power of the new technology was in its tremendous flexibility and the possibility for different uses that enabled new industrial and cultural practices for programming and viewing. While the fight over residuals was central to the relationship between actors and the rise of the videocassette, VHS technology also had profound effects on the daily practices of actors. The expansion of technologies of replay from television to VHS transformed several industry practices. In the case of actors, there were negotiations over profits. More relevant to the lived day-to-day reality of a working actor, however, it transformed how actors auditioned for roles. While the move to video auditions was slow and never fully adopted, VHS created new opportunities for recording and submitting auditions as early as the 1970s. This was one of many changes that announced the beginning of a new media landscape for performers.

Residuals also created new boundaries between the different professional tiers of actors. For regularly working actors, residuals were immensely helpful to offset periods of unemployment that are endemic to media production. For some, such as extras or women and people of color who struggled to find sufficient opportunities for workdays, issues of employment and equity in hiring remained more professionally and culturally urgent. For many actors, residuals were merely aspirational, and some of the structural problems relating to available work and casting opportunities persisted unchecked.

FOUR

NEW MEDIA, OLD
LABOR CONFLICTS

Voice Actors and Digital Professionalism

We can talk about fairness all we want, but it's really about leverage.

VOICE ACTOR SPEAKING ABOUT THE VIDEO GAME
CONTRACT NEGOTIATIONS, JULY 13, 2018

In January 2014, I sat in on an information session about SAG-AFTRA's recently implemented New Media Contract. The term "new media," which was already a bit of a misnomer by 2014, colloquially encompassed a wide array of digital media content: video on free sites such as You-Tube or Vimeo, content on subscription-based streaming sites such as Netflix, animated shows and features, and video games. This particular session was aimed at producers, directors, and actors on everything from amateur one-person shoots for YouTube to professional productions, including web series on the CW and flagship Netflix series such as *Arrested Development* (2013) and *Orange Is the New Black* (2013). The meeting, held on the first floor of the SAG-AFTRA headquarters, was free and open to any interested parties and was packed with an actively engaged audience representing a range of experience in digital narratives. Although the audience had diverse careers, they shared a question about the necessity of a union contract for new media: Why did new media producers and actors need to sign a union contract when so much new media content did not generate a profit?

In the early 2010s, SAG-AFTRA was actively in the process of establishing workplace norms for actors in digital productions. The challenge for SAG-AFTRA was to make sure that the work of its actors would be valued in any digital project at any budget. The new media contract was implemented as digitally born productions were becoming ubiquitous, and the contract itself was relatively flexible, with no minimum scale to add expenses to productions. But producers still needed to be convinced of the necessity of an agreement for these largely unprofitable projects.

The union representative in the meeting relied on a familiar justification: professionalism. The benefits of using SAG-AFTRA actors were advertised with optimistic rhetoric ("Access to world's best talent, making your production stand out"), as well as promises of financial savings ("it is also more cost-effective [fewer takes]).["] This rationale appeared to persuade the roomful of producers who had previously worked with union actors on film and television productions. Although this contract was flexible for producers and convinced them to use it, it did not suggest discernible bargaining priorities. Instead, the openness of the contract illustrated a need to forge relationships with a broad array of producers rather than a few key players.

The relatively smooth development of the new media contract and its broad acceptance by film and television professionals contrasts with the rockier experience of negotiating the video game voice actors' contract that same year. Crucial to understanding the nature of performance and the struggle over cultural status for voice actors in digital culture is the split between sound and image, or voice and body. Pamela Robertson Wojcik has discussed this split and explored how cinematic technologies (and film scholars) attempt to conceal the separation between voice and body on screen.[2] Wojcik traces the history of technological intervention in performance and concludes that neglecting technological intermediaries means ignoring the cinematic specificity of screen performance. For Wojcik, the goal is to find a language for evaluating, theorizing, and discussing screen acting that can account for all on-screen performances; she concludes, "If we can account for the technological displacements of sound-film acting, along with other technological aspects of cinematic acting, then there remains little reason to distinguish between Gollum and Frodo, or between digital performance and embodied voices, or between acting and voice acting."[3] But the problem of splitting the voice and the body is not solely one of criticism and aesthetics; it is also a production practice that is essential for creating digital performances. The split between the voice and the digitally constructed body has material ramifications for performers, specifically in the degree to which voice actors are more easily replaceable than on-screen performers.[4] From an industrial perspective, actors are often forced to specialize; they have different agents for different types of performance, and actors develop specialized networks with casting directors, producers, and directors that do not always overlap. Some performers might specialize by design, while others specialize by default, but the technological displacements of certain performance types are often accompanied by precise skill sets.

Unique to the contemporary era, though, was the need for SAG-AFTRA to negotiate a deal with an already well-established digital industry that had only recently begun to use actors: the video game industry. Video game revenue grew 18 percent between 2016 and 2017, demonstrating the importance of games within entertainment media.[5] Even though video games can be incredibly cinematic and fulfill some of the same audience needs for entertainment as film and television do, the similarities end at the level of aesthetic and textual comparisons. The creative cultures of work in games and tech has no history of unionization and is dramatically different from those of film and television. While the first decade or so of video games saw little use for professional voice work, by the 2000s, AAA games (the industry title for games with large production and marketing budgets) increasingly looked and sounded like animated motion pictures. Because the video game industry had several decades to develop its industrial practices before it began to use actors in games, the video game voice actor agreement was a particular challenge to implement.

At the core of this tension between video game companies and voice performers was a fundamental conflict between the unregulated and demanding culture of tech, coders, and Silicon Valley versus the entrenched, union-driven creative culture of Hollywood. Much of the scholarship on digital media labor focuses on workers participating in the Web 2.0 economy, addressing concerns around the free and immaterial labor endemic to digital media industries and the collapse of a line separating producers and users. While essential to theorizing some of the new social relations and economies that emerge in digital spaces, this work rarely addresses the ways in which more traditional media labor or workers also make a living in digital spheres of the media industry.[6] Angela McRobbie's *Be Creative* is a notable exception, considering the creative unions as a counterpoint to labor trends under discussion within the United Kingdom. McRobbie shows how unions have combated the de-skilling of creative labor enabled by digital media, but focuses on how unions are extraneous in the creative economy. Unions demand specialization, but the creative digital economy requires workers to acquire many skills and adapt to rapidly changing industrial trends.[7] While McRobbie suggests that unions are becoming increasingly irrelevant for creative workers in the United Kingdom, I would argue that unions remain incredibly relevant to the professional identities and careers of their membership in Hollywood. In the case of SAG-AFTRA, membership helps mark the shift from aspirant to professional, even in the current space of digital productions, by offering the advantages of a paid full-time profession such as health benefits, pension, and, in the case of the creative economy, distribution of residual checks. However, one of the ways SAG and AFTRA have stayed relevant is through their merger, which broadened the focus so that it now represents actors, dancers, extras, voice actors, journalists, broadcasters, and more. While many unions represent specialized workers, SAG-AFTRA has been increasingly attuned to a wider range of professional skills.

That workers are being asked to adopt nonspecialized skills and still relate to their union signals some of the challenges not only in understanding the contemporary production landscape, but also in assessing how digital practices have been integrated into the entertainment industry. The availability of digital tools, increased demands of "flexibility" and "multitasking" in digital workplaces, and the expansion of digital content distribution have posed significant challenges to cultural and contractual definitions of work in media union cultures. I suggest that there are four key ways to think about the rise of digital media as it impacts actors: first, in terms of the specificity of digitally born content; second, in relation to replay and residuals; third, as a new mode of performance, or, in the case of extras, a potential replacement for performers; and finally, as a set of innovations that have transformed the casting process. As with new forms of content in previous eras, actors and SAG-AFTRA have been working to understand the value of work in an era of rapid technological and economic shifts, and how to determine sound work environments and fair residual rates amid this flux. Actors and unions adjust in order to establish norms and practices for work that might circulate behind lower paywalls or freely in culture. Computer-generated imaging (CGI) has also given creators the ability to replace large crowds of actors with digital multitudes of people, thus reducing the need, in some cases, for large groups of extras.[8] Digital technologies have also transformed casting procedures and how actors look for work. Online casting sites and the increased accessibility of media-making tools and distribution platforms have created new opportunities for aspirants to maintain public visibility and connect with industry players. Actors must maintain a digital presence and own or have access to equipment that will allow them to shoot or record audition material that might need to be submitted within the hour.

The availability of digital technology has impacted all actors and placed greater demands on them to multitask and self-promote, but, as this chapter demonstrates, this transformation in auditioning, casting, and booking roles has been especially evident in the field of voice acting, where many actors work on some of the least-regulated types of projects. This chapter traces some of the origins of the deregulation that characterizes the digital media industry, beginning with the commercials strike in 2000 that resulted in fewer union commercial jobs and helped establish many of the conditions and conflicts that determine the contemporary acting profession. In addition to existing career paths in film, television, and commercials, work in video games and animated films has become more prevalent and financially significant for actors. Theoretically, actors can and do work across media, but certain trajectories are less common—for instance, there are significant silos among on-camera workers and voice workers. The result is a wider array of union content production, but with scant career pathways that lead to lucrative or middle-class acting careers.

Nonunion production has also increased as cable networks and streaming platforms generate more and more content and aspiring nonunion actors vie to get noticed alongside their union counterparts. Actors now navigate a greater array of low-paying creative and professional opportunities, and the unions are tasked with distinguishing between these types of content as they negotiate new contracts and compensation strategies. There are myriad ways to find nonunion work, including through independent films or student films, on television in reality genres and commercials, or doing voice work in video games, animation, and anime, all of which remains nonunion labor. The proliferation of content has created demands for more actors and other types of on-screen personalities and performers ("regular people," influencers, micro-celebrities, etc.) and has subsequently expanded the perpetually inflated labor pool. At various historical points, union membership can be seen as a defining characteristic that separates the amateur from the professional actor; as such, unions have been essential for determining evolving definitions of screen acting as a profession. What is and is not union work has changed, as have the various pathways from nonunion performer to union actor.

The prominence and profitability of many of these nonunion programs marks a crisis point for actors' unions, threatening the cultural significance of the professional actors who have been the focus of this book. The accessibility of technologies for making and distributing media poses challenges to the professional norms and expectations long established by a unionized profession. In the contemporary production climate, producers can drive salaries down because there is so much competition for roles, whether in film, television, or video games. This new media environment provides unparalleled access to content, but it has exacerbated worker instability. In the broadest terms I explore how digital media production (from digitally born "television" programs to video games) impacts actors and unions. I ask: How does deprofessionalization and the fact that anyone can produce content generate new challenges for professionals who seek to establish labor protocols, make a living, or even simply share in digital profits? What are the challenges facing unionized workers who regularly collaborate with nonunion workers in the notoriously grueling and exploitative digital fields?

Drawing on participant observation and interviews with actors, this chapter examines how digital media technologies reactivate key conflicts of previous eras. I spoke with twenty-five actors between 2014 and 2018, all of whom work across diverse media forms. I sourced my interviews through a snowball sample method, in which each contact generated additional contacts. In previous chapters the research and methodological challenge was to find the marginal stories of the aspirant, working, and middle-class actors within the archival collections of well-known producers, stars, and directors. Researching and writing about contemporary actors offered me the possibility to create my own archive, which drew on an array of actors at different career stages in the current moment of technological and industrial transition. Many of the actors I spoke with explicitly asked to remain anonymous as they shared details and often strong opinions about working conditions and the industry. For many actors there is an ever-present fear that speaking out about labor conditions indicates they are difficult and therefore should not be hired. The real fear of repercussions is also a fundamental difference between the evidence and stories I present in this chapter. The video game strike ended, but many of the issues remain unresolved, and, as such, the stories and interviews included here provide accounts of ongoing struggles in Hollywood.

VALUING VOICE ACTING

The addition of new narrative forms in the digital media industry has created more ways for actors (and their voices) to get on screen, and increased access to technology and channels of distribution has generated more possible entry points and career trajectories for actors. However, these new developments emerged at precisely the moment that paying acting work was diminishing. For actors, the rise of digital media technologies and the opportunities they present need to be considered in relation to the broader changes in the media landscape that have impacted the availability of roles in film, television, and television commercials.

The end of the twentieth century and the beginning of the twenty-first saw dramatic changes in television production that led to an increase in television production jobs.[9] Beginning in 2014, journalists, industry leaders, and scholars have described the contemporary moment of unprecedented television production for networks and streaming services as the era of "peak TV." That year, in which 180 shows were produced, marked the beginning of this trend, and in each subsequent year that number has ballooned; in 2017 alone there were 487 scripted shows.[10] This "peak" was not a sudden shift, but a steady trend that began with a boom in cable television production that can be traced back to as early as the 1990s or as late as 2000.[11] This increase in narrative content production in the twenty-first century was a result of more methods of distribution and more players (including Netflix, Hulu, and Amazon, as well as increasing cable networks) entering the business of original content production.

Unfortunately, the new work ushered in by digital technologies has been an inadequate replacement for the work that was dramatically transformed or lost in the same period. The headline of *Variety*'s 2016 article, "Stars' Soaring Salaries Rattle TV Business—Monster Paydays Leave Little Earnings Power for Working-Class Actors," affirms this point and boldly proclaims the reality of unbalanced earnings distribution. In the culture of star-driven television, above-the-line salaries consume much of the budget for talent, leaving many actors unable to negotiate above scale. However, *Variety*'s emphasis—that most working actors do not benefit from the changing culture of media production—is not new information. Despite the boom in television production between 2000 and 2010, the Screen Actors Guild reported that overall earnings declined while residual earnings remained largely consistent.[12]

Academic and popular press articles about the future of acting frequently explore how digitized performances challenge the cultural value of the actor.[13] Media scholar Lisa Bode considers how actors are invested in the new debates around the relationship between digital technologies and performance. Bode characterizes contemporary actors as "creative laborers and self-interested agents helping shape conversations about how we should understand and continue to value acting in the context of significant technological change."[14] Scholarship on digital performance often focuses on motion capture and computer animation that alters bodies, including actors who are completely transformed (as in many of Andy Serkis's performances) or only slightly altered. What these scholarly approaches share is a fundamental understanding of how technology and performance are intertwined and inform both our cinematic experience as well as our understanding of actors as valuable contributors to visual storytelling regardless of medium.

Voice actors have had less control over the industrial and cultural value of their performances. CGI performances would seem to have much in common with voice acting, since both feature altered bodies and vocal performances. But voice acting has a different history. In its earliest years, voice acting for the screen was less dependent on star talent, at least in part because it is disembodied. Voice acting developed through radio and became increasingly essential in the late 1930s in Warner Bros. and Disney cartoons, culminating with the Disney feature film *Snow White and the Seven Dwarves* (1938). Although voice acting was not dependent on star power for most of the twentieth century, there are some noteworthy counterexamples, including Judy Garland in *Gay Purr-ee* (1962), Bob Newhart in *The Rescuers* (1977), and Mickey Rooney and Kurt Russell in *The Fox and the Hound* (1981), but these were exceptions to the rule. As Rebecca Asherie and others have observed, the widespread practice of casting celebrities as voice actors changed in the 1990s after Robin Williams's performance as Genie in *Aladdin* (1992).[15] Subsequent Disney and studio-animated films have continued to feature star voice work and to capitalize on stars in their marketing. As animation has become more star-driven, this has pushed many trained voice actors out of contention for prominent roles in the most visible animated projects.

The use of voice actors in video games is a relatively recent phenomenon. Early arcade games occasionally featured lines of dialogue, but human voices were not a significant part of console games until the 1990s, and this work was not initially considered professional acting work. Karen Collins explains, "In the early days of game dialogue, friends of the audio developer were often drafted to record voice parts."[16] As Collins illustrates, not only was star power unimportant, but the voices were treated as an afterthought to the design of the game play. The budgets of console games increased, allowing for more aesthetically and narratively cinematic techniques in game design. The increase of in-game dialogue meant that voice work evolved into an increasingly important part of the game soundtrack. In video game spinoffs of Hollywood films, star voices remain important as they provide continuity between the film and game worlds. In a discussion of the *Spider-Man 3* video game, Casey O'Donnell notes, "New audio voice-overs were done by the original actor, Tobey Maguire, who had to be flown in to provide adequate vocal isolation for Spider-Man's lines. Bruce Campbell, who has appeared in all of the Spider-Man movies as a cameo actor, returned as the narrator on only the PS2, Wii, and PSP games."[17]

Although stars might be worth the price for these marquee roles, especially in games that extend the narrative experience of well-known film titles, the remaining characters, dialogue, and lines are typically delivered by professional voice actors who rarely, if ever, appear as actors on screen. There are many AAA games that are original properties and do not rely on movie star voices as part of their appeal.[18] The fact that video games are not (yet) tethered to the star system means that voice actors can get the jobs, but they are often replaceable and cannot demand star salaries for these performances. By their very nature, games challenge conventional notions of stardom within game play. In films and television shows the protagonist is frequently played by a star actor, but in games the protagonist is the player. As players move between settings or levels, they interact with different characters. Beloved characters can generate a significant fan base, especially in popular games. Although it does not result in the same level of recognition as on-screen performances, certain video game performances might be more clearly identifiable, and actors can leverage this popularity into convention appearances or more work in the future. In a podcast interview with Kaili Vernoff (*Red Dead Redemption 2*, *The Path*, and *House of Cards*), Vernoff commented that she is primarily recognized for her role in *Red Dead Redemption 2*.[19] In the case of *Red Dead Redemption 2*, however, the physicality of the character might contribute to her character recognition. Vernoff's entire performance was motion-captured, which differs from the voice work she did for a popular character in *Grand Theft Auto V*.

The absence of a star system for voice actors, however, should not be confused with the absence of specialization in the profession. Some voice actors do on-camera work, but it is possible to make a living solely on voice work. As one actor bluntly explained, "nobody who's very successful in VO [voice-over] dabbles in it."[20] Based on my interviews, contemporary actors who do voice work typically make a living through some combination of commercial voice-over, animated films and programs, looping (background vocals), and video games. Voice actors have separate agents and need to maintain a professional network that does not necessarily overlap with on-screen work. Even if producers are able to replace voice actors because they are not on camera, the specialized gatekeeper networks benefit those who maintain consistent work in voice-over.

For some actors, voice work is liberating, allowing them to play roles that they may not be physically suited for. As many voice actors will explain, the skill set, training, and expectations for voice actors differ from stage or screen work, or, as one actor told me, "it's pure creativity."[21] Most of the working voice actors I interviewed like to stay behind the camera, in part because they do not have the same pressures regarding physical appearance that on-camera actors face. One voice actor unlovingly remembered her experience doing casting calls for on-camera work, telling me, "I hated walking into a room and seeing 20 other mes that had better makeup or better bodies. I know I'm not supposed to care but my soul did not do well with that. It made me think too much about how I look all the time."[22]

Rather than thinking about physicality and authenticity, actors consider their vocal range and type. In practice this has meant that animated shows, films, and video games can cast white actors to voice characters of color, making it challenging for voice actors of color to find work.[23] Animated shows such as *The Simpsons* have been openly criticized, most notably in the 2017 documentary *The Problem with Apu*, for casting white actors to voice characters of color. In 2020 several actors, such as Jenny Slate, Kristen Bell, and Mike Henry, announced that they would no longer work on the shows where they voiced characters of color. These announcements were accompanied by statements from producers on *Big Mouth* (2017–), *Central Park* (2020–), and *The Simpsons* (1989–) that they would no longer hire white actors to voice characters of color. Although these announcements create some notable new roles for nonwhite actors, this potentially limits options for black voice actors who have found work voicing a diverse array of characters. For black voice actors like Dave Fenneroy, who has voiced hundreds of white and nonwhite video game characters in his career, he wants to continue to be considered for an array of roles. Although Fenneroy supports more work for black actors, there are few black characters in video games, so it would be difficult for him, or anyone, to make a career solely out of voicing black characters. Although voice acting could provide opportunities for actors to play an array of different roles regardless of race, the possession of a versatile voice is typically a privilege of white actors.

The lack of reliance on an actor's physical presence contributes to a voice actor's versatility. Rather than being limited by physical persona, voice actors are often cast to voice multiple roles in the same project. As one actor explained about her day auditioning for animation, "Today my audition was playing grandma, a 15-year-old and an 8-year-old. Where else can I do that?"[24] Starr Marcello's characterization of voice acting sums up the core challenge, saying, "Noncelebrity voice actors are presumed to have a talent and 'proclivity for voice-changing,' which prevents direct correspondence between the characters they play and their real-life personalities."[25] For voice actors, the craft is in the process of creating unique characters or variations on a theme. This "proclivity for voice-changing" contributes to the expectation that skilled voice actors should also ideally be able to do multiple distinct voices (for multiple roles or characters) on a project.[26] In reality, many voice actors have types, and as voices change, so do the opportunities for roles. As one actor explained, "there are things that are more a stretch for me that weren't ten years ago. My voice has gotten deeper, and I can still do the kids' stuff but in my opinion it's not nearly as sharp as it used to be."[27] Since actors are not physically associated with voice, and voice changing lends itself to imitations, many voice actors are replaceable. Thus while the work of the voice actor requires skillful characterization, it is ultimately anonymous, with the same character being potentially voiced by different actors in life or, as in the case of famous voice performers like Mel Blanc and Jim Henson, after death.

On a given production, voice actors are expected to be able to offer multiple variations on a given take and run through numerous lines in a session. In video games, as Karen Collins explains, there are several different types of dialogue: ambient dialogue (also known as *walla*, background ambience for environments where there are background people, such as crowds at a baseball stadium, shop, or market); scripted events (which are in-game scenes in which the player can typically walk away, but if he does so, he or she will miss some important information); cinematics (also known as "cut scenes"); AI cues (also known as *barks*, which are nonverbal lines such as screaming); voice-over narration; and in-game lines.[28]

The wide array of dialogue types can contribute to thousands of lines of dialogue. AAA Games like *Halo 2* had over sixteen thousand lines, a substantial amount of work for performers.[29] Within these sixteen thousand total lines, however, an individual actor might deliver over a hundred per session. Although the amount of cut scenes in the *Halo* games essentially constitutes a feature-length movie run time, this is actually significantly lower than for other AAA games; for example, *God of War* includes three and a half hours of cinematics or "cut scenes." As video game worlds grow, they present more opportunities for actors, but what is essential for actors and SAG-AFTRA is a culture that values actors' contributions to these worlds and offers opportunities for actors to invest in the creation of their characters.

For actors performing in games, the content is often less relevant than the context of the line. In film or television, actors know how their line contributes to a story narrative (even though scenes are shot out of sequence), but in video games the motivation and narrative placement can be less clear for AI cues (since the computer characters are responding to game play), or possibly for certain in-game lines. Voice actors often have to read lines without the contextual cues that can help them anchor their performances. In my interviews, some voice actors lamented the lack of information in scripts. As one actor explained, "I've auditioned for games where we were given a stock page and a half back story about the universe and all the dialogue is "incoming!" "frag out!" etc. Sometimes you're just a grunt in the military. Cool I got that. That's fine. I don't know why you bother with a page and a half of like 'in 140 years in the future or a bunch of space marine combat an alien force on Jupiter 7 whatever.'"[30] Beyond the general lack of description or context, scripts for voice work in games can vary wildly, ranging from conventional scripts to Excel sheets with lists of short lines, explanations, and grunts.[31]

On the surface, performing short lines of dialogue in enormously profitable games seems like it would be a particularly lucrative and easy form of work for voice actors. However, the risks are significant, including the inability to work for several days and possibly permanent voice damage. Battle chatter, or the expletives, warnings, and words shouted during video game combat, are a common part of the sound design in AAA games that creates significant vocal strain for actors. As one actor explained, "I don't do battle chatter anymore. And that was a choice that I made because I would book every battle chatter audition I did because I know exactly how to do it and I can go for pretty long. The problem is you're done [unable to perform in other jobs] for a day and a half at least—some people for three or four [days]."[32] Production practices for recording and capturing game performances have not been regulated by a union or other overseeing body; thus the experience of performing for a video game can vary from company to company. As one actor explained in a description of two different sessions: "When I went in for *Call of Duty: Infinite Warfare* with Infinity Ward, they were great. I loved them. I went in like ten or eleven times. The first one I think was 270 [lines] and they went 'OK bye. Have your tea and go away.' The next day they would say, 'OK we have dying civilian one, we have a phone sex operator, we have blah blah, and then we have 50 battle chatter loops.'"[33] Although the first session this actor described was fairly standard, her description underscores that actors are frequently cast before they know exactly which roles they will voice. A day might include numerous lines of grunts, but also dialogue for a phone-sex operator. The opacity of the industry in regard to casting and dialogue expectations means that they might not be expected to precisely communicate their expectations. The same actor recalled another session experience, relating: "This [unnamed] company wanted me to do 600 [lines] and I had prenegotiated because I went in once. So, I went in once and they booked me for three hours. And I said 'wow that's a lot. I've never booked for more than two hours for battle chatter.' They said 'Oh don't worry. You've got an hour of normal VO and then you've got a battle chatter loop.'"[34] Although the company initially asked for an inordinate amount of battle chatter, what was prenegotiated was the time and amount of lines, which meant that there could be (and were) changes to her expectations in the session.

"When I went in and they said 'oh we have you now 370 battle chatter loops, one-hour normal VO.' And I said, 'wow that's a lot I've never done that many' and they said, 'oh you should see what we make the guys do.' So, I did it, and I left, and my throat was wrecked. They wanted to bring me in again a few weeks later. . . . I said, 'OK fine.' So, I went in 9 a.m. on a Monday morning and they went 'oh, we found new scripts we have 670 battle chatter loops for you but it's ok because we don't have any normal VO for you to do. So, it like evens out.' And I on the spot refused."[35]

In this example the actor had to use her judgment of the situation and advocate for her own health and well-being. Later in the interview she was forthcoming that she felt secure enough in her career to walk away from a job that could potentially take her out of work for days at the risk of permanent damage to her voice. She was fortunate enough to feel empowered to make this choice—other actors might not be in the same position to walk away from a paying job.

This story demonstrates some of the differences between employers in an unregulated industry. While some game studios are efficient and professional, others operate on a model of trying to wrench as much work as possible out of an actor. Given the wide disparity between workloads, it is clear that what constitutes "strain" should not be left to the decision of game studios with a vested interest in cutting costs. As the poststrike contract reveals, consensus about vocal strain can be difficult to regulate. As of 2019, unions and video game studios were still looking for a solution to minimize vocal strain, but some actors might also experience this differently. As one actor explained: "I can bang out 370 battle chatter loops in 30 minutes. But the reason I do that is because I know once you start screaming your throat starts swelling it's not going to sound the same in 45 minutes or an hour. They go 'oh well, take breaks.' No. It doesn't help."[36] For these labor practices to change, voice actors need to agree upon what works best for minimizing vocal stress and need more leverage at the bargaining table. If voice actors use the model of screen actors before them, this means increasing cultural capital and forcing game designers to see them as essential contributors to the creative endeavor of video game production.

INDUSTRIAL FOUNDATIONS OF DEREGULATION

The deregulation of media ownership has been instrumental in reshaping the culture of actors' labor. Media scholars such as Jennifer Holt have traced industrial deregulation in the media industry, concluding that the Telecommunications Act of 1996 completed years of deregulation initiated in the 1980s.[37] The 1996 bill eliminated broadcast station ownership caps, broadcast/cable cross-ownership rules, and cable/telephone system cross-ownership bans. Concurrent with the beginning stages of deregulation in the 1970s were a number of other changes related to media content, labor, and technology, including: the rise of reality television; the collapse of the SEG, which had a lasting impact on SAG; and the increase in distribution platforms. Each of these developments contributed to the expansion of low- or no-pay work for actors and paved the way for how more recent screen actors have been initiated into digital labor cultures.

Ownership regulations did not have an immediate and direct effect on how actors were paid or hired, but this gradual unraveling of regulations changed the landscape of television production and distribution and produced ripples that would be felt in subsequent decades. From the perspective of audiences, the main transformation of television in the latter half of the twentieth century was an increase in networks and channels. By the end of the 1980s, US homes had access to anywhere between 12 and 140 channels, a far cry from the domination of the big three networks (NBC, CBS, and ABC) during the network era.[38] Industrially, greater competition from cable networks led to a more dispersed viewership across channels. Cable networks created competition for broadcast, but they were primarily licensing existing content to fill their programming time rather than producing substantial original programs.

As discussed in the previous chapter, numerous unions were concerned with the revenue being generated from older content and went on strike for residuals in the 1980s. SAG, AFTRA, the Writers Guild of America (WGA), and the Directors Guild of America (DGA) all went on strike over residuals, and SEG followed with a strike over extras' daily wages. Television was getting more expensive to produce due to the rising demands from and cost of union labor. At the same time, network profits declined as cable networks expanded, creating more choices for consumers but smaller shares per program. As a result, individual programs were no longer able to generate the same level of advertising revenue and producers, studios, and networks began to look for additional ways to exploit free or nonunion labor for media programming.

These economic changes set the industrial conditions for new forms of inexpensive, nonunion, and nonlicensed programming, most notably reality television. From its inception, reality TV has been at odds with unions, or as Andrew Ross more sharply states, it has been "an assault on" organized labor.[39] When networks and production companies looked to labor for their budget cuts, they found aesthetic solutions that minimized the use of union talent—especially writers and actors. Early reality programs such as *America's Most Wanted* (1988–2011) and *Cops* (1989–) used drama and suspense derived from real-life crimes and presented the material with found footage and nonunion talent. The landscape of reality TV subgenres rapidly expanded in the 2000s to include competition (*American Idol* [2002–], *The Voice* [2011–], *Survivor* [2001–]); makeover shows (*Extreme Make-Over* [2002–2007], *What Not to Wear* [2003–2013], and *Queer Eye for the Straight Guy* [2003–2007]); and shows that build drama through surveillance and confessional interviews (starting with MTV's *The Real World* [1992–] and notably including *Big Brother* [US 2000–]). These shows were less connected to documentary traditions and instead adopted many of the structures of fiction television programs. Although reality conformed to some conventions of entertainment television, the production practices were dramatically different.

As Mark Andrejevic points out, reality TV often costs a third as much to produce as scripted television programs, with the potential of enormous returns if the franchise can be spun off internationally (like *Big Brother*).[40] This is possible because most of the people working on these shows (both on- and off-screen) are not part of television unions. The same reality shows that bypass unions often become platforms for actors looking to revive their dwindling fame, or entrepreneurial people and aspiring celebrities looking to use television to launch careers or product lines. The number of people vying for work on screen for reasons beyond a desire to act only served to diminish the value of union talent for television programs. Reality television's tendency toward showcasing products meant that it increasingly became a long-form commercial. Reality television offered some solutions to industrial problems, such as the rising costs of television productions, but also offered other avenues for fame. Essential to reality television's ability to solve a number of problems is its reliance on nonunion labor—a solution also applied to the production of television commercials.

The rising cost of television commercials was concurrent with increased costs across the board in television programming in the 1970s. Like television producers, commercial producers began to look for ways to cut costs. Between 1970 and 1978, production costs for commercials rose 15 percent per year on average.[41] In the 1990s production costs continued to rise, and in 1993 the advertising trades lamented that the cost of making a national television commercial had exceeded $200,000, due to rising facility costs rather than labor costs.[42] Television commercials, like films and television shows, were produced under union agreements and often provided a living for working actors. This backdrop of consistently rising commercial production costs fueled producers' decisions to take the easy route of using nonunion labor, even if this was not the most effective way to reduce costs in commercial productions.

The changing culture of media content took a particularly tough toll on extras. In the midst of rising labor costs, multiple union strikes over residuals, and producers making reality TV as a means to cut costs, extras struggled to maintain relevance and negotiating power in the media landscape of the 1980s and 1990s. From the perspective of producers, union extras were simply an expense that could be cut. As I mention in chapter 3, in the late 1980s SEG was trying to figure out whether to merge with the Teamsters or SAG. Although the Teamsters welcomed them, the extras wanted to be part of an actors' union. With respect to hiring, there are some essential differences between entertainment unions and more traditional unions. Like traditional unions, the entertainment unions use collective bargaining to focus on wages, workplace conditions, pensions, benefits, etc. Unlike many blue-collar unions, however, the entertainment unions cannot produce or guarantee stable employment. As attorney Mark Grunewald points out, "traditional, full-time, long term employment . . . has been at the core for the development of collective bargaining."[43] This marks a key difference between more traditional unions, which can take up job stability as a key bargaining point, and entertainment unions, which are unable to place restrictions on hiring that would hinder the creative process of casting. As the other entertainment unions shifted their bargaining priorities toward residuals, it became increasingly clear that even though SEG did not want to be part of the Teamsters, in reality it had aspired to be more like a blue-collar union than either SAG or AFTRA. Extras have never been able to achieve stable or long-term employment, partially because there were too many extras available for roles, and given the minimal skills required, producers could and would always be able to obtain extras from many sources.

In 1990, when SEG failed to reach an agreement with the Association for Motion Picture and Television Producers (AMPTP), all extras work in California became nonunion by default. After extras had worked for two years without a union, SAG finally agreed to annex them.[44] Since extras had been working without a union contract, this takeover benefited extras by providing them with representation and a new contract. SAG in turn benefited by collecting more membership fees without taking on additional liabilities or providing extras with a seat on their board. But folding extras into SAG changed the balance of voting power and priorities within the union and did what many feared would happen with a merger in the 1950s. The union was now responsible for a wide range of voting members with even more divergent interests and values at a time when the union needed to focus and shore up its demands in the changing industrial culture. The reintroduction of extras into the broad population of working actors created new inefficiencies and meant that SAG would need to manage new levels of worker stratification within the union. Although the union always had many unemployed or underemployed members, and there were always actors who had dual SAG and SEG memberships, SAG would now be wholly responsible for a different type of performer. Combining the unions did not change the nature of extras work, but now union extras gained additional power (or at least greater union stability) through their association with a union with a stronger bargaining position. Working actors (especially those who previously were not members of SEG) did not gain the same types of benefits, and instead struggled to make sure their interests were heard and addressed in this larger union.

SAG ended the twentieth century with a diverse and often unwieldy population as it prepared for a bitter negotiation on behalf of commercial actors. During the 1999 SAG presidential election, *Variety* reported that many actors had criticized SAG president Richard Masur (a longtime working actor with credits including *One Day at a Time*, *It*, and *L.A. Law*) for dismissing the possibility of a commercials strike.[45] In November 1999, SAG members elected William Daniels (*St. Elsewhere* and *Boy Meets World*) as president, based on the promise of tougher negotiations. With wages stagnating in recent years, Daniels entered the commercials negotiation asking for a 20 percent pay raise.[46] The SAG and AFTRA joint commercial strike in 2000 began on May 1 after several months of failed negotiations. At stake for actors in these negotiations was a change in the rate for cable TV commercials as well as jurisdiction over and a monitoring system for internet advertisements. As cable and internet advertising became more significant, the unions sought better rates for all forms of advertisements. Advertisements on broadcast television guaranteed actors a daily rate and a "pay per play" residual ($50 to $120 per network play), while in contrast actors received $1,000 for every thirteen weeks an ad ran on cable.[47] On the surface, many of these demands seem to be simple extensions of existing agreements, but advertisers wanted to dramatically change the union contract. Not only were advertisers unwilling to grant an extension of the "pay per play" for cable, but they were trying to change the terms of the broadcast rate so that actors would be paid a flat fee for unlimited use of all commercials (network and cable). Although the terms for legacy media were particularly contentious, as one SAG member noted during the strike, "A lot of members believe the Internet is the key issue because it will eventually become even bigger than network or cable."[48] With the unions and advertisers at odds and actors positioning this negotiation as one with high stakes that would be significant for the digital era, the failure to generate a mutually agreeable contract resulted in a 175-day strike—the longest in SAG's and AFTRA's respective histories at that point.

When the strike came to an end on October 22, 2000, both sides had made some clear concessions. The contract that emerged out of the strike gave SAG and AFTRA several noteworthy gains, including jurisdiction over internet commercials. SAG president William Daniels declared, "I believe that the deal we got is better than we could have hoped for."[49] In contrast, the advertising industrial trade paper *Ad Age* cited several victories for advertisers, including no increases in broadcast costs and the retention of the same model for cable commercial production (fees would increase, but actors would not receive "pay per play" residuals). In summary, neither side made the significant gains that they initially hoped for, and this heated round of negotiations more or less maintained the status quo.

Although the new contract was in place, advertisers found a number of different ways to continue to conduct business as usual with nonunion actors. Even though the new contract seemed to restore order for actors, it had fundamentally changed the culture of commercial production. During the strike, commercial producers embraced a tried-and-true Hollywood strategy for reducing costs and avoiding unions: overseas location shooting. In the immediate aftermath of the strike, writers for *Ad Age* were already speculating that producers had grown accustomed to working with nonunion talent in non-US locations.[50] According to the president of the Association of Independent Commercial Producers, "the strike was a catalyst for speeding up the comfort level overseas. . . . Because of the attraction of lower costs, it would have happened eventually, but it's occurred much faster than many anticipated."[51] The transition of many commercials to nonunion productions was a blow to actors who had come to rely on commercial work as a means of survival.

For many working actors in the latter half of the twentieth century, union commercials (both on television and radio) paid the bills so they could continue to pursue additional training or more creatively fulfilling roles. As one actor I interviewed explained, if you booked one national commercial, you could be good for the year.[52] After the commercial strike in 2000 there were fewer commercial opportunities for US actors, which made a significant financial impact on the acting population. Things got even worse in subsequent years when commercial producers would simply abandon union agreements while continuing to shoot in the United States, preferring to cut costs and work with nonprofessional actors. Analyzing the 2000 commercial strike from a legal perspective, Craig J. Ackerman notes, "The unions' positions . . . were heavily influenced by SAG/AFTRA's prior failure to capitalize fully on the trend toward cable in terms of negotiation of a residual formula."[53] This observation in the specific instance of the commercial strike underscores one of the reasons negotiations around digital media have been so contentious: the institutional memory of past failures influences both the tone of subsequent negotiations and the perception that labor needs to win better terms.

While there were different catalysts for changes in the content landscape, what emerged from the rising costs of production and the SAG and AFTRA strike was a series of union avoidance strategies, such as the continued shift to reality television and the diminution of union commercials. The increase in distribution venues (and the need for more content) that came from the cable era set the stage and expectations for work in the digital era. The decrease in more lucrative on-screen acting options, such as scripted television and commercials, took away important sources of income for actors and made significant contributions to the shape of their career options in the twenty-first century. Those options became increasingly challenged by the arrival of digital technologies and the conditions of digital media production.

HOME/OFFICE CONVERGENCE

Convergence—the blurring of boundaries between technology, corporations, and aesthetic forms—characterizes many of the changes in the digital era. The changing functions of media technology (such as a computer or mobile device) and the type of media we can access on that device (films, television programs, games, etc.) has destabilized traditional understandings of the relationship between technology and content, not to mention the very notion of media texts as discrete forms (such as the labels "film" or "television"). The labor perspective on digital culture and media production has been largely left out of scholarship on convergence in media studies, which has been more focused on how audiences and consumers negotiate technology and their increased access to media content. As Henry Jenkins anticipated in his landmark work *Convergence Culture*, the result of more methods of content delivery has been more mobile audience members who traverse various media to seek out entertainment. Jenkins's interest in how audiences use technology nuances the conceptualization of technology as a tool and complicates discussions of access to account for the messier terrain of conversation about "cultural protocols and practices."[54] Yet cultural protocols cannot simply be reduced to audience engagement; for industrially produced media to thrive and grow for audiences, professional workers need to develop their own protocols and practices.

As I outline in the introduction, we have analyzed the protocols and practices of technology from the perspective of creators and consumers, but rarely have workers been central to digital media industry studies. Scholarly treatments of consumers, especially those scholars focused on fans, often embrace subversive or unconventional uses of technology, while histories of creators tend to focus on innovation. The lack of diversity in histories of technology resembles similar issues that plague histories of media workers, which have similarly focused on Hollywood decision-makers who are credited with innovation within the industry. By focusing on earliest instances or those quick to use new technologies, we run the risk of ignoring the slowness that is often part of technological transitions. Jenkins readily admits that his sample of culture relies on educated, white, affluent early adopters who are also fans and content producers. Thus his use of the term "producer" describes fans who create content, corporations that own intellectual property and possess means of distribution, and sometimes the collapse between the two.[55] Left out of this characterization of "producer" are those aspirants, workers, and creatives who are making media and trying to earn a living from that work. Actors might like the films, shows, or games they work on, but they do not necessarily have the same kind of affective relationship to their creative output as many of the subjects of Jenkins's work. Histories of workers' practices provide an essential (and often unromanticized) perspective on the implementation of new technologies and how these processes have shaped professional life in the media industries.

Considering convergence from the perspective of workers who rely on media for their livelihoods shifts the focus from the celebration of agency toward a consideration of how convergence reflects a driving trend toward despecializing media workers. In the twenty-first century, actors experience technological transformations in the production and distribution of the texts in which they appear, but the effects of technological convergence have been especially prominent in the audition process. For much of Hollywood history, actors seeking roles have had to travel to the studio, production office, or agency where they auditioned, recorded screen tests, or received direction and guidance on a performance. The practices of auditioning and submitting for roles has gone through tremendous changes that accompanied the arrival and ubiquity of home video technologies in the 1990s, the convergence of media technologies, and later high-speed home internet. The audition process can now be the work of actors, who become directors, producers, and editors of their own audition videos. This gives actors more individual control over some aspects of their own career management, but it also eliminates the valuable informal training that accompanied auditions and requires actors to take on additional responsibilities previously held by an array of industry professionals.

Self-taped auditions use the tools and technologies of media production, but in service of a clear industrial purpose. Whereas fans might produce content that brings them creative satisfaction, cultural capital within fan communities, and conceivably financial capital if their work garners enough views, actors produce their own auditions as a stepping-stone to obtain paying work. Auditions have a limited audience and a clear function—the satisfaction of a good audition is being cast, or in industry parlance, "booking" a role. Fans might see the creative possibilities of new technologies to be exciting and creatively liberating, but these same home technologies add to the work (and required technological competencies) of aspiring or working actors. This points to the larger reality that media workers experience convergence differently than media audiences.

Convergence has influenced the professional practice of actors such that actors are now responsible for a much wider array of tasks beyond the audition process. Mark Deuze examines convergence from the perspective of an array of media workers and identifies what he sees as the two key processes of convergence: "the convergence of *place*—as in the workplace and the home office—and the convergence of *technology*—as in the digital, networked hardware and software available to set the parameters of creative endeavors."[56] For actors, these types of convergence reflect material changes that have fundamentally reshaped the tasks, pace, and activities of an average week. Convergence of place and technology have contributed to new sets of professional expectations for actors, especially in the casting and audition process.

The business of casting has transformed since the studio era from an in-house production process to an outsourced practice featuring many private contractors and entities. Agents and sometimes actors find out about smaller roles through casting directors, interpersonal industry connections, or posted casting breakdowns, which are brief descriptions of actors needed to fill various nonstar roles. Beginning in the 1970s, these breakdowns have been produced by companies such as Breakdown Services that employ script readers to generate descriptions of the roles that need to be cast.[57] After looking at the breakdowns, agents could figure out where to submit actors for auditions. Actors would then drive directly to auditions, and voice actors would drive to their agent's office to record with the in-house engineer and director. In the 2000s, companies like Breakdown Services began to use the internet to revamp some of these established business practices. In 2003, rather than delivering casting breakdowns to casting directors who would try to fill available roles and agents who would try to place clients, Breakdown Services started posting the casting breakdowns online and allowed actors to upload videos and headshots.[58] Although this did not completely eliminate in-person auditions or casting, by 2020 many auditions were submitted and cast online.[59]

The path toward booking a role involves several gatekeepers before an actor even has the opportunity to be cast or rejected, and targeted solicitation and agency specialization can lead to a predictable talent pool for auditions. All of the working actors I interviewed explained that auditions were often filled with familiar faces: "You see the same people at auditions especially if you're in the improv world. A lot of the same improv performers have the same agents and stuff like that."[60] For many actors, this experience of seeing the same faces at auditions allows them to form a community with which to share advice and professional news, and potentially to help each other in the auditions. Shifting away from these in-person encounters eliminates potential venues for collaboration, network building, or potential organizing.

Screen tests and taped auditions have long been a staple of the film and television casting process, but digital technologies have transformed the speed and frequency of this practice. From the 1970s onward it was common for agents and casting directors to ship tapes of auditions to directors and producers. By 2011, however, *Variety* was reporting on the increasingly mediated casting process: "casting is getting tech savvy; auditions recorded by digital camera, submitted by via email or Vimeo, followed by callbacks over Skype."[61] Self-recorded auditions are enabled by the convergence of home technologies—now that many actors have access to home internet and recording devices, it is relatively easy for them to film and send their audition. Home technologies allow for actors to complete auditions and submissions from their residences. Actors can now submit headshots and audition tapes on any number of casting websites such as Actorsaccess.com, Backstage.com, Breakdownservices.com, castingfrontier.com, voices.com, etc., all of which facilitate casting for union and nonunion jobs.

For voice actors in particular, a shift toward self-recording auditions has changed some of the culture of collaboration involved in creating a character or honing a performance. To best accommodate these industrial norms, actors have had to acquire different skill sets to become amateur sound engineers and competent self-directors, whereas in-person auditions allowed actors to focus strictly on the performance. Additionally, studio auditions, as one actor explained to me, can occasionally offer up opportunities for spontaneous decisions and changes. In a lengthy anecdote, he offered up an example of the kinds of connections and improvisation possible with an in-person audition:

> It's frustrating because during the four or five years I was at William Morris very few people had recording studios at home because it was just too expensive and the Internet was around but it was pricey. More importantly they [William Morris] felt that they wanted to direct you because you'd be a better performer. So, they have booth directors who've been there and done that and know all these people out there and all the quirks of the different casting directors. And so I learned a lot from the booth directors. The other thing was that you didn't have hours. You came in, they gave you your faxed copy to look over or you did your work on it, you made your choices, and you went into the booth, and you got two takes and maybe more if the booth director liked you and if they had time. That was how I learned how to do this stuff on the fly, making big choices quick, but I was getting direction. . . . It also allowed you to do some stuff that you might not otherwise be allowed to now or don't think you're allowed to. For example, I remember my first gig auditioning William Morris. It was for eBay actually

as a radio spot, eBay L.A. of all things because they broke it down into areas at the time. The schtick of the spot was a man who was way too old to be driving gets pulled over by a cop, and the man demonstrates his inability to drive by the fact that he can't tell what's going on. "Well, time to sell the car" was the bit. So, there are two roles: the cop and the old man. I was brought in to read for the cop. I'll tell you straight up I never book cops. I don't sound like what people imagine a cop to sound like. . . . So, I went in to read the part. They were bringing in men in their seventies to read for the old man. So, I knew I wasn't going to book this. I'm reading and I see the other guys in the waiting room and have worked with them enough now to know what they sounded like and knew who was going to book it. So, I asked the casting directors or the booth director. I know this sounds crazy but to me this doesn't read like they want an actual older man. They want Grandpa Simpson. Can I give it a shot? It sounds crazy to us but sure why not. I read with my pal Todd. . . . If you want a guy who sounds like everyman, you got Todd. . . . He read the cop, I read the old man, and I booked it. And nowadays that would be a total shot in the dark without anybody coaching it, framing it, or possibly even allowing it to be listened to. And that's just an example. There are still agencies that use booth directors but for the vast majority of working voiceover actors it's all self-directing.[62]

This story demonstrates a number of key elements of in-person auditions, including the ability to take time to make performance choices, receive direction, learn about the various quirks and preferences of casting directors, and, finally, collaborate with directors and possibly other actors as part of the audition process. The eBay radio bit was relatively simple, but the auditioning process offered a wide array of creative and collaborative moments. For the actor, this process provided valuable lessons and experiences that could be applied to roles and auditions in the future. These interactions, as the actor points out, are much less frequent as casting agents increasingly expect actors to record and submit auditions from home and personal devices.

The shift toward self-recording voice auditions best represents the increased isolation of media production and the diminution of opportunities for professionalization. For many voice actors, audition waiting rooms offered opportunities for conversation, camaraderie, and potentially work. Several actors made similar comments about the supportive nature of the voice acting community; as one explained, "people are not as cutthroat with one another. Like my first [thought] when someone says, 'Hey can you do this?' is to name off 10 people that can do it better."[63] Beyond the financial benefits, auditions also helped actors create networks. One actor explains,

> It's not what it used to be when I used to have to go into my agents. I made a lot of friends that way, some of whom got me work. . . . A couple of them have gone on to do casting, a couple of them have gone on to form production companies, and they'll just contact me directly. Or get me very, you know, "we're only asking five people to read for this audition" [opportunities]. Casting directors also sometimes request me directly. It's a lot of personal contact. So, when I was there in the room making friends things seemed to happen. Nowadays I'll see them at union meetings occasionally.[64]

Despite all the formal networks, such as agents and managers, that position actors to get work, these individual interactions are essential for helping actors create professional networks. As this actor pointed out, it was a way to make friends, as well as a great way to network and book roles. For this actor, the only other venue for professional interactions is the union meeting. As more acting work becomes nonunion, there is an entire class of actors that has no access to any form of interaction with other professionals. Online auditions limit the possibility of personally and professionally rewarding interactions, deemphasizing interpersonal relationships in favor of digital tools and the development of technical skills.

Traveling to record auditions at agencies helps actors to distinguish working hours from nonwork time. One actor explained that booth direction not only helped her performance, but also helped her structure her day:

> I go to my booth at the agency as often as I possibly can. There's a booth director there who is very actor minded, very smart, and that was actually honestly a huge part of the quality of life piece that I really relied on, because like it gives me an excuse to get dressed, to get out of the house, to warm up my car, to like start the day and having something like a normal day, . . . working with another person who I trust, and then doing whatever with the rest of my day. Even in just the last six months as my agency's been like sending more auditions, they're like "we don't have time for this [booth auditions]. You have to send this from home." That's been [difficult] because that was a huge part of staying sane and building a routine to help me transition into a city.[65]

This actor is particularly thoughtful about the benefits of going into an agency to record an audition. Not only does it offer a more collaborative experience, but it helps her to delineate work time (which takes place in a recording booth) from personal time.

Beyond the audition and casting process, a voice actor's skill set now requires basic competence with recording equipment. All of the voice actors I spoke with owned equipment to record and mix audition tapes, which meant they had all spent at least $300—and up to $1,200—on microphones and audio software (although many used the same free version of Audacity that I used to record my interviews). All the voice actors I interviewed made their livings working as actors (with one supplementing his income by recording demos for other voice actors), so this was an essential expense that they could recuperate through work. Auditions have always required some degree of financial output—in-person auditions required actors to have sufficient money and access to fund car maintenance and/or transportation costs. Contemporary actors now need to spend money to produce demos and build websites to help them create a profile that will get them in the door for auditions. As auditions increasingly move online, the financial consequences are significant. The online auditions require actors to know how to make appropriate creative choices, without the benefit of a director or casting director providing performance notes, and they require actors to have basic competencies as sound recorders and mixers.

Honing professional abilities as a voice actor involves a combination of creative and technical skills—many actors find themselves learning how to become more-attuned listeners and acquiring basic audio-mixing abilities. Developing an ear and learning how to make adjustments is more of an embodied process than an intellectual one. Understanding the relationship between sound and body is at the core of what actors need to be able to identify in their own work. One actor remembered auditioning in college at the beginning of her career, recalling: "I trained myself. . . . It was half learning how to have an ear . . . training your ear to hear these things. You know, you hear the noise, the text in your voice trying to . . . you know, developing sensitivity to what's good sound quality and what isn't."[66] For voice auditions, the quality of the voice is the most important aspect, because, as many actors explained, it is important to keep the recording clean and representative of an actor's abilities. Or as one actor analogized, "you don't want to present someone with a heavily Photoshopped headshot, it's just not helpful."[67] The same actor explained that she only utilizes a few audio-cutting and pasting functions. In her opinion, "there are people who are way more skilled at making things sound good. I send clean, dry stuff, because that's kind of the client's call."[68] While actors position listening as a skill tied to sound production, honing the ability to hear and to recognize intangible qualities of sound combines the aptitudes of the critic, artist, and technician, and greatly expands the expectations for what an actor must bring to a project.

For actors, the home has now become the site of auditions, a fact that concretely demonstrates the convergence of home and workplace in the twenty-first-century gig economy. Every consistently working actor I spoke with has some kind of setup that allows them to film, record, edit, and email or upload auditions to casting directors or casting websites. Screen actors can film auditions with video equipment, but voice actors need to transform their homes to create a studio space for audio recording. Since many professional voice actors live in bustling cities, constructing a soundproof (or "neutral") recording space can prove to be a challenge. Every voice actor I interviewed had a story about recording auditions (and sometimes actual dialogue) in a Los Angeles or New York closet. As one actor explained, "Minimum, you need a quiet place to record and unless you live in a neighborhood that somehow doesn't have motorcycles and leaf blowers and airplanes, oh my, then you might need to pad it. A lot of actors I know use their closet because it's crammed full of soft clothing that eats up sound. Makes it a very dead space."[69] Surrounded by fabric in a small space, actors are able to absorb ambient noise and capture a relatively clean piece of audio.

While some actors purchase insulating foam to line closets, others make the more substantial investment to install in-house recording booths. These booths can range in size and can occupy the entirety of a home office or a portion of a bedroom. As one actor described, "I have a six-foot booth in my bedroom. . . . I don't have a whisper room, which is really expensive. . . . I don't have broadcast quality, but I'm not cutting promos in my booth."[70] These booths can be incredibly expensive, but voice actors frequently explained to me that they sold their old booths or mics to other actors when they upgraded their equipment. These rooms provide physical reminders of how contemporary audition practices require professional space to encroach upon personal space, thus further eroding the boundaries between work and home life.

Portable technologies, ubiquitous data networks, and Wi-Fi hotspots have also made it possible for actors to turn any space into a workspace. The quality and portability of microphone and recording technologies can vary; as one actor I spoke with explained, "I used to have an apogee mic that I plugged directly into my iPad. But it's a little too sensitive. It's a good mic but it picks up kind of everything in the room which isn't always ideal."[71] But as the same actor noted, recording technologies have dramatically improved, allowing for more control and higher quality recordings. He explained, "These days I have a sure shotgun mic that I plug into a zoom recorder, which is a portable. It's [the mic] kind of what they use these days on most sets because it's super advanced and digital."[72] The availability of high-quality recording equipment enables actors to reproduce studio-quality sound. That this equipment is now small and portable also means actors can audition and record while they traverse the city on gigs or simply while they are doing other jobs.

If the home can become a workspace, then there is little preventing the world from becoming a studio or office. Voice actors can bring their office with them if they are out of the house for the day or on vacation for a week and need to submit an audition with a quick turnaround. For some, the closet might be the best option on vacation as well: "One of my very favorite places to record is my brothers walk-in closet [in] Manhattan because the door for some reason is like three inches thick. Makes me wonder what it was designed for originally. It's nothing but sweaters and suits. I put my microphone in there, shut the door and Manhattan, which you can hear from other rooms, disappears. And you kind of need to do that wherever you are."[73] One actor I interviewed explained that he often recorded auditions with his portable microphone kit and iPhone in the backseat of his car. "Well, it depends where you're parked, but if you're parked somewhere not terrible, there's a lot of sound-absorbing material in there. The angle of the window is not directly back at you, if it's at an angle. The back seat tends to be a really good place to record. And I've gotten a couple of gigs actually recording auditions in my car."[74] Another actor laughed about recording an audition in the backseat of a car dealership showroom car while she waited for a friend who was car shopping. Another recounted an important audition that came up while she was out to dinner with her husband: "I recorded an audition under a jacket, in a bathroom, in a Chicago restaurant and I booked it. That's the weirdest craziest success story. It was for a huge film. I realized I forgot to do my name slate and I literally recorded it under the table and edited while we were eating. I asked the restaurant if they would turn the music off in the bathroom, and they did. We were on vacation and I didn't have enough time to go back to the hotel."[75] What is noteworthy about this story is not only that this actor was willing to bend over backward for this audition, but also that her husband and the restaurant employees were supportive in this endeavor. To some extent, this anecdote indicates a generalized understanding of what it takes to "make it work" within the creative gig economy. Although this audition was infringing on her personal vacation time, for her, the end result, a role in *The Incredibles 2* (Bird, 2018), made it worth the effort and the lost vacation time.

Conditions that protect workers from exploitation and guarantee compensation are often a problem in the speculative world of new media production. The unions have long relied on specialization and clear differentiation to help establish professional norms and to make acting a viable profession for those below the level of the star. In her discussion of precarious and creative work, Angela McRobbie defines the features of creative workforces, two of which are useful in considering the unique characteristics of voice actors and performance in digital fields. First, McRobbie posits that the new sped-up work culture leaves "little possibility of a politics of the workplace, little time, few existing mechanisms for organization, and no fixed workplace for a workplace politics to develop."[76] We can see this in the audition process for actors: moving some of the audition process online takes away physical locations where they come together, wait, chat, and potentially commiserate and develop identities as part of a group of professionals. McRobbie continues along this point to describe a second characteristic of creative labor, positioning it as a place where we see "a manifest tension for new creative workers, highly reliant on informal networking but without the support of these being underpinned by any institutional 'trade association.' They can only find individual . . . solutions to systemic problems."[77] The interpersonal connections McRobbie sees between twenty-first-century creative workers are born out of a need for a network to achieve financial success rather than a commitment to resolving systemic worker problems. Even though actors have a union to help mitigate some of these cultural changes, the conditions of voice acting would seem to support McRobbie's points.

Shifting auditions online has meant that actors have found themselves taking on new roles and acquiring new aptitudes and skills. Taking on new responsibilities that were previously covered by other workers or career sectors is another salient characteristic of the twenty-first-century economy. As McRobbie observes, creative workers experience a collapse of previously distinctive roles, speculating, "we can propose that where in the business side of things was an often disregarded aspect of creative identities best looked after by the accountant, now it is perceived as integral and actively incorporated into artistic identity."[78] In the contemporary landscape, aspiring or working actors not only have to manage their own finances, but they are often directing, recording, and submitting their own auditions. Taken together, the convergence of home and office and the expectation that creatives are also adept at business and financial matters are undoubtedly significant aspects of convergence for media workers, and voice actors especially.

One of the key functions of a union is to maintain a high level of professional standards among workers, but in the digital age one of the challenges is the erosion of quality control. SAG-AFTRA, like its membership, is in the position of having to adapt and accommodate some of the industrial changes that are shaping performance in the digital age. In an effort to train and educate actors on the future potential of new media content, SAG-AFTRA and the SAG-AFTRA Foundation (the nonprofit wing that provides resources and assistance to SAG-AFTRA members) offer discounted or free courses on a wide array of topics of interest to actors looking to hone or acquire skills. Sessions include workshops in the voice-over lab, Twitter basics, how to create a reel, and website building.[79] Others, such as the July 2018 workshop on "The Social Media Advantage," focus on digital media. This particular workshop offered to teach actors to "grow your social media pages exponentially and use them for your career, and monetize your newfound following or current following through lucrative partnerships and sponsorships."[80]

While I do not want to diminish the reality that the SAG-AFTRA workshops fill a real demand from actors, the existence of sessions that help actors acquire technical skills and round out their abilities as personal career managers aligns with all of the other impulses of the digital age. As McRobbie has observed, "Capital finds novel ways of offloading its responsibility for a workforce, but this relinquishing process no longer is confronted by traditional and organized 'labour.'"[81] This observation is relevant for certain changes in casting and acting, but its assumption that unions and management have a wholly antagonistic relationship fails to account for the often cooperative relationship between the two in the media industries. In the case of acting, unions are not confronting these changes or resisting these business trends; they are helping take responsibility for training actors into these new dimensions of the career. However, by helping actors become more entrepreneurial, SAG-AFTRA is also helping to normalize the expectation that actors are all one-person businesses expected to self-direct, self-produce, and self-promote.

As my interviews indicate, voice actors need to acquire and hone many skills beyond performance to help them find continuous work. One challenge with digital media for actors is the need to develop multiple sets of protocols for many different media and modes of delivery. Actors who

self-produce content and work on films and television shows that are replayed on digital devices, as well as voice actors who work in commercials,
video games, and animation, are simultaneously integrated into widely
varying cultural norms and standards. These demands have required actors
to become, in a sense, more flexible and "entrepreneurial." Voice actors
have been the focus of much of this discussion because the changes to
voice acting have been unique. Many of the changes, such as the reliance
on self-submission through digital platforms and the quick turnarounds
for auditions, are the result of industrial changes and the rise of more
nonunion voice work. At the audition stage, acting embodies many of the
characteristics of freelance and digital work cultures. While these abilities, such as learning to self-direct and turning a critical eye to auditions,
are acquired with time and practice, some of the more technical elements
have been self-taught or honed through classes as actors try to stay relevant in the changing workplace. As actors acquire more skills to stay
relevant in the profession, websites that enable people around the country
to audition for voice work have made competition for nonunion commercial work more intense. The isolation of voice performances, coupled with
the growth of home recording technologies, has also meant that this type
of work has been the easiest to outsource to less-expensive amateurs and
aspiring actors. Where acting positions differ from many of the trends in
digital work cultures is in the actual performance work. Once an actor has
been cast, the union workplace is regulated and protected by collective
bargaining agreements, which marks it as a unique form of freelancing.

THE VOICE ACTORS STRIKE

The year 2014 was significant for actors working in digital media. In addition to the implementation of the new media contract, SAG-AFTRA's
video game contract expired, sending the union to the bargaining table
with negotiators for nine companies: Activision Publishing, Blindlight,
Corps of Discovery Films, Disney Character Voices, Electronic Arts Productions, Formosa Interactive, Insomniac Games, Interactive Associates,
Take 2 Interactive Software, VoiceWorks Productions, and WB Games.
In addition to representing a significant proportion of video game production, these companies are significant employers of voice actors. At
stake for voice actors were three key issues: residuals based on the number
of game units sold, transparency in performance expectations and hiring,
and the risks associated with vocal strain. Residuals and vocal strain in

particular were essential issues that impacted a voice actor's professional longevity.

Like many media makers in Hollywood, game developers are often deeply connected to the content they are creating, entering the industry as a means to pursue a career path rooted in personal fandom and passion. Identifying as a "gamer" is, as Casey O'Donnell points out, "often considered to be a job requirement."[82] The similarities between these impulses across creative industries help us understand the culture and motivations of workers in the video game industry; however, the differences between film and television production and video game production are meaningful and indicative of larger trends in an increasingly deregulated media industry. In his discussion of the labor conditions in reality television production, Andrew Ross explains, "The labor infractions in these old media sectors are conspicuous because they take place against the still heavily unionized backdrop of the entertainment industries."[83] Although Ross makes this claim with regard to network television, it is broadly applicable to how unregulated digital sectors have interacted with the unionized entertainment industries.

The labor practices and the social and cultural world of video game design reveals more connections to Silicon Valley than to Hollywood. Scholarship on the relationship between Northern California tech companies and Southern California entertainment companies has been limited. Stuart Cunningham and David Craig describe Silicon Valley (or "NorCal") business practices as fast-paced and in a state of "permanent beta," meaning they are highly sensitive to change and willing to make rapid adjustments. In contrast, Cunningham and Craig characterize the "SoCal" business practices as possessing "time-honored business models of talent-driven mass media and premium content."[84] For Cunningham and Craig, who are considering the rise of social media entertainment on platforms such as YouTube and Facebook, they find that the relationship between NorCal and SoCal work cultures is best defined as an "interdependent clash of industrial cultures."[85] I argue that the core of these issues is not simply practices and protocols, but some fundamentally different relationships toward their respective labor cultures. The video game industry has long been able to coexist with the legacy entertainment companies without clashing, but as video games attempt to use more Hollywood talent, these once-separate industries are becoming increasingly imbricated.

Video games are produced by engineers and coders who frequently work long hours to meet deadlines. These spurts of long hours are called "crunch" and have been the source of conflict in the game industry for decades.[86] As O'Donnell explains, in 2004 a LiveJournal account from someone identifying as "ea_spouse" gave voice to the specific qualities and impact of the grueling hours and work conditions at Electronic Arts.[87] Revealing the working conditions of the game industry, as O'Donnell explains, did very little to actually change the culture of video game development, which remains intense and demanding. Media workers in film and television also work long hours, but if it is a union production they are compensated with overtime and, in particularly dangerous situations, they have recourse to their union representatives. Game designers and coders are paid salaries or hourly rates for work completed over a period of time. By comparison, actors work for shorter periods of time and receive residual payments because their individual performances contribute to the longevity of the property. Silicon Valley and Hollywood both employ a tremendous number of people who identify as creative and innovative workers, but the primary difference between the two cultures is that Hollywood workers have a history of labor protections that they can lean on to improve working conditions and build lifelong careers.

Institutionally, the unions recognize that collective bargaining has been the only way to achieve gains for actors, and actors understand that they have the power to strike to strengthen their position. On the eve of the video game strike, a union spokesperson explained the stakes of the negotiations: "It is about fairness and the ability of middle-class performers to survive in this industry. These companies are immensely profitable, and successful games—which are the only games this dispute is about—drive that profit. . . . We have proposed a fair payment structure that enables the sustainability of a professional performer community."[88] Like many conversations, debates, and negotiations in past decades, the struggle for the union was to find a way to help actors make a reasonable living from their craft. As this comment notes, of paramount concern in the 2010s is the "middle-class performer." This class of working actor has struggled the most in the growing digital landscape, in part because sources of reliable income, particularly commercial work, have largely shifted to become nonunion. In the absence of sufficient well-paying work, residuals offer a route toward a living wage and the ability to maintain health insurance benefits, but negotiating residuals for digital content has and continues to be contentious. Reaching an agreement with game companies, where creative and technical workers are employees who earn annual salaries as compensation, presented a unique wrinkle in negotiations. Within Hollywood, residuals have been hotly contested, but they are readily understood as a form of compensation that helps to offset long periods of unemployment. The perception on the part of video game employees, as it was in the film and television industry in the 1950s, was that residuals were another way for actors to be paid multiple times for the same job.

As has been the case for other forms of digital media, SAG-AFTRA wanted to establish a precedent for residuals. SAG-AFTRA was not seeking residuals for all games, just the highly profitable AAA games. In the case of video games, while the content is digitally generated, AAA games are sold as units and follow a more conventional formula that resembles the unit-based models of VHS or DVD. In the union's discussion of transparency, the lack of clear script cueing in video game performance was problematic, as was the general lack of information for actors about the overall project. Several actors I spoke with explained that frequently they did not even know what game they were working on. As one actor explained, "on the smaller roles I'll just get my scenes. I'll have no idea where they fit into the rest. I don't even get them before I go in [to the recording booth]. I get them when I go in."[89] From the perspective of professional and career development, the effect of not knowing a project is twofold: first, it means that actors could not use the budget or reputation of the project to aid in negotiations; and second, they frequently do not have enough information to see their performances or even to update their credits appropriately. As one actor jokingly recounted: "people look at your IMDB page and you're like, 'I'm missing twenty credits but also I don't even know what those twenty credits are! Nobody told me!'"[90] The same actor explained that while it might be possible to track down or accidentally hear yourself in game play, it is nearly impossible to account for credits on foreign games. Those productions, she said, are even more opaque: "They don't give you a title, they just put the production company. I'll ask the production company 'hey what is this?' [and they respond] 'We don't know.' It's so strange, but as long as I'm getting paid [it's] ok."[91] Her willingness to accept these conditions demonstrates one of the struggles in organizing actors; even though many recognize the value of more information for their performance for their professional résumé, for some it is not worth risking the loss of the paycheck.

The cultural expectations and norms of the video game workplace contributed to how these workers perceived the demands of actors. The video game industry, which only has a short history of voice acting dating to the 1990s, does not pay residuals to the designers or the programmers who create the vast visual landscapes of games; they instead receive bonuses that are determined in a nontransparent fashion. SAG-AFTRA was fighting for a very common contract condition in media fields, but the union was waging this battle against a nonunionized industry rife with labor abuses. For the strike to be effective, actors had to disseminate material online, since the isolated nature of voice acting did not create opportunities for spontaneous in-person conversations at auditions. Many of the striking performers helped create and maintain a strong digital presence with a website that collected information and summarized talking points and videos about key issues. In November 2016 game performers launched a strike campaign on Twitter that the union called a "virtual picket-line" under the hashtag #performancematters. In preparation for the strike, actors posted a notice on the strike website providing information about the hashtag, sample tweets, and images.[92] This dual approach attempted to generate greater national awareness for the strike and its key issues. As striking actors on the Game Performance Matters website explained, "developers SHOULD get bonuses. . . . The reason we're able to go after secondary payments for actors is because we have an established union. . . . In order to fight for fair treatment, we feel developers need to organize as well."[93] The lack of precedent for residuals or unions within the game industry meant that actors not only were battling management, but were doing so without the benefit of sympathetic strikes from other industry workers. In an industry where no one has union protections or residuals, they found few allies willing to stand up for them.

SAG-AFTRA and the video game companies finally reached an agreement on September 23, 2017, which, from the actors' perspective, made progress with respect to transparency but not with what the union has termed secondary payments (as opposed to residuals). Video game companies are now required to provide actors with information about productions. There is also a clear structure for how actors can be paid for additional sessions. The union had to drop the topic of residuals, and there were no clear decisions about how to address vocal strain. As the new agreement stipulated, "The deal also contains an employer commitment to continue working with SAG-AFTRA on the issue of vocal stress during the term of the successor agreement."[94] For actors, this means that there is no consensus regarding safe and fair labor practices, but this tentative language establishes contractually that these concerns will need to be addressed at a later date.

Of all the digital media negotiations and conflicts, the video game strike is unique because it shows the struggles of SAG-AFTRA as it confronted a profitable digital media business working outside of traditional Hollywood labor structures. Whereas many previous problems in the digital era arose from the union attempting to account for lower-budget productions and projects with dubious profitability, the business of AAA games is extremely visible and profitable. The video game industry, like the film industry in the 1910s and 1920s, is unchecked by unions, a fact that made the negotiations with SAG-AFTRA particularly unhospitable. But the force of Hollywood talent can be persuasive and influential. In the wake of the SAG-AFTRA strike, unionization talks among video game developers has escalated.[95] As the video game industry grows and its connections with Hollywood become more entrenched, these Silicon Valley cultures will undoubtedly need to cede ground to the talent, whether that means actors or game developers, who help elevate the craft of video games.

CONCLUSION

Technologies have converged, audience members traverse media forms, and conglomerates produce for multiple platforms, but historically separate industries still retain their unique and distinct labor cultures. The challenges facing actors and unions with digital media is that this umbrella of technology encompasses a clutter of production practices, some that look like traditional media production, but others, such as video games, that bear little resemblance to conventional narrative media production. Although unions are equipped to deal with technological transitions, convergence has ushered in changes to acting that go beyond contracts and on-set working conditions. As the business and regional cultures of Silicon Valley and Hollywood become more intertwined and tech companies seek Hollywood talent, not solely in video games, but also for content produced by streaming services such as Apple, YouTube, Netflix, Amazon, and Hulu, workers and scholars alike should be attuned to cultural shifts in media production and labor practices.

CONCLUSION

Living a creative life in the media industry often reduces actors from artists performing roles to workers hustling for them. Actors need to be resourceful and inventive: shaping a character and a performance involves a high degree of artistic craft, but making a living as an actor also requires creative thinking. For many actors and extras, juggling jobs is a necessity until they achieve that elusive big break, and, as many actors know, even if achieved, fame and consistent work might only be temporary. An actor's career is not a linear path toward success, and work can diminish at any moment.

The fickle nature of acting as a profession was on display in 2018 when Fox News picked up a story from the *Daily Mail* that featured actor Geoffrey Owens, a former household face on *The Cosby Show* "caught" working in a Manhattan Trader Joe's.[1] A story criticizing anyone who works multiple jobs in 2018 reveals the source to be not only wholly dismissive of twenty-first-century labor conditions but also clearly unaware of the long history of acting as a freelance profession and certainly naïve to the minimal opportunities for Black actors. More noteworthy than the story was the social media outpouring that accompanied it, with a litany of actors posting descriptions of their experiences working multiple jobs under the hashtags #GeoffreyOwens and #ActorsWithDayJobs.

Tweets in solidarity with Owens demonstrated a wide array of jobs that supplement the work of an actor, and they foregrounded how common it is for actors to maintain multiple jobs. The tweets ranged from critiques of Fox and the *Daily Mail* for shaming Owens, to a demonstration of pride over how actors balance acting with other jobs. For example, actor Kerri Sheragy tweeted: "Performed in 30+ plays, 22 of them lead roles, two commercials and 1 indie film. . . . I work in a corporate billing dept."[2] Other actors joked about their other work experience and various odd jobs over the years. Prior to listing several different examples of past day jobs, actor Jacqueline McKenzie tweeted that most actors have PhDs in waiting tables.[3] Implicit in the public outpouring of these tweets and explicitly stated in others was the point that there is no shame in the ups and downs of an actor's career, and no surprise at an actor having a day job.

In the context of the struggles documented in this book, the Twitter campaign also represents a rare moment of professional solidarity within this heterogeneous and dispersed workforce. When actors took to Twitter to share stories about their work, they did so in a way that differed from the ways they are expected to use social media in their professional lives. As noted in the previous chapter, there is increased pressure on actors to boost their social media profiles and establish an online presence so that producers and casting directors can quantify their worth. Tweeting about new projects, showcasing jokes and humor, and sharing industry tips and tricks are just a few of the ways that actors might use social media to expand their professional online presence. Social media are often carefully curated to project the image of one's most confident self, but in the case of this hashtag campaign, they offered access into deeply personal stories and challenging experiences of working actors (and all in 280 characters or less). In contrast to more curated posts, the #ActorsWithDayJobs tweets complicate an actor's online presence and demonstrate the truths of a messy professional life and the sacrifices necessary to make a career as an actor.

As I have shown throughout this book, there are many things that have remained consistent for actors across the twentieth and twenty-first centuries—like any capitalist enterprise, Hollywood consistently strives to keep labor costs low and profits high. There are natural ebbs and flows to labor conflicts in the media industries as new forms of technology present new revenue streams, which in turn generate new challenges for workers trying to share in the profits and make a sustainable living. The changes wrought by digital media are only the most recent in a long history of instances of industrial and technological transformations. Changes in the digital age, however, have been mercurial and not always profitable—industry leaders, workers, and unions (not necessarily working together) have all tried to figure out the future of media production and profits with varying degrees of success, and the battle over control and compensation for new media is far from over. Contract renegotiations since 2008 have been particularly contentious as actors (as well as writers, editors, and directors) attempt to improve working conditions for new media work, increase residuals, and improve contributions to pensions and health care plans.

Focusing solely on the present-day lives of actors obscures the reality that labor's present is the culmination of past events and struggles. History matters to workers in real and material ways. As I have learned conducting research, the archival documents that sit in files have directly affected the lives of workers. Decisions made in the past, historical documents, and precedents fuel contemporary conditions and practices. At SAG-AFTRA there is a tremendous amount of material archived and used to generate content for union publications, but there is even more material contained in the negotiating files. These files, which are not available to researchers, contain documents that have helped negotiators understand the cost of doing business in Hollywood (such as the cost of shooting a television show) and are used to help the negotiating team understand and establish precedent for agreements. The files also contain documents that can help staff members in contract compliance to advise on best practices when actors are on set. Staff members have to be well-versed in these decisions and agreements that do not always make it into the Minimum Basic Agreement. Labor practices always bear the marks of battles won or lost.

Old forms of exploitative agencies and services also have a way of continually resurfacing in Hollywood. Although the exploitation of extras seems like a relic of 1920s scandals and outdated perceptions of endangered young women, it is not. In 2011 the Los Angeles city attorney forced Central Casting to stop charging registrants for headshots as a condition of registration.[4] There are many businesses that still offer support, but often end up exploiting extras in film and television, such as casting bureaus and call services (which act as a middle-man between extras and casting services such as Central Casting). For those looking for more substantial roles in film and television, casting workshops ask actors to pay for time with a casting director for the chance of being discovered. Significantly, the women who have come out to tell their stories about the powerful men in the industry, from producer Harvey Weinstein to Warner Bros. ex-CEO Kevin Tsujihara, reinvigorate the sense that Hollywood is a dangerous place of sexual predation. All of these examples indicate that even though technologies change and production values improve, labor conditions and modes of exploitation stay the same.

Hollywood screen labor functions as it does because passionate people are willing to do whatever it takes to stay in the industry and keep creating. Although freelance work has always been an integral part of the acting profession, the number of freelancers has greatly expanded. Speaking of his other gigs beyond Trader Joe's, Owens explained: "Teaching has been a little bit more consistent than acting in my last five to 10 years."[5] In 2020 a Hollywood freelance career might look similar to what Owens has been doing: teaching on an adjunct salary and helping students hone their craft, working at Trader Joe's, and, when possible, acting. As an instructor, Owens undoubtedly encourages students, as he does in the *New York Times* interview, to pursue acting if it is their passion and "do whatever you need to do to stay in touch with the art and the craft that you love."[6] This is a common message in programs that train students for creative careers, but it is also one that perpetuates the existing culture of Hollywood. Passion is supposed to override the challenges of working in a competitive and volatile labor market. Those who don't have the passion to survive the difficult working conditions, as Owens explains, should "do something else."[7] When actors see their work as purely rooted in love and passion, they undermine their position as workers.

ACTORS AND COVID-19

What the Pandemic Teaches Us about
Film and Television Labor

In early March 2020, Tom Hanks and Rita Wilson announced from the set of a Baz Luhrmann production in Australia that they both had tested positive for the coronavirus. Their announcement led to an immediate production shutdown, but it was only the beginning, as many productions followed suit by declaring that shooting would be delayed or halted. The virus, which had been identified only three months earlier, quickly began to sweep around the world and through the United States, resulting in shelter-in-place orders and business closures in an attempt to flatten the curve of infections and prevent mass death. As the pandemic wore on, delayed productions became shutdowns, and unemployment benefits, which were recently made available to gig workers, skyrocketed to record heights. The pandemic certainly did not start with stars, but Hanks's and Wilson's announcement, and later positive test results for Daniel Dae Kim and Idris Elba, made it clear the coronavirus would be a major disruption to film and television production around the world.

The pandemic reminds us that even though the media business is driven by technology, Hollywood is an industry that is run on face-to-face meetings and physical productions that gather large groups of people from around the world into close proximity with little attention to sanitization. In this book, I have demonstrated how SAG and AFTRA shifted their collective bargaining priorities from set conditions to residuals in the 1960s, but this was largely because their set safety protocols had largely been established. Revenue streams and distribution platforms for media changed, but this has had little effect on how media are made. The coronavirus pandemic made set conditions central to union conversations once again.

The pandemic disrupted our sense of safety in space and our relationship to each other in the physical world. Some aspects of the business, such as pitch meetings, postproduction, and animation, could all pivot online. As I discussed in chapter 4, some industry practices, such as auditions and even voice recording, had already been shifting out of studios and into the home. In the pandemic, when all auditions needed to shift online, this was not a difficult transition. There is, however, a limit to how much production work can be done online from remote locations: pitches for films and shows can be handled virtually, but they will not be produced, and editors working remotely will have nothing to edit. Studios and networks might be able to provide some original content, but audiences will lose patience (if they have not already) if they are forced to watch too much media produced as a Zoom call. As of this writing, productions have been given the green light to resume around the world, but many are still figuring out how to execute the safety protocols. When productions fully resume, there will likely be fewer people on set, there will be significant changes to people's jobs, productions will favor the controlled environment of the backlot over location work, and all this will undoubtedly affect the aesthetic of the films and television shows produced.

The Hollywood pipeline ensures that there are plenty of films and television shows that will be released on streaming sites and in theaters (when they reopen), but the pandemic had an immediate impact on the livelihood of workers. In the weeks following the nationwide shutdown in March, millions of people were laid off or furloughed. Many actors lost both their screen work and their other jobs in the service sector. Working actors and extras are accustomed to breaks between jobs and often have other part-time jobs or side hustles to help pay the bills, but in the wake of the pandemic, many of these other jobs were also eliminated. In an interview for *The Business* podcast, actor David Saucedo explained how his side hustles, selling old records and vintage clothes, had dried up along with his acting work at the start of the pandemic.[1] Although scholars of labor and precarity have long been aware that these kinds of work arrangements leave many people in a tenuous situation, the pandemic revealed the shaky foundation of the gig economy.

Actors are not working during the pandemic, but their performances continue to generate revenue, and SAG-AFTRA continues to process hundreds of thousands of residual checks each week. During the shutdown, films and television shows became essential for audiences to stave off boredom, keep children occupied while parents attempted to sneak in a few hours of work or rest, and perhaps even provide some background chatter for lonely people in quarantine. Netflix reported a strong first-quarter performance due to the pandemic, but not all services fared as well. The shutdown also coincided with the launch of numerous new streaming services, including HBOMax, Peacock, and the expansion of Disney+ into India. None of the new streaming services were able to launch with their new programs, which meant that some of these streaming services went searching for content to license and bolster their offerings.[2] With viewers and streaming services searching for more content, actors could still count on their residual checks. But for some actors, these residual earnings were a curse: they were not large enough to pay the bills, but they were sufficient to make some ineligible for unemployment.[3] Residuals, which provide an essential supplement to income between acting jobs and other gigs, pose problems for an unemployment system that was not built to accommodate a gig economy.

Reopening businesses and the economy required us to rethink our relationship to other people and our work environment, which now seemed to contain myriad threats. On film sets, intimate moments between actors, shared props, party scenes with a hundred extras, craft service buffets, and ventilation systems in production offices all posed potential threats to cast and crew. Developing a safe way to return to production was the subject of widespread conversation and public speculation. In April and May there were proposals, provocations, and drafts of production protocols circulating as *Variety* think-pieces, studio instructions, or individual state guidelines.[4] Film and television production was able to resume in Korea in May, and US producers began to explore Iceland as an option for productions that were able to contain the virus and continue to implement rigorous testing.[5] As of July, the first major studio film (*Jurassic World: Dominion*) resumed production at Pinewood Studios in the United Kingdom.[6] At this early reopening stage, each production provides important information about what will work best in the future.

In the United States, the plan to resume production was the product of collaboration between producers and all the guilds. On June 1 a committee consisting of the AMPTP, all of the unions and guilds, and several health officials released their white paper of best practices for set safety. *Variety* reported that the release of this document was delayed due to conflict between the AMPTP and unions and speculated that some of the conflict stems from the fact that the AMPTP wants to eliminate some jobs to keep crews small, while the unions want to protect jobs.[7] The document itself is fairly broad, offering a bird's eye overview of the general changes required for physical distancing and the expectations regarding sanitization. Almost two weeks later, the unions released an additional document called "The Safe Way Forward," which expanded on the white paper protocols with some additional "organizing principles," specific recommendations regarding testing, further explanation of the role of the health safety supervisor and their teams, and some specific departmental protocols.[8] Both documents deconstruct set practices, highlighting the many ways COVID-19 can be contracted on set and providing a new set of practices that will shape the creative conditions and aesthetics of film and television for the foreseeable future.

The prominence of the Zoom grid in pandemic-produced media has been one of the visual developments of the pandemic, but when production resumes there will likely be new changes to the visual landscape. Media scholars such as Janet Staiger have explained how the production process influences film aesthetics and "signifying practices."[9] However, concern with broader structures of management that transcend cultures of labor and workers frequently underlies these arguments about the relationship between production and film form. The pandemic by necessity has pulled the focus away from management decision-making and forced us to focus on media workers and the way production processes shape texts. Arguably, we can already identify a pandemic aesthetic. Media produced under shelter-in-place clearly reflect the often DIY conditions of production: shows have finished their season through Zoom calls, late night shows have been produced by teams of two people, actors have produced Sweded (remade on a low-budget aesthetic) versions of films, and others have shot documentaries for Netflix within the confines of their homes. Likewise, films and television shows that will be produced under new safety guidelines will also bear the traces of their labor conditions in unexpected ways.

Working in front of the camera means that actors will be working without masks that can prevent the spread of the virus. As "The Safe Way Forward" states in bolded text: "It's important to remember that performers are the most vulnerable people on the set."[10] In addition to the lack of PPE, actors have to work close to other actors and cannot physically distance from other characters in the scene. Some productions, such as soap operas, have proposed creative workarounds to try under these circumstances. Bradley Bell, executive producer of *The Bold and the Beautiful*, explained that soap operas have devised a few means to create physical distancing on set: "[Actors will] shoot eight feet apart, following all the safety standards, but use the tricks of the business. We'll shoot one side of the couple in a romantic scene alone in the room, but looking at a spot very close to them, and then shoot the other side alone. When we edit it together, it will look like they're nose to nose."[11] In order to safely include intimate moments of people touching, Bell explains that they have settled on using "love-scene" doubles:

> We're also bringing in, in some cases, the husbands and wives of the actors as stand-ins for their [characters'] significant others. So if you see hands touching faces in close proximity from a wide shot, instead of a stunt double we'll have a love-scene double, where it will be the husband or the wife doing the actual touching.[12]

There are a few obvious questions about this approach: Is it a problem to bring new people on set, and will these "love-scene" doubles be paid? And this is not to mention that this strategy seems to assume that all the cast members have spouses who align with the race and gender of their on-screen love interest. Implicit in this solution is that *The Bold and the Beautiful* will be trying to minimize on-screen human contact. These measures are necessary to keep actors safe, but these cheats will likely be noticeable, a characteristic of the pandemic visual style.

In the effort to reduce the number of people on set, many productions will also inevitably reduce the number of background actors on set. Historically, cutting extras was a cost-saving measure (which is certainly important given the rise of costs associated with the new safety precautions). In the pandemic, reducing the number of people on set is simply one of the important COVID-19 prevention measures. Cutting or reducing extras or relying on digital crowds will change the look of films and television shows, potentially making them resemble the more sparsely populated environments we all occupy during the pandemic.

For actors working at a safe physical distance, shooting scenes by themselves or with stand-ins will also place different kinds of demands on their creative process. Not every production will take this approach, and soap operas, which shoot hundreds of episodes per year, might feel compelled to take extra precautions, but this solution shows how actors will need to adapt and adjust to very different on-set practices.

The current goal for the film and television industries is to resume as much production as soon and as safely as possible. As of July 2020, cases of COVID-19 remained high in US production hubs like California and Georgia, and a widespread return to set seemed ill-advised. Despite the risks, production has already begun and will continue, with producers implementing various quarantining, sanitizing, and distancing procedures to bring films and television shows to our screens. Hollywood leadership has made very thoughtful suggestions for what it will take to restart production safely, but we have yet to see whether this will be enough. Among all of the plans, "bubbles," such as the NBA bubble and Tyler Perry's Camp Quarantine, in which people live and work in a monitored and enclosed area, have been the most successful method of keeping COVID-19 cases low.[13] However, not all productions have the money and space to set up a contained environment. Amid all the specific advice in these documents, perhaps the most important point is buried in a list of different departmental considerations. The section on actors offers: "Actors/performers may benefit from extra tender loving care. Remember, they have to give an on-screen performance in the midst of all of this."[14]

Much of *Below the Stars* situates actors as labor, and the pandemic has been effective at revealing these unglamorous aspects of acting. Even though production shut down, unions had to continue to find ways to protect vulnerable workers. In the case of Hollywood, the importance of stars on set will likely result in a cautious return to work for film and television shows that need to be able to insure talent as part of their investment. The protection of stars on big productions will likely contribute to greater vigilance on set and potentially help protect other actors and workers on set. Keeping everyone safe and healthy on set will be a team effort, but the unique challenge for actors will be that they need to be cognizant of their personal safety and their status as labor as they try to perform a normal and pandemic-free world.

NOTES

INTRODUCTION

1. On reformers for newsboys in the nineteenth century, see Jon Bekken, "Newsboys: The Exploitation of 'Little Merchants' by the Newspaper Industry," in *Newsworkers: Toward a History of the Rank and File*, ed. Hanno Hardt and Bonnie Brennen (Minneapolis: University of Minnesota Press, 1995), 197. As I will discuss in chapter 1, several organizations sought reform for extras in the 1920s.

2. Estimates on the number of newsboys and extras appear in Bekken, "Newsboys," 190, and Charlene Regester, "African American Extras in Hollywood during the 1920s and 1930s," *Film History* 9 (1997): 109.

3. See Richard DeCordova, *Picture Personalities: The Emergence of the Star System in America* (Urbana: University of Illinois Press, 2001); Richard DeCordova, "The Emergence of the Star System in America," in *Stardom: Industry of Desire*, ed. Christine Gledhill (London: Routledge, 1991), 17–29; and Richard Dyer, *Stars*, 2nd ed. (London: British Film Institute, 2008).

4. Emily Carman, *Independent Stardom: Freelance Women in the Hollywood Studio System* (Austin: University of Texas Press, 2016), and Adrienne McLean, *Being Rita Hayworth: Labor, Identity, and Hollywood Stardom* (New Brunswick, NJ: Rutgers University Press, 2004).

5. Eric Smoodin, "The History of Film History," in *Looking Past the Screen: Case Studies in American Film History and Method*, ed. Jon Lewis and Eric Smoodin (Durham, NC: Duke University Press, 2007), 2.

6. Gerald Horne, *Class Struggle in Hollywood, 1930–1950: Moguls, Mobsters, Stars, Reds, and Trade Unionists* (Austin: University of Texas Press, 2001); Michael Nielsen, "Labor Power and Organization in the Early U.S. Motion Picture Industry," *Film History* 2 (1988): 121–131; and Janet Staiger, "The Hollywood Mode of Production: Its Conditions of Existence," in *The Classical Hollywood Cinema: Film Style and Mode of Production to 1960*, ed. David Bordwell, Janet Staiger, and Kristin Thompson (New York: Columbia University Press, 1985), 87–89.

7. Vicki Mayer, *Below the Line: Producers and Production Studies in the New Television Economy* (Durham, NC: Duke University Press, 2011).

8. Erin Hill, *Never Done: A History of Women's Work in Media Production* (New Brunswick, NJ: Rutgers University Press, 2016).

9. Horne, *Class Struggle in Hollywood*; Mike Nielsen and Gene Mailes, *Hollywood's Other Blacklist: Union Struggles in the Studio System* (London: British Film Institute, 1995); David Prindle, *The Politics of Glamour: Ideology and Democracy in the Screen Actors Guild* (Madison: University of Wisconsin Press, 1988).

10. Miranda Banks, *The Writers: A History of American Screenwriters and Their Guild* (New Brunswick, NJ: Rutgers University Press, 2015), and Maya Montañez Smukler, *Liberating Hollywood: Women Directors and the Feminist Reform of 1970s American Cinema* (New Brunswick, NJ: Rutgers University Press, 2018).

11. Miranda Banks, "Unequal Opportunities: Gender Inequities and Precarious Diversity," *Feminist Media Histories* 4, no. 4 (Fall 2018): 109–129; Kate Fortmueller, "Time's Up (Again?): Transforming Hollywood's Industrial Culture," *Media Industries* 6, no. 2 (2019); Smukler, *Liberating Hollywood: Women Directors and the Feminist Reform of 1970s American Cinema*, 63-76.

12. Danae Clark, *Negotiating Hollywood: The Cultural Politics of Actors' Labor* (Minneapolis: University of Minnesota Press, 1995), 10.

13. Banks, *The Writers*; Hill, *Never Done*; Luci Marzola, "Engineering Hollywood: Technology, Technicians, and the Science of Building the Studio System, 1915–1930," PhD diss., University of Southern California, 2016; Mayer, *Below the Line*.

14. Clark, *Negotiating Hollywood*, 16.

15. Hugh Lovell and Tasile Carter, *Collective Bargaining in the Motion Picture Industry* (Berkeley: Institute of Industrial Relations, University of California, 1955), 4.

16. Nicole Cohen, *Writers' Rights: Freelance Journalism in a Digital Age* (Quebec: McGill-Queens University Press, 2016), 12.

17. William Bielby and Denise Bielby, "Organizational Mediation of Project-Based Labor Markets: Talent Agencies and the Careers of Screenwriters," *American Sociological Review* 64, no. 1 (1999): 64–85; Candace Jones, "Careers in Project Networks: The Case of the Film Industry," in *The Boundaryless Career: A New Employment Principle for a New Organizational Era*, ed. Michael B. Arthur and Denise M. Rousseau (New York: Oxford University Press, 1996), 58–75.

18. Carman, *Independent Stardom*.

19. Robert Castel, *From Manual Workers to Wage Laborers: Transformation of the Social Question*, trans. and ed. Richard Boyd (New Brunswick, NJ: Transaction Publishers, 2002), 45–46.

20. For more discussion of the term "precarity" and its many theoretical connotations, see Isabell Lorey, *State of Insecurity: Government of the Precarious*, trans. Aileen Derieg (New York: Verso, 2015), 11–15.

21. Brett Neilson and Ned Rossiter, "Precarity as a Political Concept, or, Fordism as Exception," *Theory, Culture & Society* 25, no. 7–8 (2008): 54.

22. David Thomson, "The Lives of Supporting Players," in *Movie Acting: The Film Reader*, ed. Pamela Robertson Wojcik (New York: Routledge, 2004), 207.

23. Janet Hirshenson and Jane Jenkins, *A Star Is Found: Our Adventures Casting Some of Hollywood's Biggest Movies* (Orlando, FL: Harcourt, 2006), quoted in Paul McDonald, *Hollywood Stardom* (Malden, MA: Wiley-Blackford, 2013), 21.

24. Vincent D'Onofrio, *"Don't Go in the Woods* Q&A," interview by David Lerner, University of Southern California, April 2010.

25. Vincent D'Onofrio, December 11, 2018, 4:42 p.m., https://twitter.com/vincentdonofrio/status/1072607505723899905?lang=en.

26. Misty Upham, "She Worked Hard for the Money," *Daily Beast*, January 17, 2014, now available at https://portside.org/2014-01-21/she-worked-hard-money.

27. Abaki Beck, "Remembering Misty Upham in the Era of #TimesUp and #MeToo," *Wear Your Voice Mag*, January 11, 2018, https://wearyourvoicemag.com/remembering-misty-upham-era-timesup-metoo/.

28. Dan Reilly and Lila Shapiro, "An Oral History of *Game of Thrones*, as Told by the Soldiers, Wights, and Wildlings," *Vulture*, May 21, 2019, https://www.vulture.com/2019/05/game-of-thrones-oral-history-bit-players.html#_ga=2.15006718.93155620.1558401927-1880977735.1548638291.

29. "Central Casting—An Interview with Mr. Campbell MacCulloch General Manager of Central Casting Corporation," March 27, 1939, Central Casting Subject Files, Margaret Herrick Library, Academy of Motion Picture Arts and Sciences, Beverly Hills, CA.

30. For examples of histories that trace the cooperation between film and television industries, see Christopher Anderson, *Hollywood TV: The Studio System in the Fifties* (Austin: University of Texas Press, 1994), and Michele Hilmes, *Hollywood and Broadcasting: From Radio to Cable* (Urbana: University of Illinois Press, 1990).

31. Mayer, *Below the Line*, 66.

32. Martin Oppenheimer, *White Collar Politics* (New York: Monthly Review Press, 1985), 137.

33. Jane Gaines, *Contested Culture: The Image, the Voice, and the Law* (Chapel Hill: University of North Carolina Press, 1991), 145.

34. Lois Gray and Ronald Seeber, "The Industry and Unions: An Overview," in *Under the Stars: Essays on Labor Relations in Arts and Entertainment*, ed. Lois Gray and Ronald Seeber (Ithaca, NY: ILR Press, 1996), 46.

35. Lisa Gitelman, *Always Already New: Media, History, and the Data of Culture* (Cambridge, MA: MIT Press, 2006), 7.

CHAPTER I. HOLLYWOOD FREELANCE

1. Electricity Magazine Corp., *Motography*, January 2, 1915, 29, Media History Digital Library, www.mediahistoryproject.org.

2. Tino Balio, *Grand Design: Hollywood as a Modern Business Enterprise, 1930–1939* (New York: Scribner, 1993), 146.

3. Carman, *Independent Stardom.*

4. Two articles from 1928 cite conflicting data on the population of extras. See "Brows to Lose Wrinkles," *Los Angeles Times,* December 9, 1928, and Fred Beetson, "What the Association of Motion Picture Producers Has Accomplished for the Industry," *Los Angeles Times,* April 18, 1928.

5. Jordan R. Young, *Reel Characters: Great Movie Character Actors* (Beverly Hills, CA: Moonstone Press, 1975), 30.

6. Tom Kemper, *Hidden Talent: The Emergence of Hollywood Agents* (Berkeley: University of California Press, 2010), 5.

7. For more on the "Hollywood extra girl," see Hilary Hallett, *Go West, Young Women! The Rise of Early Hollywood* (Berkeley: University of California Press, 2013); Heidi Kenaga, "Making the 'Studio Girl': The Hollywood Studio Club and Industry Regulation of Female Labour," *Film History* 18 (2006): 129–139; Denise McKenna, "The Photoplay or the Pickaxe: Extras, Gender, and Labour in Early Hollywood," *Film History* 23, no. 1 (2011): 5–19; Shelley Stamp, "'It's a Long Way to Filmland': Starlets, Screen Hopefuls and Extras in Early Hollywood," in *American Cinema's Transitional Era: Audiences, Institutions, Practices,* ed. Charlie Keil and Shelley Stamp (Berkeley: University of California Press, 2004), 322–352.

8. Adrienne McLean, "Introduction," 1–26, in *Headline Hollywood: A Century of Film Scandal,* ed. Adrienne McLean and David Cook (New Brunswick, NJ: Rutgers University Press, 2001), 2.

9. Allen John Scott, *On Hollywood: The Place, the Industry* (Princeton, NJ: Princeton University Press, 2005), 30.

10. Andrew Dawson, "Labouring in Hollywood's Motion Picture Industry and the Legacy of 'Flexible Specialization,'" in *Working in the Global Film and Television Industries,* ed. Andrew Dawson and Sean P. Holmes (New York: Bloomsbury, 2012), 35.

11. Stanley Aronowitz, *False Promises: The Shaping of American Working Class Consciousness* (Durham, NC: Duke University Press, 1992), 217.

12. Horne, *Class Struggle in Hollywood,* 51–52.

13. Anna Christian, *Meet It, Greet It, and Defeat It: The Biography of Frances E. Williams* (Los Angeles: Milligan, 1999), 160, quoted in Horne, *Class Struggle in Hollywood,* 52.

14. As of 2019, Entertainment Partners owns Central Casting. Randee Dawn, "Entertainment Partners' Central Casting Unit Changes with the Times," *Variety,* October 25, 2016, https://variety.com/2016/artisans/news/entertainment-partners-central -casting-unit-changes-with-the-times-1201898965/.

15. Leo Rosencrans, "Los Angeles—October 21, 1916," Leo Rosencrans Collection, Margaret Herrick Library, Academy of Motion Picture Arts and Sciences (hereafter AMPAS), Beverly Hills, CA.

16. "Nash" is the only identifying information in the letter.

17. Rosencrans, "Los Angeles—October 24, 1916," Leo Rosencrans Collection, AMPAS.

18. Rosencrans, "Los Angeles—October 29, 1916," Leo Rosencrans Collection, AMPAS.

19. Rosencrans, "Los Angeles—December 12, 1916," Leo Rosencrans Collection, AMPAS.

20. Rosencrans, "Los Angeles—November 2, 1916," Leo Rosencrans Collection, AMPAS.

21. Rosencrans, "Los Angeles—November 2, 1916," Leo Rosencrans Collection, AMPAS.

22. Rosencrans, "Los Angeles—November 15, 1916," Leo Rosencrans Collection, AMPAS.

23. Sean Holmes, *Weavers of Dreams, Unite! Actors' Unionism in Early Twentieth-Century America* (Urbana: University of Illinois Press, 2013), 152.

24. "Central Casting Corporation—Facts about Extra Work," August 1, 1936, Alliance of Motion Picture and Television Producers Collection, AMPAS.

25. Dyer, *Stars*, 28.

26. Pamela Robertson Wojcik, "Typecasting," in *Movie Acting: The Film Reader*, ed. Pamela Robertson Wojcik (New York: Routledge, 2004), 171.

27. "Hays Lauds Film Bureau," *Los Angeles Times*, January 24, 1926.

28. Leonard Levinson, "Bigger but Cheaper Mobs," *Variety*, January 31, 1933, 19.

29. Murray Ross, *Stars and Strikes: Unionization of Hollywood* (New York: Columbia University Press, 1941), 225.

30. Ross, *Stars and Strikes*, 85.

31. Nicolas Rosenthal, "Representing Indians: Native American Actors on Hollywood's Frontier," *Western Historical Quarterly* 36, no. 3 (2005): 332.

32. Regester, "African American Extras," 96.

33. Leigh R. Smith, Date books, Series III—Date books and professional resources (1910–1929), CalArts Library and Information Resources, Department of Special Collections, Valencia, CA.

34. For detailed discussion of these scandals, see Denise McKenna, "The City That Made the Pictures Move: Gender, Labor and Los Angeles, 1908–1917," PhD diss., New York University, 2008.

35. "Extras Charge Illegal Ways: Methods of Payment and Discount Cited," *Los Angeles Times*, January 26, 1923.

36. "Extras Charge Illegal Ways," 154.

37. Wedgwood Nowell to Frank Gillmore, July 30, 1924, Actors' Equity Association Records, Tamiment Library, New York University Library and Robert F. Wagner Archives (hereafter NYU-TL), quoted in Holmes, *Weavers of Dreams, Unite!*, 154.

38. Young, *Reel Characters*, 123.

39. Wedgwood Nowell to Frank Gillmore, July 30, 1924, Actors' Equity Association Records, NYU-TL.

40. Fred Beetson, "Letter to Will Hays," July 19, 1927, Document ID #464, MPPDA Digital Archive, https://mppda.flinders.edu.au/records/464.

41. See Mike Davis, "Sunshine and Open Shop: Ford and Darwin in 1920s Los Angeles," in *Metropolis in the Making: Los Angeles in the 1920s*, ed. Tom Sitton and William Deverell (Berkeley: University of California Press, 2001), 96–122; Nielsen and Mailes, *Hollywood's Other Blacklist*, 2–7; Nielsen, "Labor Power and Organization in the Early U.S. Motion Picture Industry"; Louis B. Perry and Richard S. Perry, *A History of the Los Angeles Labor Movement, 1911–1941* (Berkeley: University of California Press, 1963).

42. Steven Joseph Ross, *Working-Class Hollywood: Silent Film and the Shaping of Class in America* (Princeton, NJ: Princeton University Press, 1998), 131.

43. Ross, *Working-Class Hollywood*, 62.

44. Ross, *Working-Class Hollywood*, 131.

45. Ross, *Working-Class Hollywood*, 132.

46. Neilsen and Mailes, *Hollywood's Other Blacklist*, 5.

47. "Agitators Busy: Recently Organized Motion Picture Players Union Holds Meeting," *Los Angeles Times*, September 16, 1918.

48. "Agitators Busy," *Los Angeles Times*, September 16, 1918.

49. "Motion Picture Players' Union Resolution—October 27, 1919," Triangle Film Collection, Harry and Ray Aitken Papers, Box 20, Folder 2, Wisconsin Center for Film and Theater Research (hereafter WC), Madison, WI.

50. Sam Stoloff, "Fatty Arbuckle and the Black Sox: The Paranoid Style of American Popular Culture, 1919–1922," in McLean and Cook, *Headline Hollywood*, 67.

51. "M.O. Players Union Gets a Separate Four A's Charter," *The Billboard* 32, no. 6 (February 7, 1920).

52. "M.O. Players Union Gets a Separate Four A's Charter."

53. "Change Extras' Booking Rules: State Demands Clean-Up by Service Bureaus," *Los Angeles Times*, March 25, 1923.

54. For more details on the riot, see Kerry Segrave, *Extras of Early Hollywood: A History of the Crowd, 1913–1945* (Jefferson, NC: McFarland, 2013); "Actors Shot by Guard; Police Halt Lynching: Five Film 'Extras' Wounded after Controversy over Wages at Service Bureau," *Los Angeles Times*, March 16, 1923; "Movie 'Extras' in Riot, Five of Them Are Shot," *New York Times*, March 16, 1923.

55. As Denise McKenna points out, sex scandals were common in the 1910s and beyond, but according to the *Oxford English Dictionary*, the term "casting couch" did not enter into popular usage until the 1940s. See McKenna, "The City That Made the Pictures Move," 90.

56. McKenna, "The City That Made the Pictures Move," 15.

57. For an extensive account of the Fatty Arbuckle and Virginia Rappe scandal, see Greg Merritt, *Room 1219: The Life of Fatty Arbuckle, the Mysterious Death of Virginia Rappe, and the Scandal That Changed Hollywood* (Chicago: Chicago Review Press, 2013).

58. Hallett, *Go West, Young Women!*, 184.

59. Fred W. Beetson, "Letter to all members—April 22, 1925," Document ID #234, MPPDA Digital Archive, http://mppda.flinders.edu.au/records/234.

60. Heidi Kenaga, "Promoting Hollywood Extra Girl (1935)," *Screen* 52, no. 1 (Spring 2011): 84.

61. "Hays Lauds Film Bureau," *Los Angeles Times*, January 24, 1926.

62. According to Murray Ross, many of the makeup schools actually worked with the employment bureaus. See Ross, *Stars and Strikes*, 70.

63. Kenaga, "Promoting Hollywood Extra Girl (1935)," 84.

64. Kemper, *Hidden Talent*, 35.

65. Claude S. Fischer, *America Calling: A Social History of the Telephone to 1940* (Berkeley: University of California Press, 1992), 108–111.

66. Fischer, *America Calling*, 112.

67. "Central Casting—An Interview with Mr. Campbell MacCulloch General Manager of Central Casting Corporation," March 27, 1939, Central Casting Subject Files, AMPAS.

68. California Bureau of Labor Statistics, *Nineteenth Biennial Report, 1919–1920* (Sacramento, 1920), 118–119.

69. Rosencrans, "Los Angeles—October 29, 1916," Leo Rosencrans Collection, AMPAS.

70. For detailed examples of exploitation in the theaters, see Kerry Segrave, *Actors Organize: A History of Union Formation Efforts in America, 1880–1919* (Jefferson, NC: McFarland, 2008), 3–17.

71. Segrave, *Actors Organize*, 3.

72. Young, *Reel Characters*, 102.

73. William Gazecki, director, *Screen Actors Guild Foundation Presents: Behind the Masks—The Story of the Screen Actors Guild—Part 1* (Los Angeles: Screen Actors Guild Foundation, 2007), DVD.

74. Morton Thompson, "Hollywood Is a Union Town," *The Nation*, April 2, 1938, 381.

75. Sympathetic strikes and union agreements were, and continue to be, one of the most valuable negotiating weapons for unions and have been the source of strength (or failure) in SAG and AFTRA negotiations well into the 2000s.

76. Perry and Perry, *A History of the Los Angeles Labor Movement*, 342.

77. Balio, *Grand Design*, 153.

78. John Scott, "Central Casting Bureau Extras' Only Hope for That Long-Awaited 'Break,'" *Los Angeles Times*, April 8, 1934.

79. Scott, "Central Casting Bureau Extras' Only Hope for That Long-Awaited 'Break.'"

80. "Central Casting—An Interview with Mr. Campbell MacCulloch," AMPAS.

81. Central Casting Corporation, "Facts about Extra Work."

82. Prindle, *The Politics of Glamour*, 20.

83. Prindle, *The Politics of Glamour*, 20.

84. Untitled Board of Directors Memo, February 19, 1940, Stephan Vaughn Collection, Box 3, WC.

85. Gazecki, *Screen Actors Guild Foundation Presents: Behind the Masks—The Story of the Screen Actors Guild—Part 1*.

86. Leo Rosten, *Hollywood: The Movie Colony, the Movie Makers* (New York: Harcourt, Brace & Co., 1941), 336.

87. Regester, "African American Extras," 111.

88. Regester, "African American Extras," 111.

89. "News of the Screen: Three Openings Here Today—Four Films at Venice Exhibition—DeMille Birthday Celebration," *New York Times*, August 13, 1937, 12.

90. Carman, *Independent Stardom*, 9.

91. "Central Casting—An Interview with Mr. Campbell MacCulloch," AMPAS.

92. "Central Casting—An Interview with Mr. Campbell MacCulloch," AMPAS.

93. The 1935 freelance contract explicitly writes extras out of the category of "day players," stating "the term 'day player' . . . shall be construed only in the manner in which said term is generally understood in the motion picture industry and shall not include 'extras.'" See Frank Lloyd, "The New Free-Lance Actor Contracts and Minimum Conditions," February 11, 1935, *Academy of Motion Picture Arts and Sciences Bulletin*, SAG-AFTRA Archives (hereafter SAA), Los Angeles, 9.

94. Lloyd, "The New Free-Lance Actor Contracts."

95. Balio, *Grand Design*, 155. For specific contract details on these freelance stars, see Carman, *Independent Stardom*, 149–161.

96. Carman, *Independent Stardom*, 40.

97. Carman, *Independent Stardom*, 78.

98. Carman, *Independent Stardom*, 78.

99. Carman, *Independent Stardom*, 78.

100. Young, *Reel Characters*, 61.

101. Carman, *Independent Stardom*, 79.

102. Carman, *Independent Stardom*, 82.

103. Carman, *Independent Stardom*, 90.

104. Lugosi, "Letter to Kenneth Thompson," February 2, 1938, SAA.

105. Gregory Peck, "Letter to Dore Shary," May 28, 1946, Gregory Peck Files, AMPAS.

106. Arnett Williams, "Letter to Gregory Peck," May 20, 1947, Gregory Peck Files, AMPAS.

107. "Screen Actors Guild Minutes—May 26, 1947," Stephan Vaughn Collection, Box 3, WC.

108. Anthony Slide, *Hollywood Unknowns: A History of Extras, Bit Players, and Stand-Ins* (Jackson: University Press of Mississippi, 2012), 209.

109. "Guild Defends Its Effort for Screen Extras," *Los Angeles Times*, April 4, 1944.

110. "Film Extras Vote to Break from Screen Actors' Guild: Defeated Union Pans Fight for Bargaining Power," *Los Angeles Times*, December 18, 1944.

111. "AAAA Backs Film Extras' Guild in Row with Screen Players Union," *New York Times*, May 18, 1945.

112. Jeffrey Sayre, "Minutes from a Special Meeting of Board of Directors of Screen Extras Guild, Inc.," June 29, 1945, SEG Files, SAA.

CHAPTER 2. ACTORS AND THE MAKING OF TELEVISION'S FIRST GOLDEN AGE

1. Ron Becker, "'Hear-and-See Radio' in the World of Tomorrow: RCA and the Presentation of Television at the World's Fair, 1939–1940," *Historical Journal of Film, Radio, and Television* 21, no. 3 (2001): 361–378.

2. Orrin E. Dunlap Jr., "Act I Reviewed: Television's First Week at World's Fair Teaches No End of Lessons," *New York Times*, May 7, 1939.

3. Albert Abramson, *Electronic Motion Pictures: A History of the Television Camera* (Berkeley: University of California Press, 1955), 94.

4. Abramson, *Electronic Motion Pictures*, 94.

5. Ida Jeter, "The Collapse of the Federated Motion Picture Crafts: A Case Study of Class Collaboration in the Motion Picture Industry," *Journal of the University Film Association* 31, no. 2 (Spring 1979): 44.

6. Jonathan Sterne, "Television under Construction: American Television and the Problem of Distribution, 1926–62," *Media, Culture & Society* 21, no. 4 (1999): 505.

7. Hilmes, *Hollywood and Broadcasting*.

8. Bradley Page, Letter to Ralph Morgan, July 20, 1933, SAA.

9. Susan Murray, *Hitch Your Antenna to the Stars: Early Television and Broadcast Stardom* (New York: Routledge, 2005), 41–43.

10. Kenneth Thomson to Frank Gillmore, June 29, 1938, Folder 31: Associated Actors and Artistes of America Records, NYU-TL.

11. Thomson to Gillmore, June 29, 1938.

12. Paul Turner, Memo: Jurisdiction over television, May 4, 1939, Folder 31: Associated Actors and Artistes of America Records, NYU-TL.

13. Frank Gillmore to Paul Dullzell, July 28, 1938, Folder 31: Associated Actors and Artistes of America Records, NYU-TL.

14. Frank Gilmore to Emily Holt (AFRA), May 17, 1939, Folder 31: Associated Actors and Artistes of America Records, NYU-TL.

15. Ron Rodman, *Tuning In: American Narrative Television Music* (Oxford, UK: Oxford University Press, 2010), 9. For more on the AFM's actions in the 1940s, see Michael James Roberts, *Tell Tchaikovsky the News: Rock 'n' Roll, the Labor Question, and the Musicians' Union, 1942–1968* (Durham, NC: Duke University Press, 2014).

16. Anderson, *Hollywood TV*, 2.

17. Sterne, "Television under Construction," 508.

18. Scott, *On Hollywood*, 61.

19. Scott, *On Hollywood*, 7.

20. For more discussion of these scandals, see Hallett, *Go West, Young Women!* and McKenna, "The City That Made the Pictures Move."

21. Holmes, *Weavers of Dreams, Unite!*, 13.

22. Holmes, *Weavers of Dreams, Unite!*, 13.

23. Alan Hewitt, "Report to Council Meeting of September 15, 1942. Recommending revision of Amendment concerning eligibility for Senior membership, with

additional reference to results of recent employment survey," September 15, 1942. Alan Hewitt Papers, Box 1, New York Public Library for the Performing Arts.

24. Alan Hewitt, "For the Proposed Amendment," 1947(?), Alan Hewitt Papers, Box 1, New York Public Library for the Performing Arts.

25. Hewitt, "For the Proposed Amendment," Alan Hewitt Papers, Box 1, New York Public Library for the Performing Arts.

26. Paul Dullzell, "Letter to Robert Henderson—February 6, 1940," National Broadcasting Corporation Records, Box 103, WC.

27. Norman Lloyd, interview by Steven Scheuer, March 16, 1998, Los Angeles, 15, Courtesy of the Steven S. Scheuer Television History Collection, SCRC, Syracuse University, in Glenn D. Smith Jr., "'The Guiding Spirit': Philip Loeb, the Battle for Television Jurisdiction, and the Broadcasting Industry Blacklist," *American Journalism* 26, no. 3 (Summer 2009): 93–150.

28. "Florine Bale to Hyman Faine," 1948, Folder 22: Associated Actors and Artistes of America Records, NYU-TL.

29. Murray, *Hitch Your Antenna to the Stars*, 43.

30. Murray, *Hitch Your Antenna to the Stars*, 43.

31. Irving Bernstein, *Hollywood at the Crossroads: An Economic Study of the Film Industry* (Hollywood, CA: Hollywood AF of L Film Council, December 1957), 28.

32. For more on this topic, see Anderson, *Hollywood TV*.

33. Michele Hilmes, *Only Connect: A Cultural History of Broadcasting in the United States*, 3rd ed. (Boston: Wadsworth Cengage Learning, 2011), 185–188.

34. Hilmes, *Only Connect*, 187.

35. For more on methods of the relationship between film and television recording and transmission, see Leo Enticknap, *Moving Image Technology from Zoetrope to Digital* (London: Wallflower Press, 2005), 174–175.

36. Screen Actors Guild Executive Board Minutes, April 4, 1949, Stephan Vaughn Collection, Box 3, WC.

37. Daniel Steinhart, *Runaway Hollywood: Internationalizing Postwar Production and Location Shooting* (Berkeley: University of California Press, 2019), 9.

38. Eric Hoyt, "Hollywood and Income Tax, 1929–1955," *Film History* 22, no. 1 (March 2010): 5–21.

39. Kate Fortmueller, "Encounters at the Margins of Hollywood: Casting and Location Shooting for *Bhowani Junction*," *Film History* 28, no. 4 (Winter 2016): 100–124.

40. Cecil Smith, "Runaway Films Tide Turns as Hollywood 'Comes Home': Big Studios Revive with Help of TV," *Los Angeles Times*, June 14, 1964.

41. Bernstein, *Hollywood at the Crossroads*, 23.

42. Summary of TV Producer Survey, April 3, 1950, SAG-AFTRA Negotiating Files, SAA.

43. This kind of data is illuminating, but it is limited in its usefulness in that it speaks to jobs rather than quality of employment. This number only accounts for people employed and does not indicate whether these are all discrete workers or how many actors were working consistently.

44. Christine Becker, *It's the Pictures That Got Small: Hollywood Film Stars on 1950s Television* (Middletown, CT: Wesleyan University Press, 2008), 40.

45. Becker, *It's the Pictures That Got Small*, 40.

46. Jack Gould, "Matter of Form: Television Must Develop Own Techniques if It Is to Have Artistic Vitality," *New York Times*, October 31, 1948, in *Watching Television Come of Age: The New York Times Reviews*, ed. Lewis Gould (Austin: University of Texas Press, 2002), 36.

47. Aronowitz, *False Promises*, 218.

48. Aronowitz, *False Promises*, 218.

49. Meeting of Four A's Television/Committee on Wages, Hours and Working Conditions, April 7, 1947, Folder 32: Associated Actors and Artistes of America Records, NYU-TL.

50. William Boddy, "The Studios Move into Prime Time: Hollywood and the Television Industry in the 1950s," *Cinema Journal* 24, no. 4 (Summer 1985): 30.

51. Stanley Rubin, "A (Very) Personal History of the First Sponsored Film Series on National Television," *E-Media Studies* 1, no. 1 (2008), DOI:10.1349/PS1.1938-6060.A.312.

52. Thomas Schatz, *Boom and Bust: American Cinema in the 1940s* (Berkeley: University of California Press, 1999), 438.

53. For more on television performance style, see James Bennett, "The Television Personality System: Televisual Stardom Revisited after Film Theory," *Screen* 49, no. 1 (Spring 2008): 32–50; John Caughie, "What Do Actors Do When They Act?" in *British Television Drama: Past, Present, and Future*, ed. Jonathan Bignell, Stephen Lacey, and Madeline MacMurraugh-Kavanagh (New York: Palgrave, 2000), 162–174; and Philip Drake, "Reframing Television Performance," *Journal of Film and Video* 68, no. 3–4 (Fall/Winter 2016): 6–17.

54. For more on these comedic styles of performance, see Rob King, *Hokum! The Early Sound Slapstick Short and Depression-Era Mass Culture* (Berkeley: University of California Press, 2017).

55. Meeting of Four A's Television/Committee on Wages, Hours and Working Conditions, April 7, 1947, NYU-TL.

56. Meeting of Four A's Television/Committee on Wages, Hours and Working Conditions, April 7, 1947, NYU-TL.

57. Meeting of Four A's Television/Committee on Wages, Hours and Working Conditions, April 14, 1947, Folder 32: Associated Actors and Artistes of America Records, NYU-TL.

58. Thomas Brady, "Film Extras Agree to a New Contract," *New York Times*, December 17, 1948.

59. Internal NBC memos about television production succinctly indicate that terms will be resolved and spend tremendous detail about clearances for music. See Robert Meyers, Television Recording of Live TV Programs, July 14, 1948, National Broadcasting Corporation Collection, Box 106, WC.

60. Meeting of Four A's Television/Committee on Wages, Hours and Working Conditions, April 7, 1947, NYU-TL.

61. Conference Meetings of President's Committee of Associated Actors and Artistes of America, and Board of Directors of Screen Actors Guild, and Representatives of Screen Extras Guild, commencing Saturday July 30, 1949 at 8:00 pm in Redwood Room of Roosevelt Hotel, SAA, 2.

62. Proposed Recommendations of Joint Committees for Merger of Equity, AFRA, AGMA, and Chorus Equity, 1948, SAA, 1.

63. Margaret Webster, "Memo to Council on A.E.A. on Merger," January 20, 1949, SAA, 2.

64. Webster, "Memo to Council on A.E.A. on Merger," January 20, 1949, 6.

65. Alan Hewitt, "Merger—For the Minority," *Equity Magazine*, April 1949, p. 21, Alan Hewitt Papers, New York Public Library for the Performing Arts.

66. Proposed Recommendations of Joint Committees for Merger of Equity, AFRA, AGMA, and Chorus Equity, 1948, SAA, 5.

67. Proposed Recommendations of Joint Committees for Merger of Equity, AFRA, AGMA, and Chorus Equity, 1948, SAA, 5.

68. Pierre Bourdieu, *The Field of Cultural Production: Essays on Art and Literature* (New York: Columbia University Press, 1993), 42.

69. Bourdieu, *The Field of Cultural Production*, 42.

70. Philip Loeb, Statement, February 14, 1949, Associated Actors and Artistes of America Records, NYU-TL.

71. Loeb, Statement, February 14, 1949, NYU-TL.

72. Jack Dales, "Letter to the Four A's," August 16, 1949, SAA.

73. Conference Meetings of President's Committee of Associated Actors and Artistes of America, and Board of Directors of Screen Actors Guild, and Representatives of Screen Extras Guild, commencing Saturday July 30, 1949 at 8:00 pm in Redwood Room of Roosevelt Hotel, SAA, 1.

74. Conference Meetings of President's Committee of Associated Actors and Artistes of America, and Board of Directors of Screen Actors Guild, and Representatives of Screen Extras Guild, commencing Saturday July 30, 1949, SAA, 4.

75. Conference Meetings of President's Committee of Associated Actors and Artistes of America, and Board of Directors of Screen Actors Guild, and Representatives of Screen Extras Guild, commencing Saturday July 30, 1949, SAA, 17.

76. SAG and SEG Statement to Membership, October 13, 1949, SAA.

77. SEG Membership Meeting Transcript, May 9, 1951, SEG Files, SAA.

78. Conference Meetings of President's Committee of Associated Actors and Artistes of America, and Board of Directors of Screen Actors Guild, and Representatives of Screen Extras Guild, July 30, 1949, Executive Dept. Files—Television Authority (Four A's), Box 2, SAA, 9.

79. SEG Proposed 4As Regional TV Council Plan, SAA.

80. Notes on SEG Proposal, n.d., SAA.

81. SEG Membership Meeting Transcript, May 9, 1951, 50.

82. Richard Gordon to Paul Dullzell, Telegram, November 2, 1949, Folder 32: Associated Actors and Artistes of America Records, NYU-TL.

83. SEG Membership Meeting Transcript, May 9, 1951, 41.

84. SEG Membership Meeting Transcript, May 9, 1951, 68–69.

85. Untitled, *Variety*, February 22, 1952, 8.

86. Untitled, *Variety*, February 22, 1952, 8.

87. "Actors and Unions Break over Television," *Los Angeles Times*, April 20, 1950.

88. Buck Harris, Intelligence Report to Members of Screen Actors Guild from the Board of Directors, December 13, 1950, vol. 4, no. 8, December 13, 1950, SAA, 2.

89. Rita Morley Harvey, *Those Wonderful Terrible Years: George Heller and the American Federation of Television and Radio Artists* (Carbondale: Southern Illinois University Press, 1996), 124.

90. As Michele Hilmes asserts, "when broadcast's seriality met the possibilities inherent in film's visuality and permanence . . . television programs as we know them today began to take place." Hilmes, *Only Connect*, 192.

91. C. E. Butterfield, "It's a Pleasure to Watch That Alan Young Show," *Washington Post*, March 20, 1953.

92. Thomas F. Brady, "Hollywood TV News: 'Musical Comedy Time' Presents 'Rio Rita,'" *New York Times*, November 12, 1950.

93. Anderson, *Hollywood TV*, 56.

94. William Boddy, *Fifties Television: The Industry and Its Critics* (Urbana: University of Illinois Press, 1993), 72.

95. Conference Meetings of President's Committee of Associated Actors and Artistes of America, and Board of Directors of Screen Actors Guild, and Representatives of Screen Extras Guild, commencing Saturday July 30, 1949 at 8:00 pm in Redwood Room of Roosevelt Hotel, SAA, 3.

96. Chester Migden, "Interview with SAG Foundation," SAG Foundation, Los Angeles, May 1989.

97. Outline of evidence to be prepared for New York NLRB Hearing—Audio Productions, Inc. and Screen Actors Guild, n.d., SAA, 5.

98. Television Film Producers Association, 93 NLRB 932 (1951).

99. Television Film Producers Association, 93 NLRB 932.

100. Television Film Producers Association, 93 NLRB 929.

101. Television Film Producers Association, 93 NLRB 932.

102. H. O'Neil Shanks, "Minutes of the Regular Meeting of the Board of Directors of the Screen Extras Guild," August 15, 1951, SEG Files, SAA, 2.

103. There would not be another performers' union merger until SEG dissolved into SAG in 1992 and SAG and AFTRA merged in 2012.

CHAPTER 3. REUSE AND REPLACE?

1. Jennifer Holt, *Empires of Entertainment: Media Industries and the Politics of Deregulation, 1980–1996* (New Brunswick, NJ: Rutgers University Press, 2011); Amanda Lotz, *We Now Disrupt This Broadcast: How Cable Transformed Television and the Internet*

Revolutionized It All (Cambridge, MA: MIT Press, 2018); Frederick Wasser, *Veni, Vidi, Video: The Hollywood Empire and the VCR* (Austin: University of Texas Press, 2001).

2. Holt, *Empires of Entertainment*, 6.

3. Andrew Dawson argues that prior to 1950, below-the-line unions were more radical than the above-the-line unions that were largely content with their industry status. For Dawson, above-the-line unions became more active after 1950. Although SAG's first strike was in 1952, I would argue that the 1960 strike and a stronger commitment to bargaining for residuals is the most important turning point for actors. See Andrew Dawson, "Strikes in the Motion Picture Industry," in *The Encyclopedia of Strikes in American History*, ed. Aaron Brenner, Benjamin Day, and Immanuel Ness (New York: Routledge, 2009), 652–664.

4. Brooks Barnes, "In Hollywood, a Sacred Cow Lands on the Contract Table," *New York Times*, August 5, 2008.

5. Charles Acland, *Screen Traffic: Movies, Multiplexes, and Global Culture* (Durham, NC: Duke University Press, 2003), 4.

6. Alyssa Ribeiro, "'We Want Both! Pressuring Philadelphia Unions for Inclusion and Equity during the Long 1970s," *Labor History* 60, no. 5 (October 2019): 559.

7. Ribeiro, "We Want Both!," 559.

8. For more on the efforts of the WGA and the DGA, see Miranda Banks, "Unequal Opportunities: Gender Inequities and Precarious Diversity," *Feminist Media Histories* 4, no. 4 (Fall 2018): 109–129; and Smukler, *Liberating Hollywood*.

9. See Aronowitz, *False Promises*, and Jeter, "The Collapse of the Federated Motion Picture Crafts," 38.

10. Aronowitz, *False Promises*, 218.

11. Eric Hoyt, *Hollywood Vault: Film Libraries before Home Video* (Berkeley: University of California Press, 2014), 145.

12. Jennifer Porst, "United States v. Twentieth Century-Fox, et al. and Hollywood's Feature Films on Early Television," *Film History* 25, no. 4 (2013): 114–142.

13. E. A. Hungerford Jr., "Film Roundup," November 28, 1940, National Broadcasting Corporation Collection, WC.

14. Wasser, *Veni, Vidi, Video*, 35–36.

15. Conference Meetings of President's Committee of Associated Actors and Artistes of America, and Board of Directors of Screen Actors Guild, and Representatives of Screen Extras Guild, July 30, 1949, Folder: Minutes of Presidents Committee SAG Conferences July 1949, Executive Dept. Files—Television Authority, SAA.

16. SAG Meeting Minutes, May 14, 1951, Stephan Vaughn Collection, Box 3, WC.

17. Robert Gilbert, "'Residual Rights' Established by Collective Bargaining in Television and Radio," *Law and Contemporary Problems* 23, no. 1 (Winter 1958): 107.

18. Grant Code, "Letter to AFTRA Board," October 8, 1958, American Federation of Television and Radio Artists National Office Records, NYU-TL.

19. Murray Schumach, "Top Studios Face a Writers' Strike: Talks Deadlocked on Issue of Sharing Income in Sales of Post-'48 Films to TV," *New York Times*, November 23, 1959.

20. This language was reiterated throughout negotiations. See "Studios Reaffirm Stand on TV Pay," *New York Times*, February 29, 1960, and T.J.H., "Talent Strike Seen Aid to Studios by Value Line," *Independent Exhibitors Film Bulletin*, April 11, 1960, 14, Media History Digital Library, www.mediahistoryproject.org.

21. Boddy, *Fifties Television*, 205.

22. Mike Mashon, "NBC, J. Walter Thompson, and the Struggle for Control of Television Programming, 1946–1958," in *NBC: America's Network*, ed. Michele Hilmes (Berkeley: University of California Press, 2007), 149.

23. Cynthia Meyers, "From Sponsorship to Spots: Advertising and the Development of Electronic Media," in *Media Industries: History, Theory, and Method*, ed. Jennifer Holt and Alisa Perren (Malden, MA: Wiley-Blackwell, 2009), 74.

24. "SAG Will Seek Higher Rates for TV Plugs," *Motion Picture Daily*, January 17, 1958, 4, Media History Digital Library, www.mediahistoryproject.org.

25. Greg Krizman and Valerie Yaros, "20th Century SAG," *Screen Actor*, January 15, 2000, 25–31.

26. Krizman and Yaros, "20th Century SAG."

27. Grant Code, "Letter to AFTRA Board," October 8, 1958, American Federation of Television and Radio Artists National Office Records, NYU-TL.

28. Howard Kennedy, "SAG, Studios Recess Talks over Week End," *Los Angeles Times*, March 19, 1960, 3.

29. For further details, see Howard Kennedy, "SAG, Studios Recess Talks over Week End," *Los Angeles Times*, March 19, 1960, and "SAG Package Plan Weighed by Producers," *Los Angeles Times*, March 21, 1960.

30. Penelope Houston, "After the Strike," *Sight and Sound* 26, no. 3 (1960): 108.

31. Bill Davidson, "Again and Again and Again: Those Reruns, the Facts behind the Complaints," *TV Guide*, June 9, 1973, 6–13.

32. Chester Migden, "Letter to Academy of Television Arts and Sciences President—Robert Lewins," December 7, 1972, SAA.

33. Derek Kompare, *Rerun Nation: How Repeats Invented American Television* (New York: Rutledge, 2005), 81.

34. Holt, *Empires of Entertainment*, 53.

35. Richard Nixon, "Letter to SAG President—John Gavin," September 12, 1972, SAA.

36. Nixon, "Letter to SAG President—John Gavin," September 12, 1972, SAA.

37. Dennis Weaver, "Address of Dennis Weaver, President of Screen Actors Guild at the Annual Membership Meeting," November 19, 1972, Dennis Weaver—President File, SAA.

38. "Screen Actors Guild Press Release—August 4," August 4, 1972, SAA.

39. Mac St. Johns, "Screen Actors Guild Press Release—May 31," May 31, 1972, SAA.

40. "Preliminary Analysis of the Causes and Effects of Rerun Programming and Related Issues in Prime Time Network Television," Office of Telecommunication Policy, Washington DC, SAA, 9.

41. "Preliminary Analysis of the Causes and Effects of Rerun Programming and Related Issues in Prime Time Network Television," SAA, 11.

42. "Preliminary Analysis of the Causes and Effects of Rerun Programming and Related Issues in Prime Time Network Television," SAA, 13.

43. Megan Mullen, *The Rise of Cable Programming in the United States: Revolution or Evolution?* (Austin: University of Texas Press, 2003), 67.

44. Dennis Weaver, "Address of Dennis Weaver, President of Screen Actors Guild at the Annual Membership Meeting," November 18, 1973, Dennis Weaver—President File, SAA.

45. "FCC Launches Investigation of Prime-Time Network Reruns," *Screen Actor Magazine*, Fall 1974, 15.

46. Weaver, "Address of Dennis Weaver," November 18, 1973, SAA.

47. Dennis Weaver, "Address of Dennis Weaver, President of Screen Actors Guild at the Annual Membership Meeting," November 17, 1974, Dennis Weaver—President File, SAA.

48. Kompare, *Rerun Nation*, 70.

49. Vance King, "SEG Pitches TV Reuse Payment for Blurbs," *Hollywood Reporter*, November 14, 1966.

50. "Screen Extras Guild Finances Need Fixing," *Variety*, May 29, 1968.

51. For thoughtful and sustained discussion of the limits of this kind of data collection, see Banks, "Unequal Opportunities."

52. "Women in Commercials: Fewer Jobs, Lower Pay," *Screen Actor Magazine*, Fall 1974, 14.

53. "Women in Commercials," 14.

54. For more detailed discussion of these committee efforts, see Banks, "Unequal Opportunities"; Fortmueller, "Time's Up (Again?)"; and Smukler, *Liberating Hollywood*.

55. Interestingly, though other studies in the same issue break down data by race and gender, this data set only focuses on gender. See "Women in Commercials."

56. Minutes from Meeting of Ethnic Minorities Committee in Actors Equity Boardroom in Hollywood, December 1, 1971, AMPAS.

57. Minutes from Meeting of Ethnic Minorities Committee in Actors Equity Boardroom in Hollywood, December 1, 1971, AMPAS.

58. Minutes from Meeting of Ethnic Minorities Committee in Actors Equity Boardroom in Hollywood, December 1, 1971, AMPAS.

59. "What the Viewers Want on TV," *Screen Actor*, Fall 1974, 1.

60. Olaf Hoerschelmann, *Rules of the Game: Quiz Shows and American Culture* (Albany: State University of New York Press, 2006), 100.

61. "Extra Trade-Off: Producers Can Hire 25 Less in TV, but Need 25 More for Features," *Variety*, August 9, 1976.

62. Bernard Weinraub, "For Film Extras, Variety Is Certain, Stardom Isn't," *New York Times*, January 2, 1970.

63. "Altman Vows He'll Never Utilize SEG," *Variety*, January 9, 1976.

64. Headlines from *Variety*, June 2, 1980, 37.

65. Paul McDonald, *Video and DVD Industries* (London: British Film Institute, 2007), and Wasser, *Veni, Vidi, Video.*

66. McDonald, *Video and DVD Industries*, 109.

67. Wasser, *Veni, Vidi, Video*, 14.

68. McDonald, *Video and DVD Industries*, 110.

69. Will Turner, "Majors Considering Rent-Sell Plans for Their Videocassettes," *Variety*, September 18, 1980, 15.

70. "SAG-AFTRA Offer No Concessions on Supplemental Market," *Variety*, June 2, 1980, 37.

71. Will Turner, "SAG-AFTRA Return to the Bargaining Table after Mulling Producers' 'Message,'" *Variety*, September 3, 1980.

72. Chad Raphael, "The Political Economic Origins of Reali-TV," in *Reality TV: Remaking Television Culture*, 2nd ed., ed. Laurie Ouellette and Susan Murray (New York: New York University Press, 2009), 128.

73. "We Urge a Yes Vote on the SAG Contract Referendum," *Variety*, October 10, 1980, 12; see also Howard Osofsky and Jan Schneiderman, "The California Gold Rush: SAG's 1980 Strike Revisited," *Journal of Arts Management and Law* 12, no. 2 (Summer 1982): 14.

74. "To the SAG and AFTRA Membership," *Variety*, October 10, 1980, 13.

75. Will Turner, "Strike's Impact Spreads; Prune Prod. Payrolls," *Variety*, August 6, 1980.

76. "We Urge a Yes Vote on the SAG Contract Referendum," *Variety*, October 10, 1980.

77. "Record Number of Actors to Okay Pact," *Variety*, October 29, 1980.

78. Sally Ogle Davis, "Battling It Out in Hollywood," *New York Times*, April 25, 1982.

79. Davis, "Battling It Out in Hollywood."

80. Harry Weinstein, "Teamsters Court Screen Extras Guild for Merger," *Los Angeles Times*, November 23, 1986.

81. Weinstein, "Teamsters Court Screen Extras Guild for Merger."

82. McDonald, *Video and DVD Industries*, 48.

CHAPTER 4. NEW MEDIA, OLD LABOR CONFLICTS

1. SAG-AFTRA New Media Contracts Meeting, SAG-AFTRA Headquarters, Los Angeles, January 14, 2014.

2. Pamela Robertson Wojcik, "The Sound of Film Acting," *Journal of Film and Video* 58, no. 1–2 (Spring/Summer 2006): 80.

3. Wojcik, "The Sound of Film Acting," 81.

4. Within fan communities, these voice actors are often well known and beloved. In some cases, replacing the voice of a well-known character has caused tremendous

controversy, as was the case when Ashly Burch was replaced in the *Life Is Strange* prequel. See Cecilia D'Anastasio, "Ashly Burch 'Heartbroken' She Won't Play Chloe in *Life Is Strange* Prequel," *Kotaku*, June 14, 2017, https://kotaku.com/ashly-burch -heartbroken-she-wont-play-chloe-in-life-is-1796111269.

5. Updated financial data on video games is available through the Entertainment Software Association report, https://www.theesa.com/resource_type/annual-report/. See Michael D. Gallagher, "An Exceptional Year of Growth, Impact, and Innovation," ESA 2017 Annual Report, https://www.esaannualreport.com/a-letter-from-michael -d.-gallagher.html (last accessed May 29, 2019).

6. For more on the relationship between traditional media labor and digital labor, see Angela McRobbie, *Be Creative: Making a Living in the New Culture Industries* (Cambridge, UK: Polity, 2016); Trebor Scholz, ed., *Digital Labor: The Internet as Playground and Factory* (New York: Routledge, 2013).

7. McRobbie, *Be Creative*, 40–41.

8. Lisa Bode, *Making Believe: Screen Performance and Special Effects in Popular Cinema* (New Brunswick, NJ: Rutgers University Press, 2017), 7; Jason Sperb, "I'll (Always) Be Back: Virtual Performance and Post-Human Labor in the Age of Digital Cinema," *Culture, Theory, and Critique* 53, no. 3 (2012): 383–397.

9. Amanda Lotz, *The Television Will Be Revolutionized* (New York: New York University Press, 2007), 99.

10. Ashley Rodriguez, "The End of 'Peak TV' Must Finally, Mercifully Be Nigh," *Quartz*, January 13, 2018, https://qz.com/999827/the-end-of-peak-tv-must-finally -mercifully-be-nigh/.

11. Joe Adalian, "Why You Feel Like There's Too Much TV to Watch, in One Graph," *Vulture*, January 22, 2015, https://www.vulture.com/2015/01/why-you-feel-like -theres-too-much-tv-to-watch.html; Lotz, *The Television Will Be Revolutionized*, 99.

12. Kate Fortmueller, "Pay to Play: Booking Roles in the Post-Network Era," *Journal of Film and Video* 68, no. 3–4 (Fall/Winter 2016): 118.

13. For discussion in popular venues, see Margaret Talbot, "Pixel Perfect: The Scientist behind the Digital Cloning of Actors," *New Yorker*, April 28, 2014, 32–38.

14. Bode, *Making Believe*, 7.

15. Rebecca Asherie, "Heavenly Voices and Bestial Bodies: Issues of Performance and Representation in Celebrity Voice-Acting," *Animation Practice, Process and Production* 1, no. 2 (2011): 230.

16. Karen Collins, *Game Sound: An Introduction to the History, Theory, and Practice of Video Game Music and Sound Design* (Cambridge, MA: MIT Press, 2008), 96.

17. Casey O'Donnell, "Games Are Not Convergence: The Lost Promise of Digital Production and Convergence," *Convergence* 17, no. 3 (2011): 275.

18. Voice actors featured in AAA games often acquire celebrity status within gaming circles, but this does not cross over to film or television fame.

19. Amin Elhassan, Stugotz, and Kaili Vernoff on Hour 2: Video Games, The Dan Le Batard Show, podcast audio, February 22, 2019, http://www.espn.com/espnradio/ play?id=26055763.

20. Interviewed by author, July 25, 2018, Los Angeles.

21. Interviewed by author, July 25, 2018, Los Angeles.

22. Interviewed by author, July 25, 2018, Los Angeles.

23. Shonte Daniels, "Black Video Game Characters Are Still Often Voiced by White Actors," *Vice*, February 2, 2016, https://www.vice.com/en_us/article/78kv5x/ black-video-game-characters-are-still-often-voiced-by-white-actors-uncharted-4 -nadine-ross.

24. Daniels, "Black Video Game Characters Are Still Often Voiced by White Actors."

25. Starr Marcello, "Performance Design: An Analysis of Film Acting and Sound Design," *Journal of Film and Video* 58, no. 1–2 (Spring/Summer 2006): 64.

26. *The Simpsons* is a great example within animation of the versatility required of voice actors. Actors such as Harry Shearer and Hank Azaria voice many of the recurring star characters, but actors such as Chris Edgerly voice a wide array of supporting characters and might even be a substitute for actors who miss table reads.

27. Interviewed by author, July 24, 2018, Los Angeles.

28. Collins, *Game Sound*, 97.

29. Collins, *Game Sound*, 96–97.

30. Interviewed by author, June 27, 2018, Los Angeles.

31. Interviewed by author, June 27, 2018, Los Angeles.

32. Interviewed by author, July 25, 2018, Los Angeles.

33. Interviewed by author, July 25, 2018, Los Angeles.

34. Interviewed by author, July 25, 2018, Los Angeles.

35. Interviewed by author, July 25, 2018, Los Angeles.

36. Interviewed by author, July 25, 2018, Los Angeles.

37. Holt, *Empires of Entertainment*, 165.

38. John Downing, "The Political Economy of Uvww."

39. Andrew Ross, "In Search of the Lost Paycheck," in *Digital Labor: The Internet as Playground and Factory*, ed. Trebor Scholz (New York: Routledge, 2013), 22.

40. Mark Andrejevic, *Reality TV: The Work of Being Watched* (Lanham, MD: Rowman and Littlefield, 2004), 11.

41. Hooper White, "Does Intelligent Cost Control Weaken the Effectiveness of Your TV Commercial?" *Advertising Age*, January 23, 1978, 44.

42. According to *Advertising Age*, the 4As only began tracking advertising production data in 1986. See Joe Mandese, "Cost to Make TV Ad Nears Quarter-Million," *Advertising Age*, July 4, 1994, 3.

43. Mark Grunewald, "Regulatory Future of Contingent Employment: An Introduction," *Washington and Lee Law Review* 52 (1995): 726.

44. Steve Coe, "Actor Groups and Alliance Reach Tentative Pact," *Broadcasting*, March 2, 1992.

45. Nick Madigan, "War of Words Propels SAG Race," *Variety*, October 18–24, 1999, 12.

46. Dave McNary, "SAG Plans Big Rally in Hollywood," *Daily Variety*, February 3, 2000, 3.

47. Chris Pursell, "SAG, AFTRA Strike Ad Industry," *Electronic Media*, May 8, 2000.

48. Dave McNary, "Actors Unions Weigh New Offer from Ad Biz," *Daily Variety*, October 20, 2000, 28.

49. John Dempsey and Dave McNary, "Returning Thesps Celebrate Ad Lib Day," *Daily Variety*, October 24, 2000, 1.

50. Wayne Friedman, "Six-Month Strike Is Over, but No Victor Declared," *Ad Age*, October 30, 2000, https://adage.com/article/news/month-strike-victor-declared/31846/.

51. Dave McNary, "Inside Move: Commercials Biz Looks Lean," *Variety*, July 20, 2003.

52. Interviewed by author, July 24, 2018, Los Angeles.

53. Craig J. Ackerman, "E-Issues Take Center Stage: The 2000 SAG/AFTRA Strike," *Jeffrey S. Moored Sports Law Journal* 8, no. 2 (2002): 298.

54. Henry Jenkins, *Convergence Culture: Where Old and New Media Collide* (New York: New York University Press, 2006), 23.

55. Jenkins, *Convergence Culture*, 23.

56. Mark Deuze, *Media Work* (Cambridge, UK: Polity Press, 2007), 70.

57. For more on Breakdown Services, see Fortmueller, "Pay to Play."

58. Gary Marsh, Personal Interview, May 8, 2015, Los Angeles.

59. During the COVID-19 pandemic, all auditions had to move online.

60. Interviewed by author, April 7, 2015, Los Angeles.

61. Peter Debruge, "Talent Finds 'Tape' Is Taking Over the Town," *Variety*, October 21, 2011, 25.

62. Interviewed by author, June 27, 2018, Los Angeles.

63. Interviewed by author, July 25, 2018, Los Angeles.

64. Interviewed by author, June 27, 2018, Los Angeles.

65. Interviewed by author, July 6, 2018, Los Angeles.

66. Interviewed by author, July 6, 2018, Los Angeles.

67. Interviewed by author, July 6, 2018, Los Angeles.

68. Interviewed by author, July 6, 2018, Los Angeles.

69. Interviewed by author, June 27, 2018, Los Angeles.

70. Interviewed by author, July 25, 2018, Los Angeles.

71. Interviewed by author, June 27, 2018, Los Angeles.

72. Interviewed by author, June 27, 2018, Los Angeles.

73. Interviewed by author, June 27, 2018, Los Angeles.

74. Interviewed by author, June 27, 2018, Los Angeles.

75. Interviewed by author, July 24, 2018, Los Angeles.

76. McRobbie, *Be Creative*, 20.

77. McRobbie, *Be Creative*, 20.

78. McRobbie, *Be Creative*, 21.

79. For a list of SAG-AFTRA Foundation workshops and panels, see https://members.sagfoundation.org/programs.

80. "The Social Media Advantage: Advanced," event advertisement, July 25, 2018, https://www.sagaftra.org/los-angeles/local-events/social-media-advantage-advanced.

81. McRobbie, *Be Creative*, 19.

82. Casey O'Donnell, "The North American Game Industry," in *The Video Game Industry: Formation, Present State, and Future*, ed. Peter Zackariasson and Timothy Wilson (New York: Routledge, 2012), 110.

83. Ross, "In Search of the Lost Paycheck," 23.

84. Stuart Cunningham and David Craig, *Social Media Entertainment: The New Intersection of Hollywood and Silicon Valley* (New York: NYU Press, 2019), 22.

85. Cunningham and Craig, *Social Media Entertainment*, 22.

86. O'Donnell, "The North American Game Industry," 110. There are also numerous popular video game-oriented websites that have published articles on crunch and video game labor conditions; for examples, see Megan Farokhmanesh, "Toxic Management Cost an Award-Winning Game Studio Its Best Developers," *The Verge*, March 20, 2018, https://www.theverge.com/2018/3/20/17130056/telltale-games-developer-layoffs-toxic-video-game-industry; David Milner, "Crunch: The Video Game Industry's Notorious Labor Problem," Gameinformer, January 16, 2018, https://www.gameinformer.com/b/features/archive/2018/01/16/crunch-the-video-game-industrys-notorious-labor-problem.aspx; Jason Schreier, "Video Games Are Destroying the People Who Make Them," *New York Times*, October 25, 2017, https://www.nytimes.com/2017/10/25/opinion/work-culture-video-games-crunch.html; and Nick Statt, "Game Developers Look to Unions to Fix the Industry's Exploitative Workplace Culture," *The Verge*, March 23, 2018, https://www.theverge.com/2018/3/23/17156472/game-developers-unionization-exploitative-toxic-workplace-culture-gdc-2018.

87. O'Donnell, "The North American Game Industry," 110–112.

88. Dave McNary, "SAG-AFTRA Rejects Final Offer for Video Game Contract," *Variety*, October 20, 2016, https://variety.com/2016/digital/news/sag-aftra-rejects-videogame-voice-actor-contract-1201895622/.

89. Interviewed by author, July 21, 2018, Los Angeles.

90. Interviewed by author, July 21, 2018, Los Angeles.

91. Interviewed by author, July 21, 2018, Los Angeles.

92. "Latest Event Information," Game Performance Matters, accessed October 11, 2018, http://www.gameperformancematters.com/events.

93. "Latest Event Information."

94. SAG-AFTRA Interactive Media (Video Games) Agreement—Referendum Booklet, October 17, 2017, Los Angeles.

95. For more on video game unionization, see "Why Organize?," Game Workers Unite, accessed May 26, 2018, https://www.gameworkersunite.org; Tim Colwill, "Why Game Developers Are Talking about Unionization," *IGN*, March 18, 2019, https://www.ign.com/articles/2019/03/18/why-game-developers-are-talking-about-unionization; Sam Dean, "As Video Games Make Billions, the Workers Behind

Them Say It's Time to Unionize," *Los Angeles Times*, April 12, 2019, https://www
.latimes.com/business/technology/la-fi-tn-video-game-union-movement-20190412
-story.html; and Aron Garst, "How Video Game Unionization Would Happen,"
Variety, December 17, 2018, https://variety.com/2018/gaming/features/video-game
-industry-union-unionization-1203091114/.

CONCLUSION

1. Dailymail.com Reporter, "From Learning Lines to Serving the Long Line!
The Cosby Show Star Geoffrey Owens Is Spotted Working as a Cashier at Trader
Joe's in New Jersey," *Daily Mail*, August 30, 2018, https://www.dailymail.co.uk/news/
article-6116357/The-Cosby-star-Geoffrey-Owens-spotted-working-cashier-Trader
-Joes-New-Jersey.html; "'Cosby Show' Actor Spotted Bagging Groceries at NJ Trader
Joe's," *Fox News*, August 31, 2018, https://www.foxnews.com/entertainment/cosby
-show-actor-geoffrey-owens-spotted-bagging-groceries-at-nj-trader-joes.

2. Kerri Sheragy, September 2, 2018, 1:20 p.m., https://twitter.com/kerrisheragy/
status/1036665175410012161.

3. Jacqueline McKenzie, September 3, 2018, 5:18 a.m., https://twitter.com/
JMcKenzie/status/1036543825127170048.

4. "Casting Companies Warned over Fees," *Deadline*, May 18, 2011, http://www
.deadline.com/2011/05/casting-companies-warned-over-fees/.

5. Sopan Deb, "Geoffrey Owens Has a Second Wind. Where Will It Take
Him?," *New York Times*, September 19, 2018, https://www.nytimes.com/2018/09/19/
arts/television/geoffrey-owens-trader-joes.html.

6. Deb, "Geoffrey Owens Has a Second Wind."

7. Deb, "Geoffrey Owens Has a Second Wind."

POSTSCRIPT. ACTORS AND COVID-19

1. Kim Masters, "Coronavirus and Hollywood: How Are Industry Workers
Faring?," *The Business*, March 30, 2020, https://www.kcrw.com/culture/shows/the
-business/jobless-hollywood-workers-cope-with-coronavirus/coronavirus-hollywood
-industry-workers-coping.

2. Alex Sherman, "NBCUniversal's Peacock Strikes Licensing Deal for Viacom-
CBS Movies and TV Shows Including 'The Godfather,' 'Undercover Boss,'" CNBC
.com, July 1, 2020, https://www.cnbc.com/2020/07/01/nbcuniversals-peacock-strikes
-licensing-deal-for-viacomcbs-content.html.

3. David Wagner, "LA Actors Are Losing Unemployment Benefits Based On
Work They Did Years Ago," *LAist*, May 7, 2020, https://laist.com/2020/05/07/actors
_SAG_AFTRA_residuals_unemployment_california_.php.

4. For examples of these early plans and discussions, see Kate Aurthur, "New Document Lays Out Plan to Resume Movie and TV Productions with Strict Quarantine Pods (Exclusive)," *Variety*, April 24, 2020, https://variety.com/2020/biz/news/production-plan-coronavirus-1234589286/; Brent Lang and Justin Kroll, "Post-Pandemic Hollywood: Inside Plans to Make Movie and TV Sets Safe Again," *Variety*, April 22, 2020, https://variety.com/2020/biz/features/hollywood-production-post-pandemic-coronavirus-1234586579/; Dave McNary, "'Contagion' Director Steven Soderbergh Leads DGA Committee on Resuming Production," *Variety*, April 16, 2020, https://variety.com/2020/film/news/contagion-steven-soderbergh-directors-guild-production-resumption-1234582940/.

5. Sonia Kil, "Film and TV Productions Make Hesitant Restart in Korea," *Variety*, May 21, 2020, https://variety.com/2020/film/asia/film-tv-productions-restart-korea-1234612971/; Stacy Perman, "Coronavirus Shut Down Production. But Iceland Could Help Hollywood Reopen," *Los Angeles Times*, April 30, 2020, https://www.latimes.com/entertainment-arts/business/story/2020-04-30/coronavirus-shutdown-filmmakers-warm-to-iceland.

6. Andreas Wiseman, "Universal's 'Jurassic World: Dominion,'" *Deadline*, June 15, 2020, https://deadline.com/2020/06/universal-jurassic-world-production-uk-chris-pratt-bryce-dallas-howard-1202958819/.

7. Cynthia Littleton and Kate Aurthur, "Industry Infighting, Union Turf Battles Slow Development of Back-to-Work Plan," *Variety*, May 21, 2020, https://variety.com/2020/film/news/production-guidelines-white-paper-amptp-iatse-1234613975/.

8. DGA, SAG-AFTRA, IATSE, and Teamsters' Committees for COVID-19 Safety Guidelines, "The Safe Way Forward," released June 12, 2020.

9. Staiger, "The Hollywood Mode of Production," 87–89.

10. DGA, SAG-AFTRA, IATSE, and Teamsters' Committees for COVID-19 Safety Guidelines, "The Safe Way Forward."

11. Rick Porter, "Bold & the Beautiful Boss on Resuming Production: 'We're Ready to Go,'" *Variety*, June 16, 2020, https://www.hollywoodreporter.com/live-feed/bold-beautiful-boss-resuming-production-were-ready-go-1298862.

12. Porter, "Bold & the Beautiful Boss on Resuming Production."

13. Kate Aurthur and Adam Vary, "Extras on Set: Inside Hollywood's Pricey Plans to Restart Production," *Variety*, May 20, 2020, https://variety.com/2020/biz/features/restarting-production-coronavirus-pandemic-hollywood-1234611125/; and Anousha Sakoui, "How Tyler Perry's 'Camp Quarantine' Fended Off the Pandemic during Filming of 'Sistas,'" *Los Angeles Times*, July 30, 2020, https://www.latimes.com/entertainment-arts/business/story/2020-07-30/tyler-perry-camp-quarantine-battled-pandemic-to-complete-shooting.

14. DGA, SAG-AFTRA, IATSE, and Teamsters' Committees for COVID-19 Safety Guidelines, "The Safe Way Forward."

SELECTED BIBLIOGRAPHY

Abramson, Albert. *Electronic Motion Pictures: A History of the Television Camera.* Berkeley: University of California Press, 1955.

Acland, Charles. *Screen Traffic: Movies, Multiplexes, and Global Culture.* Durham, NC: Duke University Press, 2003.

Anderson, Christopher. *Hollywood TV: The Studio System in the Fifties.* Austin: University of Texas Press, 1994.

Andrejevic, Mark. *Reality TV: The Work of Being Watched.* Lanham, MD: Rowman and Littlefield, 2004.

Aronowitz, Stanley. *False Promises: The Shaping of American Working Class Consciousness.* Durham, NC: Duke University Press, 1992.

Arthur, Michael B., and Denise M. Rousseau, eds. *The Boundaryless Career: A New Employment Principle for a New Organizational Era.* New York: Oxford University Press, 1996.

Asherie, Rebecca. "Heavenly Voices and Bestial Bodies: Issues of Performance and Representation in Celebrity Voice-Acting." *Animation Practice, Process & Production* 1, no. 2 (2011): 229–248.

Balio, Tino. *The American Film Industry.* Madison: University of Wisconsin Press, 1985.

———. *Grand Design: Hollywood as a Modern Business Enterprise, 1930–1939.* New York: Scribner, 1993.

Banks, Miranda. "Unequal Opportunities: Gender Inequities and Precarious Diversity." *Feminist Media Histories* 4, no. 4 (Fall 2018): 109–129.

———. *The Writers: A History of American Screenwriters and Their Guild.* New Brunswick, NJ: Rutgers University Press, 2015.

Becker, Christine. *It's the Pictures That Got Small: Hollywood Film Stars on 1950s Television.* Middletown, CT: Wesleyan University Press, 2008.

Becker, Ron. "'Hear-and-See Radio' in the World of Tomorrow: RCA and the Presentation of Television at the World's Fair, 1939–1940." *Historical Journal of Film, Radio and Television* 21, no. 4 (October 2001): 361–378.

Bekken, Jon. "Newsboys: The Exploitation of 'Little Merchants' by the Newspaper Industry." In *Newsworkers: Toward a History of the Rank and File,* edited by Hanno

Hardt and Bonnie Brennen, 190–225. Minneapolis: University of Minnesota Press, 1995.

Bennett, James. "The Television Personality System: Televisual Stardom Revisited after Film Theory." *Screen* 49, no. 1 (Spring 2008): 32–50.

Bernstein, Irving. *Hollywood at the Crossroads: An Economic Study of the Film Industry.* Hollywood, CA: Hollywood AF of L Film Council, December 1957.

Bielby, William, and Denise Bielby. "Organizational Mediation of Project-Based Labor Markets: Talent Agencies and the Careers of Screenwriters." *American Sociological Review* 64, no. 1 (1999): 64–85.

Bignell, Jonathan, Stephen Lacey, and Madeleine MacMurraugh-Kavanagh, eds. *British Television Drama: Past, Present, and Future.* New York: Palgrave, 2000.

Boddy, William. *Fifties Television: The Industry and Its Critics.* Illinois Studies in Communications. Urbana: University of Illinois Press, 1990.

———. "The Studios Move into Prime Time: Hollywood and the Television Industry in the 1950s." *Cinema Journal* 24, no. 4 (Summer 1985): 23–37.

Bode, Lisa. *Making Believe: Screen Performance and Special Effects in Popular Cinema.* New Brunswick, NJ: Rutgers University Press, 2017.

Bordwell, David, Janet Staiger, and Kristin Thompson. *The Classical Hollywood Cinema: Film Style and Mode of Production to 1960.* New York: Columbia University Press, 1985.

Bourdieu, Pierre. *The Field of Cultural Production: Essays on Art and Literature.* New York: Columbia University Press, 1993.

Caldwell, John Thornton. *Production Culture: Industrial Reflexivity and Critical Practice in Film and Television.* Durham, NC: Duke University Press, 2008.

Carman, Emily. *Independent Stardom: Freelance Women in the Hollywood Studio System.* Austin: University of Texas Press, 2016.

Castel, Robert. *From Manual Workers to Wage Laborers: Transformation of the Social Question.* Translated and edited by Richard Boyd. New Brunswick, NJ: Transaction Publishers, 2003.

Chion, Michel. *The Voice in Cinema.* Translated by Claudia Gorbman. New York: Columbia University Press, 1999.

Clark, Danae. *Negotiating Hollywood: The Cultural Politics of Actors' Labor.* Minneapolis: University of Minnesota Press, 1995.

Cohen, Nicole. *Writers' Rights: Freelance Journalism in a Digital Age.* Quebec: McGill-Queens University Press, 2016.

Collins, Karen. *Game Sound: An Introduction to the History, Theory, and Practice of Video Game Music and Sound Design.* Cambridge, MA: MIT Press, 2008.

Cunningham, Stuart, and David Craig. *Social Media Entertainment: The New Intersection of Hollywood and Silicon Valley.* New York: New York University Press, 2019.

Davis, Mike. "Sunshine and Open Shop: Ford and Darwin in 1920s Los Angeles." In *Metropolis in the Making: Los Angeles in the 1920s,* edited by Tom Sitton and William Deverell, 96–122. Berkeley: University of California Press, 2001.

Dawson, Andrew. "Labouring in Hollywood's Motion Picture Industry and the Legacy of 'Flexible Specialization.'" In *Working in the Global Film and Television Industries*, edited by Andrew Dawson and Sean P. Holmes, 21–38. New York: Bloomsbury, 2012.

———. "Strikes in the Motion Picture Industry." In *The Encyclopedia of Strikes in American History*, edited by Aaron Brenner, Benjamin Day, and Immanuel Ness, 652–664. New York: Routledge, 2009.

DeCordova, Richard. "The Emergence of the Star System in America." In *Stardom: Industry of Desire*, edited by Christine Gledhill, 17–29. London: Routledge, 1991.

———. *Picture Personalities: The Emergence of the Star System in America*. Urbana: University of Illinois Press, 2001.

Deuze, Mark. *Media Work*. Digital Media and Society Series. Cambridge, UK: Polity, 2007.

Drake, Philip. "Reframing Television Performance." *Journal of Film and Video* 68, no. 3-4 (Fall/Winter 2016): 6–17.

Dyer, Richard. *Stars*. 2nd ed. London: British Film Institute, 2008.

Enticknap, Leo. *Moving Image Technology from Zoetrope to Digital*. London: Wallflower Press, 2005.

Fischer, Claude S. *America Calling: A Social History of the Telephone to 1940*. Berkeley: University of California Press, 1992.

Fortmueller, Kate. "Encounters at the Margins of Hollywood: Casting and Location Shooting for *Bhowani Junction*." *Film History* 28, no. 4 (Winter 2016): 100–124.

———. "Pay to Play: Booking Roles in the Post-Network Era." *Journal of Film and Video* 68, no. 3/4 (Fall/Winter 2016): 115–128.

———. "The SAG–AFTRA Merger." *Television and New Media* 17, no. 3 (March 2016): 212–227.

Gaines, Jane. *Contested Culture: The Image, the Voice, and the Law*. Chapel Hill: University of North Carolina Press, 1991.

Gazecki, William. *Screen Actors Guild Foundation Presents: Behind the Masks—The Story of the Screen Actors Guild—Part 1*. DVD, 2007.

Gilbert, Robert. "'Residual Rights' Established by Collective Bargaining in Television and Radio." *Law and Contemporary Problems* 23, no. 1 (Winter 1958): 102–124.

Gitelman, Lisa. *Always Already New: Media, History, and the Data of Culture*. Cambridge, MA: MIT Press, 2006.

Gould, Jack. *Watching Television Come of Age: The New York Times Reviews*. Edited by Lewis L. Gould. Austin: University of Texas Press, 2002.

Gray, Lois S., and Ronald Leroy Seeber, eds. *Under the Stars: Essays on Labor Relations in Arts and Entertainment*. Ithaca, NY: ILR Press, 1996.

Hallett, Hilary A. *Go West, Young Women! The Rise of Early Hollywood*. Berkeley: University of California Press, 2013.

Hardt, Hanno, and Bonnie Brennen, eds. *Newsworkers: Toward a History of the Rank and File*. Minneapolis: University of Minnesota Press, 1995.

Harvey, Rita Morley. *Those Wonderful, Terrible Years: George Heller and the American Federation of Television and Radio Artists*. Carbondale: Southern Illinois University Press, 1996.

Hill, Erin. *Never Done: A History of Women's Work in Media Production*. New Brunswick, NJ: Rutgers University Press, 2016.

Hilmes, Michele. *Hollywood and Broadcasting: From Radio to Cable*. Urbana: University of Illinois Press, 1990.

———. *Only Connect: A Cultural History of Broadcasting in the United States*. 3rd ed. Boston: Wadsworth Cengage Learning, 2011.

Hilmes, Michele, ed. *NBC: America's Network*. Berkeley: University of California Press, 2007.

Hoerschelmann, Olaf. *Rules of the Game: Quiz Shows and American Culture*. Albany: State University of New York Press, 2006.

Holmes, Sean P. *Weavers of Dreams, Unite! Actors' Unionism in Early Twentieth-Century America*. Urbana: University of Illinois Press, 2013.

Holmes, Su, and Sean Redmond, eds. *Framing Celebrity: New Directions in Celebrity Culture*. New York: Routledge, 2006.

Holt, Jennifer. *Empires of Entertainment: Media Industries and the Politics of Deregulation, 1980–1996*. New Brunswick, NJ: Rutgers University Press, 2011.

Holt, Jennifer, and Alisa Perren, eds. *Media Industries: History, Theory, and Method*. Malden, MA: Wiley-Blackwell, 2009.

Horne, Gerald. *Class Struggle in Hollywood, 1930–1950: Moguls, Mobsters, Stars, Reds, and Trade Unionists*. Austin: University of Texas Press, 2001.

Hoyt, Eric. "Hollywood and the Income Tax, 1929–1955." *Film History* 22, no. 1 (March 2010): 5–21.

———. *Hollywood Vault: Film Libraries before Home Video*. Berkeley: University of California Press, 2014.

Jenkins, Henry. *Convergence Culture: Where Old and New Media Collide*. New York: New York University Press, 2008.

Jeter, Ida. "The Collapse of the Federated Motion Picture Crafts: A Case Study of Class Collaboration in the Motion Picture Industry." *Journal of the University Film Association* 31, no. 2 (Spring 1979): 37–45.

Jones, Candace. "Careers in Project Networks: The Case of the Film Industry." In *The Boundaryless Career: A New Employment Principle for a New Organizational Era*, edited by Michael B. Arthur and Denise M. Rousseau, 58–75. New York: Oxford University Press, 1996.

Keil, Charlie, and Shelley Stamp, eds. *American Cinema's Transitional Era: Audiences, Institutions, Practices*. Berkeley: University of California Press, 2004.

Kemper, Tom. *Hidden Talent: The Emergence of Hollywood Agents*. Berkeley: University of California Press, 2010.

Kenaga, Heidi. "Making the 'Studio Girl': The Hollywood Studio Club and Industry Regulation of Female Labour." *Film History* 18, no. 2 (June 2006): 129–139.

———. "Promoting Hollywood Extra Girl (1935)." *Screen* 52, no. 1 (Spring 2011): 82–88.

King, Barry. "Stardom as an Occupation." In *The Hollywood Film Industry*, edited by Paul Kerr, 154–184. London: Routledge, 1986.

King, Rob. *Hokum! The Early Sound Slapstick Short and Depression-Era Mass Culture.* Berkeley: University of California Press, 2017.

Kompare, Derek. *Rerun Nation: How Repeats Invented American Television.* New York: Routledge, 2005.

Lewis, Jon, and Eric Smoodin, eds. *Looking Past the Screen: Case Studies in American Film History and Method.* Durham, NC: Duke University Press, 2007.

Lorey, Isabell. *State of Insecurity: Government of the Precarious.* Translated by Aileen Derieg. New York: Verso, 2015.

Lotz, Amanda D. *The Television Will Be Revolutionized.* New York: New York University Press, 2007.

———. *We Now Disrupt This Broadcast: How Cable Transformed Television and the Internet Revolutionized It All.* Cambridge, MA: MIT Press, 2018.

Marcello, Starr A. "Performance Design: An Analysis of Film Acting and Sound Design." *Journal of Film and Video* 58, no. 1–2 (Spring/Summer 2006): 59–70.

Marx, Karl. *Capital, Volume 1.* New York: Penguin Classics, 1990.

Marzola, Luci. "Engineering Hollywood: Technology, Technicians, and the Science of Building the Studio System, 1915–1930." PhD diss., University of Southern California, 2016.

Mayer, Vicki. *Below the Line: Producers and Production Studies in the New Television Economy.* Durham, NC: Duke University Press, 2011.

McDonald, Paul. *Hollywood Stardom.* Malden, MA: Wiley-Blackwell, 2013.

———. *Video and DVD Industries.* London: British Film Institute, 2007.

McKenna, Denise. "The City That Made the Pictures Move: Gender, Labor, and the Film Industry in Los Angeles, 1908–1917." PhD diss., New York University, 2008.

———. "The Photoplay or the Pickaxe: Extras, Gender, and Labour in Early Hollywood." *Film History* 23, no. 1 (March 2011): 5–19.

McLean, Adrienne. *Being Rita Hayworth: Labor, Identity, and Hollywood Stardom.* New Brunswick, NJ: Rutgers University Press, 2004.

McLean, Adrienne, and David A. Cook, eds. *Headline Hollywood: A Century of Film Scandal.* New Brunswick, NJ: Rutgers University Press, 2001.

McRobbie, Angela. *Be Creative: Making a Living in the New Culture Industries.* Cambridge, UK: Polity, 2016.

Merritt, Greg. *Room 1219: The Life of Fatty Arbuckle, the Mysterious Death of Virginia Rappe, and the Scandal That Changed Hollywood.* Chicago: Chicago Review Press, 2013.

Mullen, Megan Gwynne. *The Rise of Cable Programming in the United States: Revolution or Evolution?* Austin: University of Texas Press, 2003.

Murray, Susan. *Hitch Your Antenna to the Stars: Early Television and Broadcast Stardom.* New York: Routledge, 2005.

Neilson, Brett, and Ned Rossiter. "Precarity as a Political Concept, or, Fordism as Exception." *Theory, Culture & Society* 25, no. 7–8 (December 2008): 51–72.

Nielsen, Michael. "Labor Power and Organization in the Early U.S. Motion Picture Industry." *Film History* 2 (1988): 121–131.

Nielsen, Michael, and Gene Mailes. *Hollywood's Other Blacklist: Union Struggles in the Studio System.* London: British Film Institute, 1995.

Nye, David E. *America's Assembly Line.* Cambridge, MA: MIT Press, 2013.

O'Donnell, Casey. "Games Are Not Convergence: The Lost Promise of Digital Production and Convergence." *Convergence* 17, no. 3 (August 2011): 271–286.

Oppenheimer, Martin. *White Collar Politics.* New York: Monthly Review Press, 1985.

Ouellette, Laurie, and Susan Murray, eds. *Reality TV: Remaking Television Culture.* New York: New York University Press, 2009.

Pearson, Roberta E. *Eloquent Gestures: The Transformation of Performance Style in the Griffith Biograph Films.* Berkeley: University of California Press, 1992.

Perry, Louis B., and Richard S. Perry. *A History of the Los Angeles Labor Movement, 1911–1941.* Berkeley: University of California Press, 1963.

Porst, Jennifer. "United States v. Twentieth Century-Fox, et al. and Hollywood's Feature Films on Early Television." *Film History* 25, no. 4 (December 2013): 114–142.

Prindle, David F. *The Politics of Glamour: Ideology and Democracy in the Screen Actors Guild.* Madison: University of Wisconsin Press, 1988.

Regester, Charlene. "African American Extras in Hollywood during the 1920s and 1930s." *Film History* 9, no. 1 (March 1997): 95–115.

Ribeiro, Alyssa. "'We Want Both! Pressuring Philadelphia Unions for Inclusion and Equity during the Long 1970s." *Labor History* 60, no. 5 (October 2019): 558–570.

Roberts, Michael James. *Tell Tchaikovsky the News: Rock 'n' Roll, the Labor Question, and the Musicians' Union, 1942–1968.* Durham, NC: Duke University Press, 2014.

Rosenthal, Nicolas. "Representing Indians: Native American Actors on Hollywood's Frontier." *Western Historical Quarterly* 36, no. 3 (2005): 328–352.

Ross, Murray. *Stars and Strikes: Unionization of Hollywood.* New York: Columbia University Press, 1941.

Ross, Steven Joseph. *Working-Class Hollywood: Silent Film and the Shaping of Class in America.* Princeton, NJ: Princeton University Press, 1998.

Rosten, Leo. *Hollywood: The Movie Colony, the Movie Makers.* New York: Harcourt, Brace & Co., 1941.

Rubin, Stanley. "A (Very) Personal History of the First Sponsored Film Series on National Television." *E-Media Studies* 1, no. 1 (2008), do:10.1349/PS1.1938-6060.A.312.

Schatz, Thomas. *Boom and Bust: American Cinema in the 1940s.* Berkeley: University of California Press, 1999.

———. "'A Triumph of Bitchery': Warner Bros., Bette Davis, and Jezebel." In *The Studio System,* edited by Janet Staiger. New Brunswick, NJ: Rutgers University Press, 1995.

Scholz, Trebor, ed. *Digital Labor: The Internet as Playground and Factory.* New York: Routledge, 2013.

Scott, Allen John. *On Hollywood: The Place, the Industry.* Princeton, NJ: Princeton University Press, 2005.

Segrave, Kerry. *Actors Organize: A History of Union Formation Efforts in America, 1880–1919.* Jefferson, NC: McFarland, 2008.

———. *Extras of Early Hollywood: A History of the Crowd, 1913–1945.* Jefferson, NC: McFarland, 2013.

Sitton, Tom, and William Deverell, eds. *Metropolis in the Making: Los Angeles in the 1920s.* Berkeley: University of California Press, 2001.

Slide, Anthony. *Hollywood Unknowns: A History of Extras, Bit Players, and Stand-Ins.* Jackson: University Press of Mississippi, 2012.

Smith, Glenn D., Jr. "'The Guiding Spirit': Philip Loeb, the Battle for Television Jurisdiction, and the Broadcasting Industry Blacklist." *American Journalism* 26, no. 3 (Summer 2009): 93–150.

Smukler, Maya Montañez. *Liberating Hollywood: Women Directors and the Feminist Reform of 1970s American Cinema.* New Brunswick, NJ: Rutgers University Press, 2018.

Sperb, Jason. "I'll (Always) Be Back: Virtual Performance and Post-Human Labor in the Age of Digital Cinema." *Culture, Theory, and Critique* 53, no. 3 (2012): 383–397.

Springer, Claudia, and Julie R. Levinson, eds. *Acting.* New Brunswick, NJ: Rutgers University Press, 2015.

Stamp, Shelley. "'It's a Long Way to Filmland': Starlets, Screen Hopefuls and Extras in Early Hollywood." In *American Cinema's Transitional Era: Audiences, Institutions, Practices,* edited by Charlie Keil and Shelley Stamp, 322–352. Berkeley: University of California Press, 2004.

Steinhart, Daniel. *Runaway Hollywood: Internationalizing Postwar Production and Location Shooting.* Berkeley: University of California Press, 2019.

Sterne, Jonathan. "Television under Construction: American Television and the Problem of Distribution, 1926–62." *Media, Culture & Society* 21, no. 4 (July 1999): 503–530.

Stoloff, Sam. "Fatty Arbuckle and the Black Sox: The Paranoid Style of American Popular Culture, 1919–1922." In *Headline Hollywood: A Century of Film Scandal,* edited by Adrienne L. McLean and David A. Cook, 52–82. New Brunswick, NJ: Rutgers University Press, 2001.

Talbot, Margaret. "Pixel Perfect: The Scientist behind the Digital Cloning of Actors." *New Yorker,* April 28, 2014.

Thompson, Morton. "Hollywood Is a Union Town." *Nation,* April 2, 1938.

Thomson, David. "The Lives of Supporting Players." In *Movie Acting: The Film Reader,* edited by Pamela Robertson Wojcik, 207–210. New York: Routledge, 2004.

Upham, Misty. "She Worked Hard for the Money." *Daily Beast,* January 17, 2014. http://www.thedailybeast.com/witw/articles/2014/01/17/native-american-actress -misty-upham-talks-about-her-role-as-domestic-worker-in-august-osage-county .html.

Wasser, Frederick. *Veni, Vidi, Video: The Hollywood Empire and the VCR.* Austin: University of Texas Press, 2001.

Weis, Elisabeth, and John Belton, eds. *Film Sound: Theory and Practice.* New York: Columbia University Press, 1986.

Weiss, Paul, and Robert Faulkner. "Credits and Craft Production: Freelance Social Organization in the Hollywood Film Industry, 1964–1978." *Symbolic Interaction* 6, no. 1 (Spring 1983): 111–123.

Whissel, Kristen. *Spectacular Digital Effects: CGI and Contemporary Cinema.* Durham, NC: Duke University Press, 2014.

Wojcik, Pamela Robertson, ed. *Movie Acting: The Film Reader.* New York: Routledge, 2004.

———. "The Sound of Film Acting." *Journal of Film and Video* 58, no. 1–2 (Spring/Summer 2006): 71–83.

Young, Jordan R. *Reel Characters: Great Movie Character Actors.* Beverly Hills, CA: Moonstone Press, 1986.

Zackariasson, Peter, and Timothy L. Wilson, eds. *The Video Game Industry: Formation, Present State, and Future.* New York: Routledge, 2012.

INDEX

Academy of Motion Picture Arts and Sciences (AMPAS), 42, 44, 45

Actors Equity Association, or Equity (AEA), 27, 48, 61, 62, 72, 73, 74, 78, 109; and conflict with SAG, 55–56; and jurisdiction over television, 51, 57–59; and organizing, extras, 31–32, 40; and screen actors, 40–41

#ActorsWithDayJobs, 155–156. *See also* journeymen actors

Actors Working for an Actors Guild (AWAG), 116

Adrian, Iris, 18

agents, 5, 9, 12, 37, 61, 120, 127; facilitating voiceover auditions, 143; role of, 18, 39, 140–141

Allen, Dave, 35

Alliance of Motion Picture and Television Producers (AMPTP), 13, 104, 135; COVID-19 response of, 161

Altman, Robert, 112

American Federation of Musicians (AFM), 59

American Federation of Radio Artists (AFRA), 51, 56, 57, 62, 68, 96; and discussion of merger, 72–75, 78, 86

American Federation of Television and Radio Artists (AFTRA), 13, 90, 91, 96, 97, 99, 100, 107, 134; and joint negotiations with SAG, 112–116;

origin of, 86. *See also* mergers: AFRA and TVA; mergers: SAG and AFTRA; residuals; strikes

American Guild of Musical Artists, (AGMA), 51, 57, 63, 74, 78

American Guild of Variety Artists (AGVA), 51, 61, 62, 63, 72, 74, 78, 79

American Society of Composers, Authors and Publishers (ASCAP), 59

Anger, Kenneth, 32

anti-rerun campaign, 92–93, 107; Save Television Original Programming (STOP), 104

Arbuckle, Roscoe "Fatty," 19, 22, 33–34

Associated Actors and Artistes of America (4As or AAAA), 48; and involvement in television jurisdiction dispute, 52, 55–58, 68, 75, 77–79, 82, 85

Association of Independent Commercial Producers, 136

Association of Motion Picture Producers (AMPP), 97, 100. *See also* Beetson, Fred W.; Central Casting Bureau

auditions, 8, 16, 61, 128; and convergence, 139, 144–149, 160; in person, 140–143, 153; video/digital, 118, 122, 139–141, 160; voice, 130, 141, 142, 144

background actors/performers. *See* extras

Beery, Wallace, 17–18, 28